R I P
U$D
1971 – 202X

"...and the Way Forward"

SHANMUGANATHAN. N

ISBN

Hardcase 979-8-89363-252-1
Paperback 979-8-89322-934-9

Contents

Foreword

By Doug Casey

Personal freedom is in retreat all over the world. The State - government - is growing like a cancer in every country. Citizens are increasingly told what they should believe and what they mustn't say. Universities have been transformed from educational institutions into indoctrination centers. Billions of cameras monitor everyone's activities everywhere, in the hope of preventing more crime, but crime rates continue to grow. Governments are arming, and the prospect of war is growing. The average person has to take on more and more consumer debt, mortgaging his future and consuming capital, just to keep his head above water.

Since you now have this book in your hands, I presume you see these trends and fear where they'll lead. You've probably asked yourself what can be done to turn these trends around.

There are numerous causes for what's happening, not least an upending of traditional moral values and ideas of what is right and wrong, good and evil. And perhaps there's not much you can do about these megatrends other than act correctly yourself and influence your family and friends.

But to do that, you need a foundation of knowledge. And most people lack knowledge of economics, which, if you come to think of it, is the most important and basic of studies. Why do I say that? Because economics is the study of how the world works. It gives you an understanding of what really goes on in the process of producing and consuming, saving and borrowing, investing and speculating, becoming rich, or becoming poor.

That's why this book is important and why you should read it closely. Once you've read its 200 pages and understood them, I promise you will not only know the answers to a myriad of important questions (some you may not have even thought to ask) but you'll know more about money and the way the world works than 99 out of 100 people. And almost all of those in government.

Shan approached this subject by looking at monetary inflation - which will be the root cause of the onrushing Greater Depression. I call it the Greater Depression because I believe it's going to be much worse, much longer-lasting, and much different from the unpleasantness of 1929-1946. If you read this book, you'll understand why the Depression is happening and (very important) what you can do to insulate yourself from it. And, unlike most people, emerge better off on the other side.

This is an important book. Be very glad you now have it in your hands. Read it and prosper!

Douglas Casey

April 2024

By Dr. Marc Faber

I really enjoyed reading the book *"RIP USD: 1971 - 202X ...and the Way Forward"* by Shanmuganathan, which is an outstanding read by an accomplished and libertarian economist. You won't find his views among government bureaucrats, at universities that are recipients of government subsidies, and among central bankers and Nobel Prize winners.

Whenever I read economic papers or listen to speeches by politicians or economic policymakers, what drives me nuts is that all these geniuses always know "what ought to be done," when in fact, inaction might be the most appropriate policy. (Thomas Jefferson: **"That Government is best which governs least."**)

If you study the history of great empires, a striking feature is that they all debased their currency before they decayed and fell into oblivion.

Shan does not mince his words. Already early in the book, he writes: *"Perhaps the singularly most important point for the reader to understand is the difference between the **gold standard** and **unbacked paper currency** that central banks can create at will. Most professionals today consider paper currency as an innovation while it is perhaps the most regressive and retrograde step that has happened in all of human history. For the wreck it is going to cause to the world economy in the years/decade ahead, this paper monetary system we have today is going to rival the two World Wars combined."*

I am less sure about the damage that will eventually occur, but I have two observations. Already the early Roman emperors knew what US President James Garfield wrote in the late 19th century, and that is, "Whoever controls the volume of money in our country is the absolute master of all industry and commerce. When you realize that the entire system is very easily controlled, one way or another, by a few powerful men at the top, you will not have to be told how periods of inflation and depression originate."

Moreover, we need to be aware that inflation is nothing else than a tax, imposed on you and your families by cunning and cowardly governments who are afraid to tell their citizens how much taxes they really pay for the government's poor services and senseless wars, and that, as Ludwig von Mises pointed out, "Inflationism, however, is not an isolated phenomenon. It is only one piece in the total framework of politico-economic and socio-philosophical ideas of our time. Just as the sound money policy of gold standard advocates went hand in hand with liberalism, free trade, capitalism, and peace, so is inflationism part and parcel of imperialism, militarism, protectionism, and socialism."

I am less sure that inflationism always involves socialism because to debase the currency is one of authoritarian dictators' favorite pastimes irrespective of their political affiliation. However, one fact stands out: debasing the currency allows governments to expand endlessly at the expense of the private sector. (Oscar Wilde: "The bureaucracy is expanding to meet the needs of the expanding bureaucracy.")

Shan asks rightly: "*Are there no solutions to prevent the above economic crisis? Of course, there are. The final solution, as far as the US is concerned, has to be a gold backed US dollar with a dramatically downsized US government. Whether it is done voluntarily by the US government today or is forced upon by the markets through violent disruptions and economic / currency crises tomorrow is the choice that is in front of us. At this point, the probability of the latter scenario playing out is overwhelming.*"

There two points I need to add. Above, Shan mentions the need of a "dramatically downsized US government." This is not going to happen because too many people enrich themselves through all sorts of government programs. Furthermore, once a government embarks on money printing it is practically impossible to stop. The result: more inflation in future. And as the brilliant social observer and economist John Kenneth Galbraith explained, "**People of privilege will always risk their complete destruction rather than surrender any material part of their advantage. Intellectual myopia, often called stupidity, is no doubt a reason. But the privileged also feel that their privileges, however egregious they may seem to others, are a solemn, basic, God-given right. The sensitivity of the poor to injustice is a trivial thing compared with that of the rich.**"

Furthermore, when I observe the arrogant and condescending attitude and behavior of completely irrelevant and incompetent Western leaders towards new leaders of important and "rising" nations such as India, I am concerned that Shan's "*violent disruptions and economic/currency crises*" will be accompanied by possibly horrendous military confrontations.

Shan mentions that, "*a very probable scenario, is that a group of nations issue a gold backed convertible international currency that could function as a reserve currency. If the US Dollar does not revert to its pre-1971 form in the next few years, other countries will have no option but to switch to the above alternative reserve asset."*

I agree that this is likely to occur in future but as I said above, how likely is this going to happen without serious confrontations?

I believe that you will enjoy Shan's clear economic insights and easy to read writing style, and that you will come away with the knowledge after reading the book that as the US politician Ron Paul stated, the reason why western central bankers, and the biased western media do not like gold was, **"Because gold is honest money it is disliked by dishonest men."**

Dr.Markus Faber

April 2024

Acknowledgements

My journey of learning Austrian Economics was quite an accident. The starting point was a "Jim Rogers" interview in 2002 or thereabouts where he was recommending people to buy "gold." Having been ingrained in the Buffett-Munger-Fisher style of value investing, I found it a very "unconventional" proposition. But given Jim's enviable track record in investing, I persisted with the line of inquiry and that "eventually" took me to Rothbard's "What has Government done to our Money?" Even while reading that book, I wasn't aware of the intellectual prowess of Rothbard. Truth to be told, I did not even think I was reading an Economics textbook. I was just trying to understand why gold should have any value at all.

Over the next few years, one part of the jigsaw after another fell into place. I was spending several hours a day reading and listening to Peter Schiff, Ron Paul, Jim Grant, Ayn Rand, Lew Rockwell, and of course, the pillars of the Austrian School of Economics - Ludwig von Mises and Murray Rothbard.

I started writing about "Austrian Economics / Libertarianism" with Casey Research. They were putting together a worldwide newsletter (World Money Analyst) and were looking for somebody who understood Austrian Economics and could write about the Indian economy. Similarly, Dr.Faber has carried a number of my writings over the years in his newsletter to investors. I soon realized that the world of Austrian Economists is indeed a very small one - maybe just a handful of Institutions in the world teach this.

When the idea of writing a book came to my mind, I discussed with three people - Doug Casey, Quinton Hennigh and Jayant Bhandari - about getting a co-author and all three suggested that I go "solo" on this. Given my lack of formal qualifications, industry experience and this being my first book, I was quite skeptical if I would be able to pull this one off. Not to mention the complexity of the topic and making it understandable for the common man who doesn't understand much of economics. Most of the audience of my earlier articles in newsletters were people who not only knew economics, but were followers of the Austrian School as well. But all the three gentlemen - each in their own way - nudged me towards writing it alone. I thank them for prodding me in this direction and for the other suggestions they have provided on this project.

The next set of people are the ones who worked with me on the book. When I reached out to Prof. Cristopher Lingle (one of the few Professors who teaches Austrian Economics) and requested for his help on the book, he more than readily accepted. Not only did he review my writings chapter by chapter, but he also offered several suggestions and references along the way that has made the arguments more comprehensive. More often than not, anything that I would send to Cris for review would elicit a response within 24 hours. I thank him for his extensive guidance on this project.

Another crucial part was to get a good reviewer without a background in economics to assess if the objective of conveying the message to the layperson was indeed being met. Not only did I get one in my friend, Jaishankar, but he was also practically the ideator for so many sections of the book. Another good friend, Subramanian, also did something similar. If the book is readable and devoid of jargon, it is primarily because of their inputs. The queries both of them raised ensured that I was providing sufficient clarity on issues that I would otherwise assume as known amongst the typical newsletter reader.

There are many other members whom I have to thank - more than 30 in number including my friends, family members, neighbors from my community, batch mates from B-School (IIM Lucknow, India), my Professor from B-School who got me into the reading circuit as part of the curriculum (Prof.R.K.Srivastava), my former colleagues from Infosys Technologies, my school mate Satish who has been all along part of the journey into studying Austrian Economics and newsletter editor Nitin from Nepal. All of them reviewed the book at various stages and gave their input in making it a better version.

A special mention should be made of my niece Sakthisree. She is an accounting professional and a regular reader of my columns as well. She would have prepared more than 100 graphs/images as part of this book and almost all of them multiple times in different formats. I thank her for the extensive work she did as part of this project.

Finally, it gets down to family. I need to thank my wife, Aruna, who is a medical doctor by Profession and, our son Saeyon, who is currently an Undergraduate student studying Mathematics. Our dinner conversations for a few years now have veered around the topics of Libertarianism / Austrian Economics and how freer societies lead to more prosperous ones. Both gave a number of suggestions on what I should include as part of the contents. More than anything else, it was our conversations on these topics over the years that enabled me to explain what could be complex issues in a simplified manner without making it simplistic.

In the tradition of reserving the best for the last, I do want to convey my utmost gratitude for the "Mises Institute." There is no better place if one wants to learn economics, especially if you prefer the DIY way and almost everything is free on their website. But for their shared resources and faculty extraordinaire, my journey would have been a non-starter.

Preface

The idea of this book is to explain why we are at the precipice of a collapse in the purchasing power of the US dollar, perhaps even leading to a situation similar to the hyperinflation in the German Papiermark from the period 1919 to 1923. While hyperinflation of the US dollar is by no means a certainty, it is more than a mere possibility - perhaps even a probable outcome for this decade.

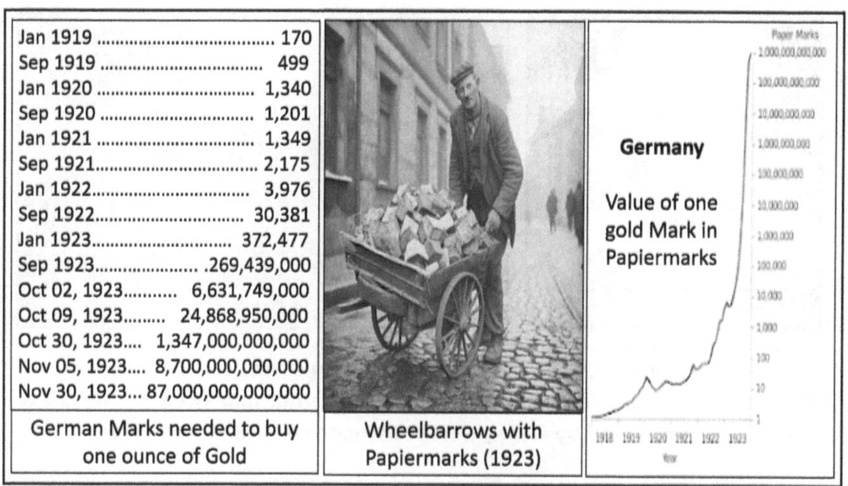

The price of a loaf of bread rose from 160 Marks at the end of 1922 to 200,000,000,000 Marks by late 1923. By Nov 1923, one US Dollar was worth 4,210,500,000,000 Marks

In the long run of history, no fiat currency (i.e. not backed by a tangible asset) has ever survived more than a few decades. So the probability of hyperinflation in the US dollar would be near 100% if we are willing to stretch the timelines, until the end of the century. For the here and now, even in the best-case scenario where the US experiences just high inflation (in double-digits and not hyperinflation), the US dollar has to go back to its pre-1971 form (where the US dollar was redeemable for gold at a fixed rate) if it is to survive the inflationary depression that lies ahead.

The depression itself is a certainty at this point. While there is no standard definition for what a depression is, we will use it to denote a period of prolonged economic contraction i.e., for a few years and where the real cumulative GDP contraction is more than 10%. The Great Depression lasted from 1929 to 1939, or more realistically, from 1929 to 1946 i.e., if we subtract the war-related goods production that did not have a meaningful market pricing or any consumer benefit. The difference between the two depressions, i.e., the forecasted one for the decade ahead and the historical Great Depression, is that the Great Depression was deflationary while the current one will be highly inflationary. Consequently, the US dollar stands to lose a substantial portion of its value not only against gold but against other currencies as well during the depression that lies ahead.

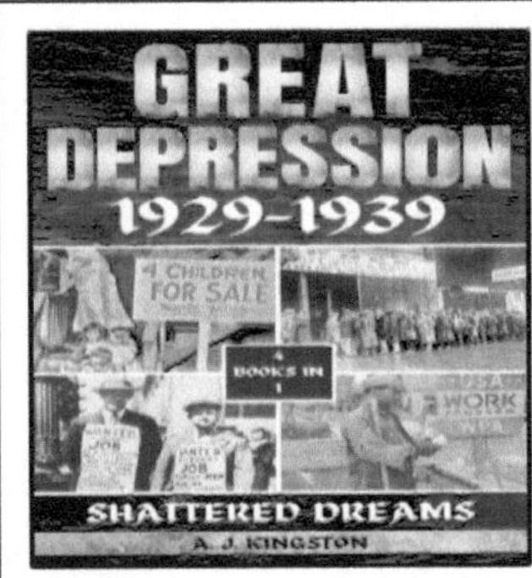

Between 1929 and 1932, worldwide GDP fell an estimated 15%. International trade fell by more than 50% with unemployment in the US at 23% and accompanied by falling personal incomes, prices and taxes.

That must indeed be a very outrageous forecast to most economists and finance professionals. For the world's reserve currency and that too for a country with the most powerful military in the world (the military budget of the US is greater than the next 10 countries combined), the forecast of an impending currency collapse should indeed be a preposterous one. What would add to the skepticism of most economists is that the Dollar Index (DXY - pronounced 'Dixie') is trading near a 20-year high. The DXY indicates the strength of the US dollar relative to a basket of currencies comprising of the significant trading partners of the US. As shown, the DXY has been below 100 for most of the last 20 years and is currently trading at a value of 104.

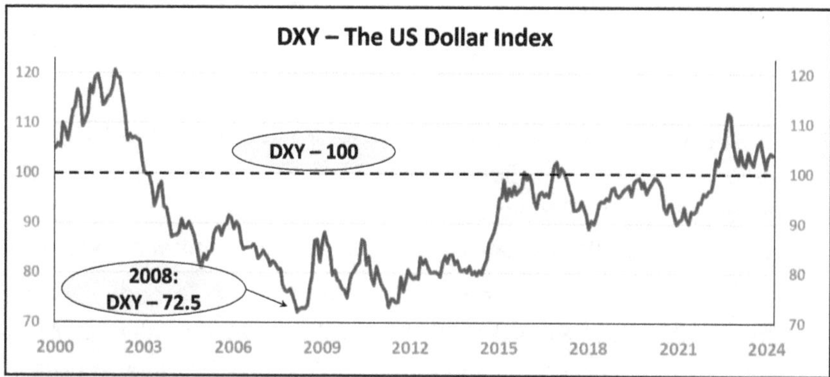

The DXY is a measure of the value of the US Dollar relative to a basket of foreign currencies. For 18 of the last 20 years, the DXY has traded below 100, with of a low of 72.5 during 2008.

Can the DXY lose 50% of its value in the years ahead? Or maybe 90%. All these are possible scenarios and it depends on whether the foreign central banks choose to untether themselves from the umbilical link they maintain to the US dollar. But even in the best-case scenario (which is a very unlikely one) where the status quo of the US dollar being the reserve currency is maintained, the DXY could easily lose 50% of its value when the crisis plays itself out.

Following the first principles, the above are the conclusions that one will come to as will be explained. Starting with first principles is indeed a must to understand the structural craters underneath a superficially sound US Economy. The US economy could best be described as being in a state of *'Unstable Equilibrium'* and a small push could send it down a path of an economic depression. As we will see in Section 4, but for the massive monetary inflation (more commonly referred to as 'economic stimulus.' The National debt added by the US government has been more than $2 trillion/year) of the last couple of years, the US would already be in a deep recession today.

We will start with the 3 most commonly used and yet misunderstood concepts in Economics - money, interest rates and inflation. These are so commonly used that everybody would assume that they know what these mean. Yet, conceptually, these remain the least understood. I am not only talking about the average reader but even within sophisticated financial circles.

To understand the above, what should be the appropriate starting point in history? Several possibilities and we will start with the most recent and go back in time.

1. **Closing of the Gold Window in 1971** - This is when the US Federal Reserve went off the Gold standard i.e., Richard Nixon 'temporarily' closes the Gold Window that enabled the exchange of US dollars for gold at a fixed rate $35 per ounce by the foreign central banks.

2. **Ban on Private Ownership of Gold in 1933** - Through Executive Order 6102, US President Roosevelt banned the holding of gold coins, bullion and certificates in 1933. This was however repealed in 1974 by President Gerald Ford though in the interim 40 years, the understanding of 'gold as money' has been forgotten by most.

3. **Formation of the US Federal Reserve in 1913** - Formation of the US Federal Reserve eventually results in a monopoly power to issue US dollars. Till that time, banks were free to issue their Dollar certificates that were convertible to gold across the counter.

4. **Money 101 - From Barter to Transactions using Money** - Starting from exchanging goods using a primitive system of barter, societies transitioned into a system with a 'medium of exchange' were all goods and services where priced in terms of this medium of exchange. Over thousands of years of experiments, gold was identified as the most ideal medium of exchange.

One could legitimately describe the above as the 'history of money.' I will start the explanations from the beginning i.e., how money emerged as a tool for commerce and what led to the standardization of gold (and silver) as the best 'forms of money' in the free market.

Perhaps the singularly most important point for the reader to understand is the difference between the *gold standard* and *unbacked paper currency* that central banks can create at will. Most professionals today consider paper currency as an innovation while it is perhaps the most regressive and retrograde step that has happened in all of human history. For the wreck it is going to cause to the world economy in the years/decade ahead, this paper monetary system we have today is going to rival the two World Wars combined.

The resolution to the above crisis has to come through a return to 'some form' of a gold standard. Why is that the case? What is the form of a gold standard that is most likely to be adopted and what are the timelines? What are other interim (and unworkable) solutions that would be tried? These are the questions that I will attempt to answer in this book.

The crisis described above is a steep loss in the purchasing power of the US dollar over a relatively short period of a few years. Are there no solutions to prevent this economic / currency crisis? Of course, there are. The final solution, as far as the US is concerned, has to be a gold-backed US dollar with a dramatically downsized US government. Whether it is done voluntarily by the US government today or is forced upon by the markets through violent disruptions and economic / currency crises tomorrow is the choice that is in front of us. At this point, the probability of the latter scenario playing out is overwhelming.

The other possibility and this is indeed a very probable scenario, is that a group of nations issue a gold-backed convertible international currency that could function as a reserve currency. If the US dollar does not revert to its pre-1971 form in the next few years, other countries will have no option but to switch to the above alternative reserve asset. The US would be forced to follow suit subsequently - either adopt the new international currency itself (as its reserve currency to pay for its imports) or issue a superior form of a gold currency i.e., offer more convenient convertibility of currency to gold at the defined price.

I do want to point out one gross caricature of the causative factors that is certain to occur as it eminently suits the government to propagate this fallacious version. The crisis when it unfolds, will be blamed on capitalism, free markets and lack of adequate regulations. The Global Financial Crisis (GFC) of 2008 that was precipitated by the bursting of the housing bubble, which could be considered as a trailer for what lies ahead, is a standing example.

The truth is anything but. Much like the GFC 2008, this is an entirely US government / Federal Reserve caused crisis - primarily due to the flawed fiat monetary system. Whether it was an engineered one or just a question of plain incompetence of the officials will be a conjecture.

A free market would have never permitted the emergence of a paper currency standard. Also, interest rates would have been determined by the laws of supply and demand i.e. the confluence of supply of money from savers and the demand for money from borrowers. The current system of decisions being made at the Eccles building (that is the headquarters of the US Federal Reserve) and not the marketplace is the primary source of these imbalances. Unless we move away from these monetary interventions, we are doomed to live with these boom-bust crises repeatedly.

US has been the beacon of capitalism since its formation in 1776 and it transitioned from a primitive agrarian society to the wealthiest country in the world following the tenets of limited government and sound money. It has veered so much away from these profound enshrined ideals, especially since the creation of the Federal Reserve in 1913 that the founding fathers must be turning in their graves.

The idea of *'individual liberty as a natural right'* was hitherto unknown in most parts of the world, as indeed was the emergence of a large middle class in societies where previously it was just the ruling class and the peasants. The US showed the world how a just and prosperous society can be created by following the principles of free markets and limited government. Individuals endowed with their unalienable rights - life, liberty, and the pursuit of happiness - could pursue their goals with industry. It was a unique experiment in world history, and as Ben Franklin put it, *"The Constitution only guarantees the American people the right to pursue happiness. You have to catch it yourself."*

For the sake of humanity, the US Government should return to its founding principles.

If there is only one takeaway message from this entire book, this would be it - Capitalism / Free Markets is NOT the source of this monetary crisis. A return to the principles of capitalism i.e., limited government and sound money is the solution to the problems caused by government interventionism on monetary issues.

How to Read this Book?

As I sit and write this section during May 2024, the most pessimistic economic forecast, at least among mainstream economists, is that of a hard landing for the US economy. There is hardly any mention of the housing bubble 2.0 (HB 2.0) though the current one is much bigger than the one that burst in 2008. In what history will record as Powell's "subprime is contained" moment, he recently remarked, "*I don't see the 'stag' or the '-flation', I don't really understand where that's coming from*".

What I am trying to convey through this book is that we should forget the hard landing outcome. If all that we get is a GFC 2008 style economic meltdown, it would be a miracle. To put it in as straightforward terms as possible, this is the end of the world as we know it.

The question then is how to make the average reader grasp the fundamental economic issues that would enable them to understand the rationale behind the above prognosis. Starting from the basics is a must, and for ease of understanding, this book has been organized into 5 chapters. The first three are an introduction to the key economic concepts that every reader needs to understand. I have tried to make the explanations as clear and simple as possible without using any technical jargon or complicated theories. The first 3 chapters also include a summary of the basic economic concepts discussed and a suggested reading list for interested readers.

A glossary of the basic financial terms used is provided at the end of chapter 5. The attempt is to make a reader without any background in economics understand the nature and magnitude of the crisis ahead. Readers who have had no formal introduction to Economics could read the glossary first before proceeding to Chapter 1.

Also, it is most important for the reader to understand that despite the similarities to the GFC 2008 in terms of the causative factors, the solutions attempted back then would spectacularly backfire in the current environment and make the situation much worse. It is, in fact, these solutions that will lead to the hyperinflation scenario for the US dollar.

The objective of explaining in very simple terms would mean that I am missing some important events/facts that might be of interest to sophisticated readers. A few examples of the above 'missed out' facts are as below.

- The formation of the Federal Reserve without mentioning the events of the Jekyll Island of 1910. Incidentally, the Federal Reserve is the only major central bank that does not have the title of 'Bank' as part of its name, and this was done deliberately due to the widespread aversion towards a central bank amongst US citizens.

- Closing of the Gold Window in 1971 without mentioning the role of the Petrodollar and the role it played in creating a demand for the US dollar despite the suspension of convertibility to gold.

- Explaining housing bubbles without discussing the reckless borrowing/ lending practices.

- Forecasting the end of the US dollar without mentioning 'Dedollarization.'

In part, because I have stuck to the fundamental causative factors and not the secondary/additional issues. In the absence of the issues that are discussed in the chapters to follow, these additional factors would be nearly irrelevant. These come into play only because of fundamental factors on account of which the foundations of the US economy are broken.

However, for interested readers in understanding the above issues, I have included a note at the end of the first 4 chapters titled 'Suggested Reading.' I certainly wish all economists, finance professionals, and central bankers not only read this book but also the entire reading list specified. For the casual reader, I would certainly encourage reading the easier ones to start with.

As mentioned in the preface, three basic concepts require explanations - money, interest rates, and inflation. Most people, including economists, have a complete misunderstanding of these concepts. So I have included a '101' explanation of these concepts. A '101' is an introductory or a beginner's course in the subject area in the American University system.

The 5 Chapters have been organized in the following manner:

1. **Chapter 1 - Money 101:** An explanation of what money is. As the reader will understand, it is certainly not the pieces of paper in our purse or the digital entries in our bank accounts. What we think of as money today i.e., US Dollar, Chinese RMB, Euro, GB Pound, Indian Rupee etc. are currencies and during the best of conditions, these are money substitutes. This distinction between money and currencies is a lesson that has been learned hundreds of times in human history, and sadly, it is time again to learn it one more time. Perhaps, at a global level, for the first time.

2. **Chapter 2 - Unbacked Paper Currencies: The ultimate retrograde step in history:** Explaining how currencies were defined in terms of fixed weights of gold/silver and how the US dollar got gradually delinked from gold over a 6 decade period. We also look at why an unbacked currency system will lead to a virtual explosion in the creation of currency. A comparison of two periods 1900 to 1971 (under various adaptations of the 'Gold standard') and 1971 to 2023 (pure fiat / unbacked paper currency system) is done to show the consequences of removing the gold backing of currencies.

3. **Chapter 3 - The State's Antagonism to Gold:** This chapter is a partial explanation of Greenspan's priceless missive 'Gold and Economic Freedom.' We start by examining the various forms of the gold standard that have prevailed starting with the 'Classical Gold Standard' during the 19th century and the progressive dilution of 'Gold in the monetary standard' culminating with Nixon closing the Gold Window in 1971. It includes 'Interest Rates - 101' and 'Inflation - 101' explaining how the gold standard even in a very diluted form restrains deficit spending by the governments and interest rate manipulations by the central banks.

4. **Chapter 4 - The Road Ahead for the US Economy:** The first three chapters were largely an explanation of historical events and a few basic economic concepts. Chapter 4 uses these concepts to make readers understand how the lack of the gold standard has resulted in the formation of many bubbles over the last few decades.

We also look at the cycles of monetary inflation and why we could potentially be at the final stage right now. An explanation of how the US has reached this end stage without too many explicit warning signals is also provided. The fundamental concepts explained in chapters 1 to 3 should make the reader understand that this crisis was foreseeable at least a decade earlier, if not even before. We also look at possible ways in which the crisis will play itself out in the years ahead.

5. **Chapter 5 - The Way Forward:** A brief introduction to the gold market is given to show how it is really small compared to the debt and equity markets today. Some possible indicators of how the gold prices would move during the decade ahead are given. We also look at alternatives to the US dollar as the reserve currency and as to why it will be gold that will replace the US dollar. Finally, some thoughts on what it would take for the US dollar and the US economy to regain its preeminent position are discussed.

The Theoretical Basis:

Almost the entirety of what I have written flows from the teachings of the Austrian School of Economics. For the uninitiated, this is the school of thought that advocates Laissez-Faire Economics / Capitalism and a very limited role for government in civil society - typically restricted to only two functions:

1. **Enforcement of contracts** - the courts and justice system.

2. **Protection of private property from internal/external aggressors** - the police and the army.

Much of the early framework and theoretical foundations were provided by a few economists from Austria - Carl Menger, Eugen von Böhm-Bawerk, Ludwig von Mises - and hence the name 'Austrian School of Economics.' My personal favorite among the Austrian Scholars who developed the theoretical framework is Murray Rothbard.

The mistakes in the interpretation of Austrian Economics as explained in this book, if any, are of course entirely mine.

Money – 101

Although *Homo sapiens* have inhabited the planet for the last 160,000 years, there was no requirement for money for most of the above period. Life was about scavenging the forests, hunting animals, and surviving the vagaries of nature. There was no surplus of anything worthwhile to trade with others. Supply was extremely limited.

Primitive agriculture started around 8000 BC, probably with the planting of barley. With the addition of other crops, the change in lifestyles and living standards was unmistakable. In about 1000 years, by 7000 BC, agriculture had become the primary occupation in many parts of the world. This led to the creation of food that could be stored and consumed subsequently. For the first time we had a surplus that could be traded for other goods and commodities.

This development of agriculture also led to the concept of 'division of labor' where people could specialize in a profession. Toolmakers who could make agricultural implements could focus and aid the farmers in their task of food production. By around 4000 BC, there were recordings of communities where people specialized in various professions such as farming, herdsmen, pottery, masonry, weaving, smithing and of course, trade.

1.A - From Barter to a Medium of Exchange:

It was agriculture that was the starting point of commerce, and different goods and services could be exchanged by members within themselves in these primitive societies. Commercial transactions started with the barter system between individuals, wherein a system of exchange of goods and services without the use of money was conducted. Simple examples could be trading a goat for 10 chickens, or paying a day's labor with a bag of wheat. This system of barter facilitated simple voluntary exchanges within a local community.

While barter worked for the limited goods that were produced, society soon ran into some of the disadvantages of the barter system:

1. **Double Coincidence of Wants:** A transaction cannot happen in the barter system unless there is an exact match of requirements between the two transacting parties, or what is referred to as the 'double coincidence of wants.' For example, Alan has goats and wants chicken, while Ben has chicken but wants rice. A transaction cannot happen unless they find Charlie who has rice and wants goats. Then Alan could trade his goat for rice with Charlie and subsequently trade his rice for chicken with Ben.

2. **Impossibility of Subdivision of Goods:** Let's say a person wants to trade their cow for a combination of rice, pencil, and paper. It will not be possible for the person to subdivide the cow and exchange it for the three goods they need. Even if the perceived valuations are acceptable to all parties, the transactions cannot occur due to the impossibility of subdivision of some goods.

3. **Time Preferences of the Traded Goods:** In another scenario, Alan might want to sell his goat to Ben for the rice he will produce the subsequent year. Ben might also want to have a goat today in exchange for the rice to be produced next year. Even under these circumstances, a transaction cannot happen as there are varying time preferences, and enforceable legal contracts are required to ensure that such transactions can occur.

The above is by no means an exhaustive list of the limitations of the barter system. But even with these simple examples, it is obvious that barter can support transactions only in primitive societies.

Solutions to the limitations of the barter system would come from the marketplace. Within the system of barter, members noticed that the exchange value of different commodities fluctuated over periods of time. It was easy to observe that goods that are needed in regular use and in short supply maintained their 'purchasing power' against other goods and services. Wheat was one such substance that maintained or gained its value vis-à-vis other goods of that era.

So, primitive people began to save required quantities of wheat as a 'reserve asset' that they could use later in barter exchanges. Since wheat was widely desired and in short supply, people began to exchange their surplus for wheat that they could, in turn, use to buy other goods they desired at a later point in time. Since wheat could be subdivided into small quantities when required, it facilitated barter for the whole range of products that were available for trade.

The period around 5000 BC is when people seem to have started using wheat as a 'medium of exchange.' Artifacts discovered around the Mediterranean Sea depict scenes of marketplaces where various items are exchanged for specified quantities of wheat. Similarly, barley was also used as a medium of exchange around 4500 BC in the southern part of Mesopotamia and southwest Asia.

1.B - The Transition from Wheat / Barley to Gold / Silver

Why are some goods more suited to performing this task of 'medium of exchange?' What are the required properties of a 'medium of exchange' to be an intermediary good for conducting transactions?

From the above historical examples, it is clear that this medium of exchange had to be a commodity that is widely desired for its utility so that all market participants would accept it willingly, and also something that will retain its value over reasonable time periods. In example (2) above, a person selling a cow will accept the medium of exchange knowing that he can use it to buy the rice, pencil, and paper he needs through 3 independent transactions. In example (3) above, Alan will sell the goat to Ben and accept the medium of exchange. In the subsequent year, Alan can use this to buy the rice from Ben, knowing that the medium of exchange will retain its purchasing power over the intervening period. There are no legal contracts required, and the two become independent transactions.

So, the medium of exchange is just an intermediary good that is used to facilitate transactions across timespan and geographical locations. People experimented with all sorts of commodities - wheat, oxen, cowrie shells, tobacco, salt (the word salary comes from salt), tea bricks, feathers, iron, copper, goat, etc. These experiments in the marketplace to choose the most preferred medium of exchange continued for thousands of years and across geographies.

By around 4000 BC, the preferred medium of exchange became metals such as iron and copper. Coins and other utilitarian forms such as arrowheads were preferred over wheat, barley for reasons of greater convenience and durability. These metals retained their property for decades or longer as compared to grains that could be stored only for a few months to a year or two. Within metals, the transition towards precious metals would start around 2800 BC with the introduction of silver as a preferred medium over copper and iron.

By 1200 BC, discs of gold and silver were the preferred medium of exchange in China. By 900 BC, there is evidence of privately issued silver coins. The earliest known gold coins issued by kings were made in 610 BC by King Croesus of Lydia. Several civilizations around this time in places such as Persia, China, and India also independently produced their coinages and this is shown in Fig 1.1. The usage of coinage spread as these cultures traded with one another and realized the benefits of trade as well as the usage of 'money' for conducting these transactions.

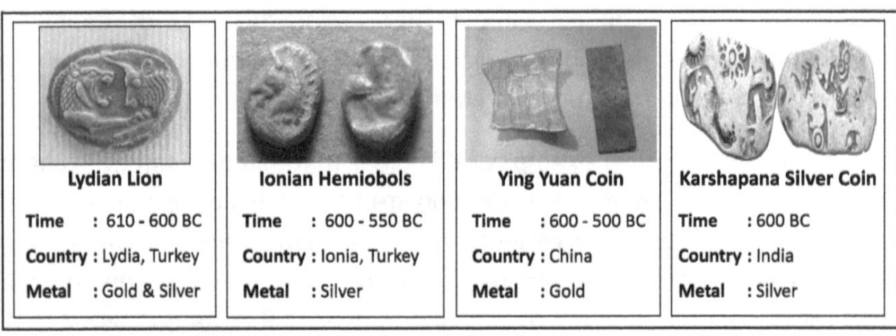

Fig 1.1 Coinages produced by civilizations and used as International trade currency.

We have summarized the 4000+ years of transition from wheat/barley to gold/silver as the preferred medium of exchange in a few paragraphs. This transition happened in the marketplace, with individual members expressing their choices for their preferred form of money.

So what were the characteristics of gold that enabled this acceptance as the best form of money across societies? Aristotle was amongst the earliest to have defined the 'properties of money,' and this was done around 325 BC. Aristotle identified the 5 properties that made gold the best form of money, and these properties were desirable, durable, divisible, convenient, and consistent.

a.   **Desirable** (i.e., has value in itself) - The commodity should be highly desired in the markets for its utility other than money. Wheat was the earliest form of money in primitive societies for obvious reasons. For a society transitioning from a hunter-gatherer lifestyle to a more settled lifestyle based on agriculture, grains were the most precious commodity. As civilizations developed, the preferred money changed first to base metals (copper, iron) and eventually to precious metals (gold, silver). Gold was extensively used in jewelry. These days, it also has many industrial applications as it is the most malleable, ductile and anticorrosive of all metals.

b. **Durable** - The commodity should be durable and retain its properties over long periods of time. Gold is virtually indestructible and even if left at the bottom of the ocean floor for hundreds of years, it retains its properties.

c. **Divisible** - Gold can be divided into as little as 0.001 grams. It still retains the essential properties when split and can easily be put back together as well. In comparison, say a diamond, virtually loses its entire value when divided into just two halves.

d. **Convenient** - Gold is a precious metal and stores enormous value in a very small volume. Houses in most parts of the developed world can be purchased for as little as 10 kg of gold.

e. **Consistent** - Every unit of gold is identical to the other piece and there's no difference whatsoever between them irrespective of where and when it was produced. This makes it very fungible and hence very attractive from a monetary perspective.

Fig 1.2 evaluates the commonly used forms of 'money' on the above 5 parameters and it is easy to see why gold & silver outranked all other commodities in having the ideal characteristics.

	Desirable[1]	Durable	Divisible	Convenient	Consistent
Gold / Silver	✓	✓	✓	✓	✓
Steel	✓	X	✓	X	✓
Diamond	✓	✓	X	✓	X
Real Estate	✓	✓	X	X	X
Salt	✓	X	✓	X	✓
Cigarette / Tobacco	✓	X	✓	X	✓
Cryptocurrency / Bitcoin	X	?	✓	✓	✓
Fiat Currency (e.g. USD)	X	✓	✓	✓	✓

Fig 1.2 - Analysis of commodities in terms of the properties desired of "Money".
Gold / Silver satisfy all the requirements and hence are the ideal form of money.
1. Why would the USD or Bitcoin not be "Desirable"? – The definition of "Desirable" in the table above is for their utility other than "money" and hence the negative score.
2. The "?" on the "Durable" property of bitcoin is explained in the section 1.C

The US adopted a bimetallic standard in 1792 with both gold and silver circulating as money with a fixed exchange ratio between gold and silver at 15:1. Article I, Section 10, Clause 1 of the US Constitution reads **'No State shall make any Thing but gold and silver Coin a Tender in Payment of Debts.'** This bimetallic standard continued till the Civil War after which it has largely been gold that has performed the function of money.

Most economic textbooks would define money as a medium of exchange, unit of account, and a store of value. But the above D3C2 (Desirable, Durable, Divisible, Convenient, and Consistent) is a more comprehensible definition for us to understand why certain commodities cannot serve the *'function of money.'* The most important takeaway from Fig 1.2 is that today's *'paper currencies'* do not fit the definition of money as it has no utility.

1.C - Competitors to Money - Paper Currency, Cryptocurrency (Bitcoin) / Central Bank Digital Currency (CBDC)

The current monetary system of 'Paper Currency' and the to-be-proposed newbie CBDC fail the 'money' test for the same reason - i.e., Desirability. There is no intrinsic value to both these commodities and there is no utility from a consumer perspective.

However, there is one major difference between paper currency and cryptocurrency. While paper currency costs nothing to produce, cryptocurrencies (e.g., Bitcoin) could be very expensive to create at the margins. The latter certainly cannot be created from thin air unlike the US dollar which the US Federal Reserve does with impunity. It, however, fails the monetary test because there is no fundamental utility to cryptocurrencies i.e., there is nothing that can be done with it and the only reason people hold is on expectations of a higher price in the future.

The fact that tens of thousands of dollars are spent on creating a new bitcoin today doesn't mean that the value of the expended factors of production (land, labor, technology, and entrepreneurship) is stored in the bitcoin. In comparison, the factors of production expended on producing gold are stored in the form of the fundamental properties of gold discussed earlier (malleable, utility in jewelry etc.) and available to the owners for eternity subsequently.

The desirability of bitcoin (or any other 'unbacked' cryptocurrency) is a figment of imagination in the minds of speculators. The only reason speculators are buying bitcoin today is the hope of selling it at a higher price tomorrow. Even in the limited use case of anonymous transfer of money, there are thousands of cryptocurrencies and there really is nothing unique about any one cryptocurrency for it to be so highly desirable. This is even after ignoring the above circular-referencing utilitarian argument that is often cited in favor of bitcoin.

But let us say, we accept the desirability argument offered by the proponents of bitcoin. Then the property of 'durability' becomes a question mark. The 'durability' has to be seen in the context of the desirability i.e. non-monetary functional utility. How can we be even sure that people will use 'bitcoin' or any other cryptocurrency for that matter just 10 years down the line for the specified purpose? Leave alone making an argument for a hundred or a thousand years down the line. All these cryptocurrencies are just mathematical algorithms and with compounding processing power, we will definitely have vastly superior algorithms a few decades down the line.

Let us consider a few other scenarios as well to illustrate the fallacious arguments put forth in favor of bitcoin.

1. Why would bitcoin or any of the unbacked-cryptocurrencies be better than a gold-backed cryptocurrency from a 'desirability' perspective? The latter would offer all of the advantages of anonymous transfer of money or whatever functional use cases the proponents can come up with and additionally have the intrinsic value of gold. These gold-backed cryptocurrencies would satisfy the property of desirability and durability better than bitcoin. Speculators who buy bitcoin instead of the gold-backed cryptocurrency today are doing so ONLY anticipating the price appreciation in bitcoin.

2. Let us consider another situation where a 'bytecoin' is introduced with exactly the same algorithm as bitcoin with some minor tweaks only for the purpose of differentiation. Should the 'bytecoin' market eventually not have the same market capitalization as bitcoin if all other properties are similar? Should the fact that El Salvador and a few other speculators gave bitcoin a head start ensure a competitive advantage for eternity when intrinsically they are the same? What if we get a 100 such identical clones tomorrow? Shouldn't the

> market capitalization of bitcoin be shared by all these near-identical cryptocurrencies?

3. Let's also consider the situation where bitcoin and dogecoin have the same market price. What would the rationale for recommending bitcoin instead of dogecoin be? At a fundamental level, there is no difference whatsoever between these cryptocurrencies and the only reason why bitcoin is recommended is because of the first-mover advantage.

Bitcoin thus doesn't have the essential properties of money and fleeing from the US dollar into bitcoin would be a case of 'jumping from the frying pan into the fire.' At least the former has the legal tender laws and the might of the US army backing its purchasing power today. While some proponents consider gold and bitcoin to be similar, I think bitcoin's immediate past & future has been and will be similar to that of the DXY. When the US dollar collapses, holders of bitcoin will realize that the bitcoin they are holding is no different from the digital entry of US dollars that they have in their bank accounts.

This should lead the reader to a follow-on question: Instead of bitcoin, can we consider the gold-backed cryptocurrencies as 'money?' The first response would be 'Which one?' There are about 9000 'active' cryptocurrencies as of April 2024 though only a handful are gold-backed. But if the idea of a gold-backed cryptocurrency gains traction, we can be assured that we will have hundreds of such cryptocurrencies within a short period of time. In addition, investors in the gold-backed cryptocurrency would still have to be concerned about the third party honoring the contract on the day of redemption.

The unique property of gold is that it is the ONLY financial asset that is not simultaneously the liability of another party. Gold was desired 3000 years ago for usage in jewelry and that continues to be the case to this day. It can be said with reasonable certainty that gold will continue to be valued in the market for hundreds or even thousands of years into the future and that no replacement will come along readily.

But aren't most people buying gold today also doing so for the same reasons as the buyers of Bitcoin / Cryptocurrency i.e., expectation of a higher price for tomorrow? Probably. But there will always be end users who will buy gold for its utility in jewelry and industrial applications. It is this utility that is lacking in bitcoin. The ONLY reason people are buying bitcoin is the expectation of a higher price.

A good comparison would be to consider the inmates of prisons where even today cigarette is the most accepted form of money. Inmates who hold cigarettes do not have to be the end consumers themselves; they just have to be convinced that there will be end users in the future for the cigarettes that they are holding as 'money' today.

1.D - The State's Antagonism to Gold – An Introduction

Incidentally, kings and governments have never willingly accepted gold as money. This aversion to gold by the rulers continues to this day and the reasons will be elaborated in Chapter 3. Technically, with gold circulating as money, we do not need a central bank, at least in their current omnipotent role. Within the US itself, there were two failed attempts at Central Banking during the 18th and 19th centuries. However, the powers of these banks pale in comparison to what the Federal Reserve has today. These banks could issue banknotes on behalf of the United States government without 100% backing by bullion. However, both these had a limited time charter and the antagonism to the concept of a 'central bank' amongst the general public was so widespread that these were not renewed.

1. The Bank of United States, or more commonly referred to as the First Bank, was given a 20-year charter from 1791 to 1811.

2. The Second Bank of United States was also given a 20-year charter from 1816 to 1836.

A more recent example of the government's antagonism to the free market system of gold as money would be the formation of the Federal Reserve in 1913 and even more tellingly, Nixon closing the 'Gold Window' in 1971. This moment marked a 'temporary intermission' to the long tenure of more than 2500 years that gold has had as 'money.' But as we shall see in Chapter 4 and Chapter 5, it's only a matter of time before gold gets reinstated into its rightful place as money. The thesis of this book is that the same will happen before the end of the current decade.

One of the best expositions of the role of gold as money and why governments / kings since time immemorial have hated gold was written by Alan Greenspan. Written in 1966 (available in Appendix I) by *The Maestro*, it explains why gold and economic freedom are inseparable and go hand in hand. But this is a very cryptic essay and a more understandable explanation of key parts of the essay will be provided in Chapter 3.

We have tried to establish how gold emerged as money in the free market and has indeed served the purpose of 'money' till 1971. How did the transition from the 'gold' to 'paper' happen? This move happened gradually over many decades and will be explained in Section 3.A 'What is The Gold Standard?'

Chapter 1 - Takeaways

1. The progression from a barter system to transactions based on money.

2. How gold evolved as the most superior form of money over other competing commodities / assets

3. The D3C2 (Desirable, Durable, Divisible, Convenient, and Consistent) characteristics required of money.

4. Why bitcoin or other cryptocurrencies cannot be money.

Chapter 1 - Suggested Reading

1. *"What has Government done to our Money?"* by Murray Rothbard

2. *"The Penniless Billionaires"* by Max Shapiro

Unbacked Paper Currency - The Ultimate Retrograde Step in History

The first recorded use of "paper currency" was in China during the 7th century AD. It was a means to reduce the requirement of carrying heavy copper coins to conduct transactions. In other words, the paper represented a certain claim on copper coins that were circulating as money. So paper money was a Certificate or a Currency that had a claim over tangible goods to be delivered by the signatory of the Certificate.

While similar isolated instances of paper currency circulated in various parts of the world, the concept arose in wide prominence in parallel with the advent of banking. During the 17th century, it was a common practice for London's goldsmith bankers to issue receipts that were redeemable for bullion. It was not until 1844 that the Charter Act was established and the Bank of England was granted a monopoly on issuing banknotes i.e., what is now commonly referred to as the "Central Bank." But even with the Bank of England and other such central banks, these notes were redeemable for gold / silver bullion. In other words, the banknotes were a liability of the issuer that had to be settled through a fixed weight of bullion. The Pound Sterling was a pound by weight of sterling silver.

The Federal Reserve Act of 1913 established the Central Bank for the US to supposedly provide a safe and flexible monetary system. Similar to the Pound Sterling, the US dollar was defined as approximately 1/20th an ounce of gold and the paper dollar was redeemable in gold bullion across the counter.

Even while the convertibility of the US dollar across the counter was suspended for US citizens with Executive Order 6102 in 1933, this option continued to remain open for foreign central banks holding US dollars. The point to remember is that even with a central bank monopoly to issue currency, these "paper currencies" were redeemable for a fixed weight of gold/silver by a few select market participants. So the paper currency, albeit in a very tenuous way, continued to represent a claim on gold/silver till Nixon closed the Gold Window in 1971.

Fig 2.1 – As printed *"Redeemable in Gold on Demand at the United Stated Treasury, or in Gold or Lawful Money at any Federal Reserve Bank"*
Signed Andrew Mellon, Secretary of the Treasury (1921 – 32)

A critical flaw in the paper certificates as well as the Federal Reserve Note above was that the value was not defined in terms of the fixed weight of gold/silver/copper that it claimed to represent. It was this omission that permitted the devaluation (from a dollar being defined as $1/20^{th}$ to $1/35^{th}$ of a gold ounce) and the eventual default on the delivery of gold against these notes by the Federal Reserve.

While "Paper Currency" (redeemable in bullion at some level) had been widely adopted for more than 100 years then, the change that happened in 1971 was astronomical. Few understood the significance of the move despite the immediate consequences of widespread stagflation (inflation combined with a recession) during the 1970s. However, the real catastrophic consequence of the 1971 move is set to play out in the years just ahead. Given that 50 years have elapsed between the cause and the consequences, very few are going to correlate the two events - at least in the initial stages of the crisis that lies ahead. This book has been written from the perspective of enabling the reader to connect-the-dots - between the economic depression / hyperinflation ahead and the closure of the Gold Window in 1971.

It would be useful to point out an event that the average reader might consider as trivia. Dr. Ron Paul, a medical doctor by profession, joins the

US Congress as a consequence of the above act by Nixon to put the US dollar back on the gold standard. Over the subsequent decades, he would go on to inspire a whole generation of individuals - in favor of free markets, limited government, sound money, and libertarianism - around the world. Including me.

2.A - The difference between Redeemable and Irredeemable Paper Currencies

For the rest of the book, the phrase "paper currency" would mean an unbacked/ irredeemable one unless explicitly stated otherwise. When economic commentators refer to paper currency as an innovation these days, they are referring to the irredeemable version indeed.

Now it doesn't matter whether the currency is backed by gold or even copper, iron, cow, salt, cigarettes, etc., or any of the other innumerable commodities that have circulated as money throughout history. The rationale remains much the same. Gold is the best form of "money" and other commodities satisfy the "requirements for being money" to varying lesser degrees. But the explanation below is valid as long as the currency is backed by something i.e. redeemable paper currency. Whether it is backed by gold or salt, it doesn't make a lot of difference for the specific purpose of the explanation below.

Let us say that an individual is buying a car for $50,000 today. Let us also assume that the US dollar is backed by gold and is defined as 1/2000th of an ounce of gold. Or as is more easily understood, gold is priced at $2000/oz. What this implies is that when a car is purchased for $50,000, the car is being exchanged for 25 ounces of gold.

But what happens when the same transaction is conducted with an unbacked paper currency? A car is being exchanged for pieces of paper (or a digital transfer of this amount) that virtually cost nothing to produce. So the producer of these pieces of paper has an incentive to create as many of these currency units as possible and buy all the cars in the world.

Thus paper currency creates a system where one entity, i.e., the creator of the paper currency - the government, gains at the expense of another i.e., the producers. The government (or the first recipient of the dole-outs) gets something for free while the other entity has to expend the factors of production to earn the same paper currency. The obvious beneficiary is the government that holds the monopoly power to create this paper currency and spend it first.

2.B - Consequences of an Unbacked Paper Currency System

A question that should arise in the minds of readers at this stage should be "What are the consequences of entrusting this capacity to create purchasing power from thin air to the Federal Reserve?"

The answer to the above question must be a very obvious one. What happens when you give the power to politicians to spend at will with little near-term consequences? Of course, they will create as many dollars as would be tolerated and spend on all populist schemes and that's exactly what we have witnessed over the last 50 years in the US. So "RIP USD" is the short easy answer to the question. The hard part is the timelines. Suffice to say at this juncture that it is not a question of "IF" but "WHEN."

Parameters	1900 to 1971	1971 to 2023
Growth in US National Debt	$2.1 B to $398 B	$398B to $34 T
Growth in US Money Supply (M2)	$287 B to $710 B	$710 B to $20.8 T
Growth in US GDP (in trillion USD)	0.59 T to $5.1 T	$5.1 T to $20.5 T
National Debt to GDP ratio	7.8% (1971)	120% (2023)
M2 to GDP ratio	13.9% (1971)	101% (2023)

Fig 2.2 - Analysis of the Gold Standard and the Paper Currency Standard to show the explosion of Debt & Money Supply under the latter.

Fig 2.2 provides a comparison of the various parameters for the 52 years post 1971 and for the 71 years before that. The debt-to-GDP which will be discussed in Chapter 4 is now at 120% while it was less than 10% by 1971. Remember that the period 1900 to 1971 had two world wars while the subsequent 50-year period witnessed the longest peacetime expansion in recorded history. As will be shown in section 3.A, in the absence of the two world wars, the national debt would have been well under $100B by 1971. Despite the overwhelmingly favorable economic conditions in the latter time period, debt has skyrocketed in absolute terms. Even as a % of GDP, the difference is staggering. It is this debt that is going to cause the eventual demise of the US dollar.

Will more Paper Currency help?

It is useful to answer these questions within a microcosm of the society as it's easier to understand the consequences. Let's just imagine that the entire world is just one island and there is no source of external trade. We can start with the amount of paper currency that the island has in circulation today and further add a condition that this quantity is going to be held constant for the next century. Will it hamper progress and development?

The key point to remember is that "paper currency" or "money" for that matter is useful not for its consumption value but only for its transaction value. To that extent, anything that we consume - food, cars, laptops, entertainment services, houses etc. - society benefits from an additional supply of these goods and services. In the case of paper currency or money, it only serves the purpose of divvying up the goods already produced and so an additional supply only serves the purpose of driving up the cost of existing goods.

So all of this additional supply of paper currency, i.e. monetary inflation (to be defined more precisely in the next chapter), causes the prices of a basket of goods to rise as compared to the earlier period.

Does this mean there are no benefits in producing more gold? Of course not. Remember that money has to be a highly desired commodity to start with for its other utilities. It is this desirability by consumers that is the primary reason why gold is money to begin with. So an additional supply of gold would mean increased jewelry, electronics and other industrial applications. Only from a monetary perspective, we don't need any more gold than what we have.

Chapter 2 - Takeaways

1. Evolution of redeemable paper certificates/currency - backed by physical assets like gold, silver, and copper.

2. Difference between unbacked/fiat and Redeemable paper currencies.

3. Consequences of the fiat currency system as can be observed in the US today.

Chapter 2 - Suggested Reading

1. "The Case for Gold" by Dr. Ron Paul.

2. "End the Fed" by Dr. Ron Paul.

3. "The Creature from Jekyll Island" by Edward Griffin.

4. "Money of the Mind: How the 1980s Got That Way: Borrowing and Lending in America from the Civil War to Michael Milken" by James Grant.

Government's Antagonism to Gold

An almost hysterical antagonism toward the gold standard is one issue which unites statists of all persuasions. They seem to sense - perhaps more clearly and subtly than many consistent defenders of laissez-faire -- that gold and economic freedom are inseparable, that the gold standard is an instrument of laissez-faire and that each implies and requires the other.

- Gold and Economic Freedom, Alan Greenspan (1967)

Greenspan wrote the article "Gold and Economic Freedom" in The Objectivist and he was a disciple of Ayn Rand at that time. Most readers would be familiar with Ayn Rand's fictions - "Atlas Shrugged" and "The Fountainhead." Rand was an American writer espousing the ideals of capitalism, the gold standard, and individual liberty. She named her philosophy "Objectivism" and advocated the same through her fictional works and other writings. Greenspan was prescient to understand that statists understood the virtues of the gold standard far better than the avowed free-market advocates. As I will explain in this chapter and the next, if we are to lay the blame on only one individual for all of the monetary imbalances and the economic crises that lie ahead, it would have to be Alan Greenspan.

Much of the intellectual cover for what Greenspan did was provided by Milton Friedman and the Monetarists through their arguments in favor of "Neutrality of Money" and "Equation of Exchange." Many Austrian Economists consider Friedman equally culpable, if not more than Greenspan, as responsible for the current bankruptcy of the US. Some details on the above-mentioned issues have been included as part of "Suggested Reading" at the end of Chapter 3. A supposed advocate of "Free Market Capitalism," Milton Friedman had long been a critic of the gold standard.

So what is it about gold that makes the governments hate and belittle the role of the same in commerce? There are three specific policies that governments love to indulge in under the guise of public welfare - deficit spending, setting artificially low interest rates, and third is a consequence of the first two i.e., creating monetary inflation. Under a gold standard, none of the above three favored instruments of public policy are possible.

It is necessary at this juncture to point out one crucial economic axiom that will be explained later in this section. All of the above three policies mentioned above are deleterious for the economy and merely serve to protect and grow the interests of the government at the expense of the common man. Essentially, gold limits the power of governments and hence the vehement opposition to "gold" by governments of nearly all persuasions.

The three specific constraints placed on the government by gold are as below:

1. **Deficit Spending:** Deficit spending is the mechanism by which a government spends more than its revenues in a given time period, typically a fiscal year. The gold standard if implemented even in a diluted form restraints deficit spending by the government. We will also show how once the restraints of gold are removed, it is only a matter of time before the deficits and the consequent debt accumulated by governments overwhelm the system.

2. **Interest Rate Manipulations:** An explanation of how the gold standard prevents interest rate manipulations by central banks. These artificially low interest rates engineered by the central banks cause malinvestments and the boom-bust cycles.

3. **Monetary Inflation:** An explanation of what monetary inflation is and why the lack of a gold standard will eventually result in the (monetary) inflationary death spiral for an economy.

Before getting into the details of how the Gold Standard achieves the above, it is useful to expand on what the Gold standard means. There have been several versions of the gold standard over the decades and most of them have not stood the test of time making the bystander conclude that "gold" failed. That is most certainly not the case as will be explained below.

3.A - What is "The Gold Standard?"

Was the US dollar on "The Gold Standard" before 1971? There are valid arguments to be presented for both answers to the above question and these differences arise out of what each individual perceives to be the correct version of *The Gold Standard.*

So it is worthwhile to explain what **The Gold Standard** is. Different forms of the gold standard that have been adopted over the course of the monetary history of the world over the last 200 years. The readers need to understand the staged dilution of the "Gold Standard" that has occurred over this period of time. So while technically the dollar was on the gold standard till 1971, it was a very different and weakened form of the free-market gold standard that prevailed before the formation of the Federal Reserve in 1913. The correct terminology for what prevailed during 1971 is the "Gold Exchange Standard."

We will start with the Classical Gold standard that was widely prevalent during the nineteenth century and explain how we eventually reached the current fluctuating fiat currency standard where the role of gold has been completely eliminated for all official purposes. In fact, gold was even referred to as a "barbaric relic" by John Maynard Keynes in 1924. By the time the reader is through with the book, I do hope it is clear that the rightful place for John Maynard Keynes is the "footnotes of history" and not the center stage of economic ideology as is the case today. Incidentally, Keynesian Economics is what is widely taught in most Economic Schools worldwide - perhaps in more than 90% of these institutions.

Why then should central banks even hold gold these days? As readers will understand over the course of reading this book, it is certainly not for reasons of "tradition" as Bernanke remarked in 2011.

3.A.I - The Classical Gold Standard (1815 to 1913)

This was the "free markets" version of the monetary system and operated on the following principles:

1. Nearly all major countries defined their currencies in terms of a fixed weight of gold. For example, the US defined the dollar as 1/20th of an ounce of gold, and the pound sterling was defined as slightly less than 1/4th of an ounce of gold.

2. The above meant that the currencies had a fixed exchange rate between them; not because of regulations but just by the definition of what these

currencies represented. For example, the exchange rate of 1 GBP was fixed at $4.86 as both these represented the same weight of gold.

3. The central banks under the classical gold standard had the predominant function of guaranteeing the convertibility of the currency to gold at a predetermined price.

4. The international balance of payments was settled through gold transfers where the countries with a trade surplus would receive gold. This was a self-correcting mechanism where countries with trade deficits would witness an outflow of gold reserves leading to a contraction in the amount of money within the economy. This would result in a decline in domestic prices and therefore an increase in competitiveness.

5. The classical gold standard provided the basis for checking the monetary inflationary motives of government as it limited the currency in circulation. It also ensured equilibrium for the trade balance amongst nations by limiting or increasing the amount of money in circulation in accordance with the trade balance. The flexibility desired of a monetary system was thus implicitly built into the classical gold standard.

It is easy to understand why the above monetary system would have allowed for the development of free international trade and investments without any of the competitive devaluations that are commonplace today.

So why did the world even move away from the system that worked so well?

The world did not move from the classical gold standard to the fiat system that we have today overnight. Readers should remember that the defining feature of the classical gold standard was the convertibility of the currency into money across the counter for the citizens.

In fact, the difference between currency and money was extremely well understood back then. Currencies (US Dollar, British Pound, German Mark, Indian Rupee, etc.) had value ONLY when they were backed by money (gold or silver) and the test of this backing was ready convertibility for its citizens. Currencies under the classical gold standard were just warehouse receipts for a fixed quantity of money, i.e., gold.

This distinction between currency and money is now lost and these words are used interchangeably when they mean very different things. This distinction was erased from the minds of people between the two World Wars through a series of steps by the US government. While the first steps may not have been initiated with the intention of completely delinking gold from the currency, it was a foreseeable conclusion if one understood the constraints that gold imposed on the governments.

It was the folly of trusting governments to not inflate their currencies that caused the failure of the classical gold standard. It was not the failure of gold - but exactly the opposite. Gold was doing an exceptional job of not allowing the governments to inflate their currencies.

Wars have always been a convenient excuse for governments. Amidst WW-I, the Federal Reserve Act was legislated during 1917 that compelled the banks to keep a minimum ratio of reserves to deposits and these reserves could only be kept at the Federal Reserve Banks. Gold could no longer be part of the legal reserves of commercial banks and had to be deposited at the Federal Reserve. In one stroke, this

> *You never let a serious crisis go to waste. And what I mean by that it's an opportunity to do things you think you could not do before.*
>
> *— Rahm Emanuel*

move took the public off the gold convertibility habit and placed it under the monopoly control of the US government. The citizens, however, came to see the Federal Reserve as performing a public service that would guarantee their gold at all times.

The US entered World War I only towards the end of 1917, and therefore the war had a limited monetary inflationary impact on the dollar as compared to most other countries. By some estimates, the world could have returned to the classical gold standard post WW-I by resetting the exchange rates of other currencies with the US dollar. For example, the British pound would have to be devalued to $3.50 from the earlier $4.86 due to the greater monetary inflation of the British pound as part of WW-I.

Whether it was for reasons of *"national pride"* in not devaluing their currencies or to just persist with their wartime-learned tactics of monetary inflation, the devaluation that would have permitted a return to the classical gold standard did not occur. As a result, over the next nearly 50 years, the world would stumble from one monetary crisis to another in experimenting with increasingly diluted versions of the gold standard.

I. **The Gold Exchange Standard (1926 to 1931):** The monetary inflation of WWI meant that most countries could not continue on the classical gold standard excepting the US. So, a scheme where the US would continue on the classical gold standard, Britain would redeem the Pounds in Gold / US dollars, and other major economies would redeem their currencies in British Pounds was devised. This was essentially done to maintain the pre-WWI currency exchange rates but was unworkable due to the interim monetary inflation. This made maintaining the exchange rates an indefensible proposition from the hard money advocates, as Britain would learn in 1931.

II. **Fluctuating Fiat Currency Standard (1931 to 1945):** With the collapse of the Gold exchange standard, the world was under monetary chaos for a couple of years. The US, which had continued on the classical gold standard till 1933, suspended convertibility for its citizens citing the Great Depression. To account for the monetary inflation of WWI as well as the roaring twenties, the US devalued the Dollar from $1/20^{th}$ to $1/35^{th}$ an ounce of gold and maintained convertibility ONLY for foreign central banks at this fixed exchange rate. Other currencies would freely fluctuate in the international markets against the US dollar.

III. **Bretton Woods and the New Gold Exchange Standard (1945 to 1971):** Towards the end of WWII, the world was looking for a restoration of monetary order of fixed exchange rates and this would happen at the Bretton Woods conference in 1944. Under this, the US Dollar was defined as $1/35^{th}$ an ounce of Gold and was redeemable for the foreign Central Banks but not for its citizens. As far as other currencies were concerned, these returned to the fixed exchange rate vis-à-vis the US Dollar at pre-WWII rates. For example, the Pound still was defined as 4.86 dollars though the gold that allowed this earlier definition was no longer available with Britain.

The Bretton Woods agreement would enable a very peculiar form of monetary inflation. The US could inflate knowing that only foreign Central Banks could ask for redemption of the dollar for gold at the fixed rate of $1/35^{th}$ an ounce of gold. But as long as the foreign currencies also inflated their currencies at a similar rate using the dollar as a reserve, the system would work fine. It seemed to work till about the middle of the 1960s, although by design this was doomed for failure from day one.

Fig 3.1 - Bretton Woods (1944), hailed as an *"Impregnable Monetary System"*, this currency standard based on fixed exchange rates was doomed from the start.

By design, Bretton Woods enabled cartelization of central banks where they could all inflate at the same rate and citizens would be powerless to insulate themselves from the adverse consequences. But all it needed was for just one or two hard money advocates to not "fall in line" and the system would stand exposed as is the case with all cartels. That's exactly what happened as well.

Incidentally, this Bretton Woods agreement was described as *"a permanent and impregnable monetary system"* by the US political and economic establishment at the time of its creation. The system would start unraveling when the hard money nations of France and Switzerland would start converting their US dollars into gold. Knowing that the stock of gold would cover just a fraction of the dollars in circulation, the then US President Richard Nixon would close the gold window in 1971 bringing to an end the Bretton Woods agreement.

IV. **Free Floating Fiat Currencies (1973 to date):** This is the current system of pure fiat currencies without any tangible "money" backing the currencies and works entirely on the confidence of the people and the legal tender laws in the system. A very misplaced confidence as we are all going to realize over the next few years as the US Dollar gets inflated well beyond the range of possibilities considered by the mainstream economists today.

I do have a request for first-time readers at this juncture. The section *"3.A - What is The Gold Standard?"* can be appreciated better after understanding the three constraints imposed by gold that are explained in sections 3.B to 3.D. So while the introductory note served the purpose of explaining the historical degradation from the classical gold standard to the current free-floating system, the rationale can be better understood if the reader is cognizant of the motives behind the movement away from gold.

3.B - Golden Hand-Cuff I - Restraining Deficit Spending

"...government deficit spending under a gold standard is severely limited. The abandonment of the gold standard made it possible for the welfare statists to use the banking system as a means to an unlimited expansion of credit. They have created paper reserves in the form of government bonds which -- through a complex series of steps -- the banks accept in place of tangible assets and treat as if they were an actual deposit, i.e., as the equivalent of what was formerly a deposit of gold."

- Alan Greenspan, Gold and Economic Freedom

3.B.I - Fiscal Deficits

Governments, especially democracies, have an insatiable appetite for expenditures that exceeds the revenues and this difference on an annual basis is the fiscal deficit. In the case of the US, this appetite for expenditures is fueled by both warfare (referred to as the Military-Industrial Complex by Eisenhower) and domestic pork barrel expenditures (euphemistically referred to as "welfare").

Under a gold standard, there is a natural limitation on this deficit as the new required money cannot be issued at the will of the governments. This is also the reason why consumer price inflation is practically non-existent under a gold standard (more on this in section 3.D). However, once the linkages to gold are removed, governments embark on the path of deficit spending under one pretext or another.

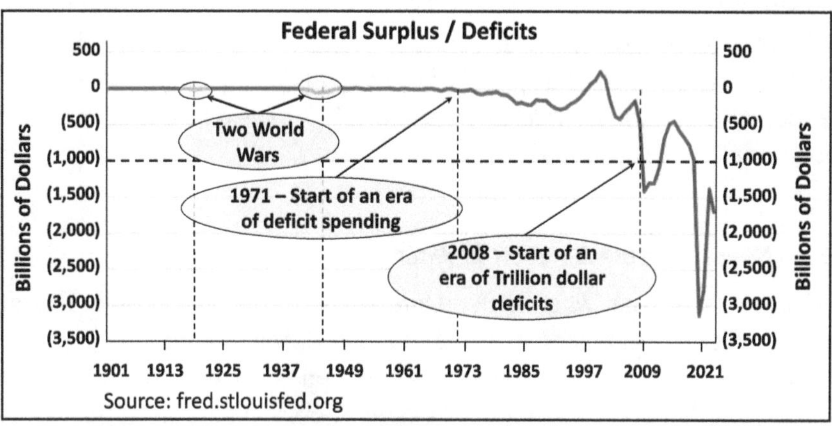

Fig 3.2 - Federal surplus / deficits from 1900 to date. Since 1971, the US has had perpetual deficits. Since 2008, it has almost routinely been trillion dollar deficits. We are close to a point where 2+ trillion dollar deficits becomes the norm.

Fig 3.2 is a graph of the annual federal surplus/deficits from 1900 to date. As can be seen, deficits were practically non-existent till the early 1970s. The tiny bump preceding the 1970s was the two World War years, and these also were reversed (the debts were not paid back; just that the size of the future deficits were dramatically reduced) once the wars ended.

The inflection point in the above graph is 1971, and as can be inferred from Greenspan's observations on deficit spending, this is not entirely a coincidence. Even under the diluted forms of the gold standard as existed between 1914 and 1971, deficit spending on a grandiose scale was confined to the World War years.

Why was the Gold Window closed in 1971? - Why not 10 years earlier, for instance?

It was in 1944 that the Bretton Woods agreement was negotiated for a supposedly "efficient" foreign exchange system. Under this, the value of the dollar was pegged at 1/35th of an ounce (or in other words, the Federal Reserve would redeem US Dollars at the rate of an ounce of gold for $35 for the foreign central banks) and other currencies were pegged to the US Dollar at fixed exchange rates. The Bretton Woods system became functional by 1958.

This Bretton Woods system of fixed exchange rates granted an enormous privilege to the US Dollar. As Economist Eichengreen summarized, *"It costs only a few cents for the Bureau of Engraving and Printing to produce a $100 bill, but other countries had to pony up $100 of actual goods in order to obtain one."*

3.B.II - National Debt - A Nation Drowning in Debt

In a given fiscal year, when expenditure exceeds the revenues, a budget or a fiscal deficit is the outcome. To pay for this deficit, the federal government borrows money by selling marketable securities typically Treasury bonds (typically 20-30 year maturity), Treasury notes (between 2 to 10 year maturities), Treasury bills (under 52 days) and Treasury inflation-protected securities (between 5 and 30 year maturities).

The national debt is the total of the above borrowings to cover the federal deficits over time. So while fiscal deficit refers to the excess of expenses over revenues in a given fiscal year, the national debt at a given point in time is the accumulation of these fiscal surplus/deficit numbers since the formation of the Republic.

To give an example, the fiscal deficit during FY2023 was $1.7 trillion. This is the excess of expenditures incurred during FY2023 over the revenues collected during the same period. The national debt was $33.17 trillion by FY2023. This is the sum of the accumulated fiscal deficits from 1789 to 2023.

How about the reported budget surplus years towards the late 1990s? Shouldn't these reduce the national debt? Technically, yes. However, there are a number of line items that do not make it to the accounting statements but still are funded by the federal government. Therefore, the growth in the national debt year-on-year is a much better reflection of the fiscal deficits than the officially reported fiscal deficit. In the example of FY2023 given above, the reported fiscal deficit was $1.7 trillion though the national debt grew by $2.24 trillion during the same fiscal year. So a decrease in national debt is a better indicator than a fiscal surplus to conclude if the government's expenditures have indeed been met with the revenues generated for a given time period. **Not coincidentally, *since 1971, we have not had a single year in which the national debt decreased when compared with the previous fiscal***

year. So even the budget surpluses of the late 1990s as shown in Fig 3.2 were more of an accounting surplus rather than a real one.

Right till the 1960s, Americans generally believed in balanced budgets as the path to prosperity. Even more so, the linear relationship between budget deficits and consumer price inflation was extremely well understood by economists and the public back then. As shown in Fig 3.2, balanced budgets were the norm and national debt was a non-issue back then. Even by 1960, the accumulated national debt was only $286 Billion. Adjusting for price inflation, it would be about $3 trillion today.

Digging deeper, the two World Wars spanning 11 years (WW I during 1914-19 and WW II during 1939-45) accounted for $242 Billion or nearly 85% of the debt of $286B accumulated between 1789 and 1960. The remaining 160 years cumulatively accounted for just $44 Billion.

However, persuaded by his economic advisors, John Kennedy (1961-63) embarked on a program of deficit spending to apparently smoothen the business cycles and lower unemployment. The economic consequence of price inflation was indeed recognized back then, but Kennedy was convinced by his economic advisors that low price inflation was a good trade-off for eliminating the business cycles. That, as with most government programs, was the proverbial "camel's nose under the tent."

Once the theoretical foundations (a very immoral one apart from being intellectually flawed) for deficit spending were established, new requirements naturally arose. Lyndon Johnson who succeeded Kennedy, almost immediately launched the Great Society programs in 1964. The Gulf of Tonkin incident in 1964 (a false flag attack) allowed for a great expansion of the Vietnam War expenditures. Within just 1 year into the Presidency, Lyndon Johnson had turned around the traditional "Guns vs. Butter" argument into "Guns and Butter." Fiscal deficits exploded and the national debt that was $317 billion in 1965 would grow by more than 25% to $398 billion in the next 6 years. While these increases raised serious concerns back then, these numbers appear to be rounding-off errors compared to the scale of increase in national debt these days. This only goes to show how much the US government has moved the needle on national debt increases over the decades.

Year	National Debt (in $ Billion)	Growth in National Debt (over 5 preceding years)	CAGR (preceding 5 years)
1945	258		
1950	257	- 1	0 %
1955	274	14	1.29 %
1960	286	12	0.86 %
1965	317	31	2.08 %
1970	370	53	3.14 %
1971	398	28	7.56 %
		(1 year 1970 - 1971)	(1 year 1970 – 1971)

Fig 3.3 - The launch of the *"The Great Society"* program in 1964 and the escalating Vietnam war expenditures lead to a significant growth in the National Debt.

By 1971, the US Money Supply had vastly increased in line with the federal budget deficits of the preceding years. This was not missed by the hard money nations in Europe, and sticking to the Bretton Woods agreement under such conditions would undervalue their currencies, resulting in price inflation in their local economies. So how did these countries respond?

In May 1971, West Germany left the Bretton Woods system as it undervalued their currency and the Deutsche Mark rose 7.5% subsequently. Realizing that the US government had indeed created too many dollars compared to the gold reserves it held, other central banks started redeeming their dollar holdings for gold. Both Switzerland and France converted a substantial portion of their dollar holdings into gold in July 1971.

With other countries threatening to follow suit, on Aug 15th, 1971, Richard Nixon announced the unilateral closure of the Gold Window such that foreign central banks could no longer exchange their dollars for gold at the fixed exchange rate of $35/ounce. This was an act of financial default by the US government, though very few economic commentators would define it as such - back then or, for that matter, even today.

The biggest losers on account of the above act by Nixon were not the foreign central banks but the US dollar and the US citizens. The Gold Window was the last restraint on deficit spending. With that out of the way, the US government would go on to indulge in deficit spending in a manner that would put the most outrageous forecasts to shame. Annual trillion-dollar deficits have been the norm for the last 5 years, and we are not far from the situation where trillion dollars a quarter becomes the standard. This could start as early as H2 of 2024 or 2025.

Fig 3.4 shows the increase in national debt and the explosion in growth after 1971 is obvious. The national debt by 1971 was less than $400 billion and out of this $240 billion happened during the two World Wars. So the total national debt accumulated inclusive of the interest payments for the 182 years leading up to 1971, excluding the two World Wars, was just $160 billion. That's the addition to the national debt in a fortnight these days.

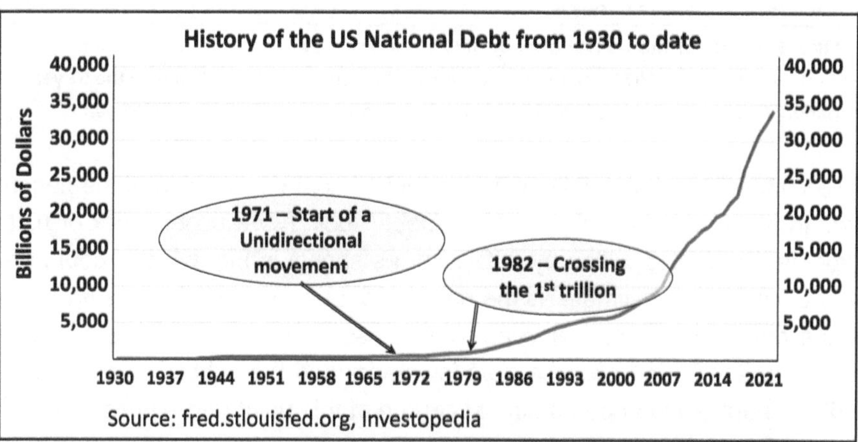

Fig 3.4 - The first $1 trillion took nearly 200 years (i.e. 1789 to 1982). The last 2 trillions (32 to 33 trillion & 33 to 34 trillion) have taken 92 days and 105 days.

i.   **Post 1971, we have not had a single year where the national debt has decreased on a year-on-year basis.**

It would be interesting to analyze the historical growth of national debt, and a summary of the same is provided in Fig 3.5. A few key events have been taken to identify the patterns of growth within the 225 years period. These events are the formation of the US Federal Reserve in 1914 (technically, December 1913), the two World Wars period, and the biggest event of all in 1971, i.e., closure of the Gold Window.

Year / Period	National Debt (in $ Billion)	CAGR of National Debt	Monetary System
1800	0.083	From $83 million to $2.91 billion over 114 years for a **CAGR of 3.17%**	**The Classical Gold Standard** 1914 had two historic events – the creation of the US Federal Reserve and World War I.
1900	2.14		
1914	2.91		
1914 – 1919	2.91 to 27.4	**CAGR of 56.5%** during WW-I	**Federal Reserve Standard*** A CAGR of 9.01% over 57 years with various forms of the Gold standard.
1919 – 1939	27.4 to 40.44	**CAGR of 1.96%** over 20 years	
1939 - 1945	40.44 to 258.68	**CAGR of 36%** during WW-II	
1945 - 1971	258.68 to 398.13	**CAGR of 1.68%** over 26 years	
1971 - 2023	398.13 to 33,167	**CAGR of 8.75%** over 52 years	**Fiat Currency Standard**
Source : fiscaldata.treasury.gov			

Fig 3.5 History of the US National Debt with milestones

*** - Between 1914 to 1971, the total expansion of the debt was $395 billion over the 57 year period. Out of this, the two World Wars alone accounted for $243 billion over 11 years.**

Projection of the National Debt: If one looks into the projection of the national debt from the popular website of "US Debt Clock" (www.usdebtclock.org), it is expected to hit $45 trillion by 2027. But as shown in Fig 3.4, this could be a very conservative estimate as the national debt is currently increasing almost at the rate of $3 trillion per year. This is assuming that the current housing bubble doesn't burst over the next few years and the bubble bursting during 2024 or early 2025 appears almost certain at this point (more in section 4.C). If the GFC 2008 and the increase in national debt during that period is any indication, i.e., more than an 18% increase between 2008 and 2009, we could well reach $50 trillion by 2026.

3.B.III - Unaccounted / Unfunded Liabilities:

Any discussion on the national debt that skips the unaccounted liabilities of the US government is missing the proverbial "elephant in the room." While the acknowledged national debt is about $34+ trillion and is unmanageable as it is, the unaccounted portion is an additional $200 trillion.

Almost 90% of this unaccounted liabilities emanate from just two federal programs - Medicare and Social Security. These two programs account for $175 trillion according to the "US Government Financial Report for the Fiscal

Year 2023." These are the official US Government estimates which have historically always been very conservative. Despite that, we are grappling with unfathomable numbers here.

The traditional term used to refer to these is "Unfunded Liabilities." This is a very misleading term as it somehow implies that the other part of the national debt, i.e., the $34 trillion, is somehow funded. The correct terminology and the one that we will use going forward is "Unaccounted Liabilities" as these do not show up in the national debt though by standards of accrual accounting, they should. Just to put this in context, had the same accounting error been committed by a private organization, the executives would be behind bars.

Medicare was started by Lyndon Johnson as part of the "Great Society program" in 1965 while Social Security was started during the Great Depression period by Franklin Roosevelt. Both have been functioning as "pay as you go along" programs. Though both these have trust funds, it has been run without the accounting discipline that would be mandatory for such large public programs.

Even with the acknowledged debt of $34 trillion, a default (the nature of default will be explained in sec 4.E) by the US Government is a certainty. So this additional $175+ trillion mentioned above has no conceivable chance of being serviced by the US Government. The nature of default remains the unanswered question. That said, politically, the US government will find it impossible to "explicitly" default on the unaccounted liabilities as these are programs for which citizens have made payments.

The Social Security program is widely recognized as the backbone of the US retirement system. In 2023, more than 57 million Americans received Social Security benefits. For the beneficiaries in the lowest quintile, the Social Security payments represented more than 80% of their total retirement income. Even for workers in the fourth quintile with a median income of more than USD 80,000, social security benefits account for more than 30% of their total retirement income.

The Social Security program is managed through the Old-Age and Survivors Insurance (OASI) Trust Fund. The OASI costs have exceeded the tax inflows into the fund since 2010 as shown in Fig 3.6. Even including the interest earned on the accumulated reserves, costs have exceeded the total receipts since 2021. This deficit is projected to continue indefinitely into the future as well.

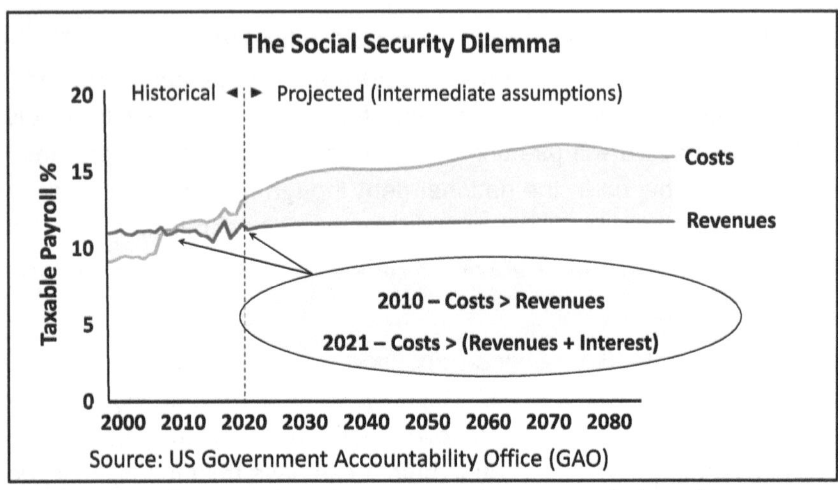

Fig 3.6 - Social Security benefit payments have exceeded total income including interest since 2021.

Payments are being made today by dipping into the accumulated surplus of the OASI Trust Fund. At the current rate, the entire fund is expected to be depleted by 2033. This, of course, is not a problem for 2033, but for the here and now. The payments are being made today by the Federal Reserve monetizing the federal deficits on account of the above payments, and this is just monetary inflation. What the Social Security program is going to put into the pockets of the retirees, the price inflation ahead is going to take away the purchasing power of those very dollars.

While we have defined the nature of the debt problem that lies immediately ahead for the US, the basic issue to understand in this section is that under a gold standard, such levels of debt could never have been accumulated. Citizens / other holders of the US dollar would have converted their dollars to gold, bankrupting the government well before the accumulation of debt of any significant magnitude. It's the fiat monetary system and the illusion of *"creating money out of thin air without adverse consequences"* that has allowed these gross structural imbalances to build within the system.

3.C - Interest Rates 101:

> ... Periodically, as a result of overly rapid credit expansion, banks became loaned up to the limit of their gold reserves, interest rates rose sharply, new credit was cut off, and the economy went into a sharp, but short-lived recession. (Compared with the depressions of 1920 and 1932, the pre-World War I business declines were mild indeed.)... But the process of cure was misdiagnosed as the disease: if shortage of bank reserves was causing a business decline-argued economic interventionists -- why not find a way of supplying increased reserves to the banks so they never need be short! If banks can continue to loan money indefinitely -- it was claimed -- there need never be any slumps in business. And so the Federal Reserve System was organized in 1913... now, in addition to gold, credit extended by the Federal Reserve banks ("paper reserves") could serve as legal tender to pay depositors.
>
> - Alan Greenspan, Gold and Economic Freedom

Before embarking on an explanation of how the gold standard prevents interest rate manipulations, ideally, we should do an "Interest Rates 101." While "interest rates" is one of the most commonly used words in business channels and circles, it is also easily the most misunderstood concept in economics.

3.C.I - What are "Interest Rates?"

Very simply put, Interest Rates are the *"price of borrowing"* and are determined by the time preference of individual borrowers and lenders.

Before explaining the above definition, let us understand how the price of a common item, say tomatoes, is set in the free markets.

Fig 3.7 illustrates how prices are arrived at by a confluence of supply and demand. There are various supply combinations (quantity produced at various price points) and demand requirements (quantity consumed at different price points). The market price is the equilibrium price at which the supply from producers is equal to the demand from consumers.

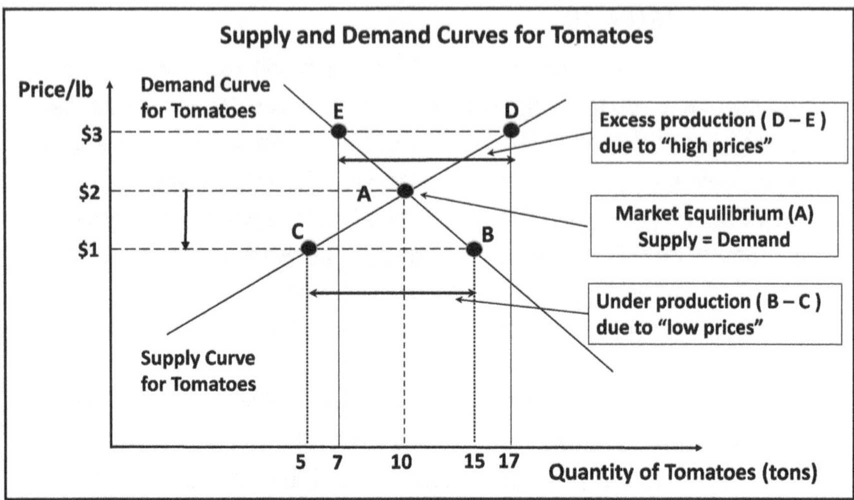

Fig 3.7 – A simple Supply - Demand graph for Tomatoes.

i.   At a high price (i.e. $3/lb), the Supply > Demand leading to "surplus of tomatoes"

ii. At a low price (i.e. $1/lb), the Demand > Supply leading to "shortage of tomatoes"

iii. At the market equilibrium price (i.e. $2/lb), Supply = Demand

1. **Supply Curve for Tomatoes** - The upward-sloping line indicates the supply (or production) of tomatoes at various price points. Points A, C, and D on the supply curve indicate that at a price of $1/lb., the production is 5t, at $2/lb., the production is 10t, and at $3/lb., the production is 17t. Naturally, at a higher price, there is a greater incentive for the marginal producer to create additional supplies.

2. **Demand Curve for Tomatoes** - The downward-sloping line indicates the demand for tomatoes at various price points. Points A, B, and E on the demand curve indicate that at a price of $1/lb., the demand is 15t, at $2/lb., the demand is 10t, and at $3/lb., the demand is 7t. Again, quite understandably, people cut back on consumption at higher prices leading to a reduction in demand.

3. **Situation of Price-Fixing by Government** - Let us think of a situation where the Government considers the price of $2/lb. to be unfair to the poor and fixes the price at $1/lb. This will lead to a situation where the supply at the fixed price is just 5t while the demand is 15t. So we will have a scenario of underproduction, and this leads to other imperfect government interventions like rationing, quotas, etc.

4. **Situation of Price-Fixing by the Producers** - Let us also consider the condition that the producers of tomatoes decide that they need a price of $3/lb. for their production. This will lead to a situation where the production is 17t while the demand is just 7t, leading to a situation of excess production / unsaleable inventory.

5. **The Market Equilibrium Pricing** - The free interactions of buyers and sellers in the markets allow the fixing of the price of tomatoes at a level that would equate the supply and demand, i.e., $2/lb. The *"invisible hand of the free markets"* works to bring about this equilibrium.

The above is a simplified version of how the Demand-Supply equilibrium happens in the free market but still works well for our purpose of understanding the process of how prices are determined in the markets.

Let us now return to what interest rates are, i.e., **Interest Rates are the** *"price of borrowing."*

While consumers prefer all commodities for their consumption, money is needed only for the purpose of buying other commodities in the present and future. Interest rates serve the all-important purpose of coordinating between current consumption and investment decisions (which enables future consumption) of individuals. Investment decisions by individuals are necessarily made from their choice to forego consumption today to have the option of greater consumption in the future, and "interest rates" are the enabling factor that coordinates the intertemporal decisions.

This coordination between the intertemporal consumption plans of consumers and the investment plans of entrepreneurs has its basis in the market for loanable funds or the Quantity of Money. Fig 3.8 shows how interest rates are determined in the markets and the consequences of artificially lowering the interest rates by the central banks. This is explained below.

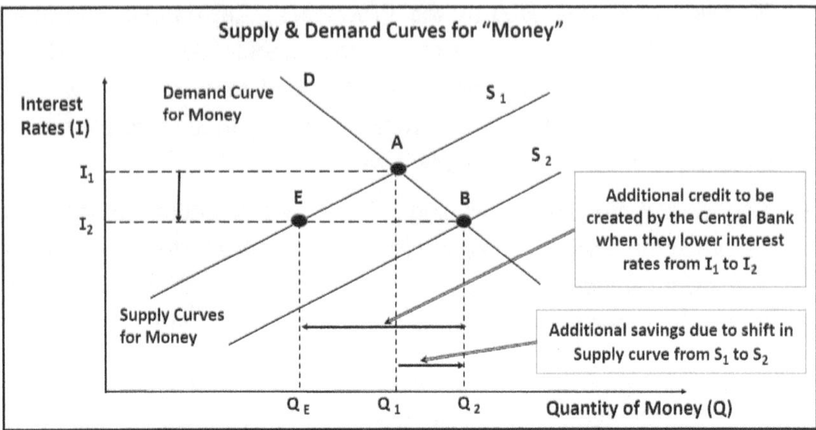

Fig 3.8 - Supply - Demand curve for Money

i. "Natural Rate of Interest" is where "Supply of savings = Demand for investments" e.g. A & B

ii. When a shift in Supply curve happens from S_1 to S_2 because of higher preference for savings, then interest rate falls (from I_1 to I_2) and greater investments are made i.e. Q_2 Vs. Q_1

iii. When Central Banks lower interest rate (from I_1 to I_2), then the Supply falls (from Q_1 to Q_E). The additional credit required (i.e. $Q_2 - Q_E$) has to be created by the Central Bank.

1. **The Supply Curves S_x** indicate the supply of money available for investments at various interest rates. S_1 and S_2 indicate different environments / timelines wherein S_2 shows a shift in the supply curve towards a greater preference for savings vis-à-vis S_1. In other words, forego consumption today with the expectation of greater consumption in the future.

2. **The Demand Curve D** indicates the quantity of money entrepreneurs are willing to borrow at said interest rates. Naturally, the lower the interest rates, the greater will be the number of projects that will be profitable. At progressively increasing rates, the marginal projects become unviable and hence the demand for money is lower.

3. **The *Natural Rate of Interest*** is the rate at which the supply of savings equals the demand for investments. Points A (I_1 and Q_1) and B (I_2 and Q_2) reflect the loanable funds or the quantity of money available for investments at different interest rates.

The two different scenarios that need to be understood are (i) when the rate of interest falls due to an increased preference for future consumption that causes a shift in the supply curve from S_1 to S_2 and (ii) when central banks artificially create a lower interest rate environment when they lower the interest rate from I_1 to I_2. The implications of these two scenarios are explained below.

4. **Shift in Supply Curve from S_1 to S_2:** This happens when the population decides in favor of delayed consumption and so a greater proportion is allocated to savings as compared to current consumption. As the quantity of money available through savings is higher, there is a decline in the interest rate as well. So previously, projects that were unviable due to the higher rate of interest now become profitable. So a greater amount of investments $(Q_2 - Q_1)$ are made that enable greater future consumption due to the natural decline in interest rates $(I_1 - I_2)$.

5. **Lowering of the interest rate by Central Banks from I_1 to I_2:** In this scenario, there is no shift in consumer preference to become more future-oriented and so the supply curve remains at S_1. So what happens is that the availability of loanable funds declines to Q_E from Q_1. At the same time, there is a greater demand for loanable funds from Q_1 to Q_2 due to the reduction of interest rate from I_1 to I_2. Therefore, the Central Banks have to create this additional credit $(Q_2 - Q_E)$ as there is no sufficient savings to meet the additional demand for funds.

6. The additional supply of goods brought about by the central bank-created credit is not backed by savings. This intertemporal mismatch between production and spending patterns eventually turns the credit-induced boom into a bust. More specifically, the artificially low rate of interest that triggered the boom eventually gives way to a high real rate of interest as committed projects bid against increasingly scarce resources.

7. The end result is liquidation of the previously marginal projects (unviable under the changed circumstances) and a market capital restructuring process occurs through which production is aligned with the consumption preferences.

8. To summarize, a fall in interest rate - whether caused by a genuine increase in savings or credit creation - translates into investment in projects where production is further into the future than the near term. The difference between the two scenarios is that in the latter (i.e., credit-induced fall in interest rates), there arises a mismatch between intertemporal resource allocation for production and intertemporal consumption preferences. This leads to what Economists refer to as malinvestments or more commonly as bubbles or the boom-bust cycles.

9. Recent examples of bubbles in the US would be the NASDAQ bubble of 2000 and the housing bubble of 2008. Following the patterns outlined above of a central bank created low-interest regime, the US has witnessed a near 0% interest rate policy (ZIRP - Zero Interest Rate Policy) for almost 15 years between 2008 and 2022. This has created a super bubble in the assets of stocks, bonds, and real estate today.

So essentially, interest rates serve the purpose of allocating resources between present consumption vs. investments (that enable future consumption). When this market allocation mechanism is altered by the central bank's creation of credit (that leads to the illusion of excess savings), it results in bubbles. This artificially low-interest rate scenario doesn't arise under a gold standard as credit creation is severely limited i.e., a central bank cannot print gold and allocate it the way they do with paper currencies.

> *Quite unlike tomatoes that cannot be printed out of thin air, the Federal Reserve can do so with US dollars to meet the shortfall between supply and demand caused by the artificially low interest rates. That's why it's NOT possible to price fix the simple tomato, but can be done so for the mighty US dollar. Albeit temporarily as the world will soon find out.*

It stands to reason from the above section that the growth in money supply would be much higher when the central banks can artificially manipulate the interest rates lower as the additional credit required would have to be created by the central banks. This is exactly what we have observed in the US as well. Fig 3.9 shows the growth in Money Supply (M2) just before and after the US went off the gold standard in 1971. As shown, the growth in the M2 during the decade after 1971 has been 9.77% as compared to 7.07% for the period before 1971.

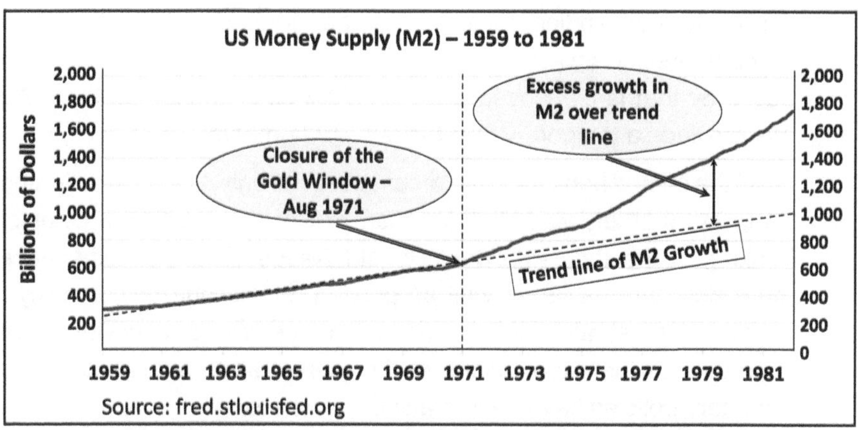

Fig 3.9 - Accelerated growth of Money Supply post closure of the Gold Window in 1971

i.   From 1960 – 1971 : Growth in M2 was from $298 to $632 billion for a CAGR of 7.07%

ii. From 1971 – 1981 : Growth in M2 from $632 to $1,606 billion for a CAGR of 9.77%

So why do Central Banks create artificially low interest rates? There are several reasons as listed below.

1.   Almost universally, the government is the biggest borrower and a lower interest rate environment facilitates the borrowers at the expense of the savers.

2.   An artificially low interest rate environment facilitates a speculative boom - in different asset classes at different points in time. The fact that artificial booms have to be inevitably followed by bubbles bursting is never acknowledged and various justifications are provided as to why the current boom is different and sustainable as compared to the previous ones e.g. "New Economy" during the NASDAQ bubble of 2000; "housing prices never decline nationwide" during the housing bubble 2008 etc. The blame on the inevitable burst is placed on the reckless speculators, greedy capitalists, and predatory lending by the banks.

     In all of the reports produced by the US government analyzing the previous boom-bust cycles, never even once has the blame been placed at where it rightly belongs i.e. the Federal Reserve and the artificially low interest rates it creates.

3. Artificially low lending rates encourage greater consumption today as compared to investments that enable future consumption. For an economy that is composed of nearly 70% consumption as the US is, this provides a temporary fillip to the GDP numbers.

4. Of all the central bankers in the recent past, the only one who really stood up to the markets was Paul Volcker. However, despite the complete backing of the then President Ronald Reagan, Volcker experienced more political attacks as well as public protests due to his policy of keeping interest rates high. In contrast, the central bankers who played according to the expectations of the market and implemented loose monetary policies have been praised for their role.

   a. Alan Greenspan who was the Fed Chairman from 1987 to 2006 presided over the NASDAQ bubble of 2000 and the formation of the HB1.0 that resulted in the GFC 2008. However, even today, he is referred to as "***The Maestro***" in the media.

   b. Bernanke was the Fed Chairman from 2006 and 2014 and he presided over the radical monetary approaches of ZIRP and QE as a response to GFC 2008. He laid the foundations for the HB2.0 that is in the early stages of bursting and yet, he was awarded the **Nobel Prize** for Economics in 2022.

Interest Rates Movements and the Impact on National Debt as a % of GDP - We have seen that the growth in national debt has been a one-way street almost right from the formation of the Federal Reserve. There have been the occasional reductions or stabilization periods especially after the World Wars but none outside of those periods. If the national debt goes up anyway, what do the interest rate hikes even achieve?

While the national debt has shown only an increasing trend, what the interest rate increases have done is to ensure that the national debt as a % of the GDP declines. Higher rates have partly helped to flatten the rate of increase in debt, though in absolute terms the debt still has expanded. But even this decline in the debt-to-GDP is within an overall pattern of increasing trend for the last 50 years as shown in Fig 3.10.

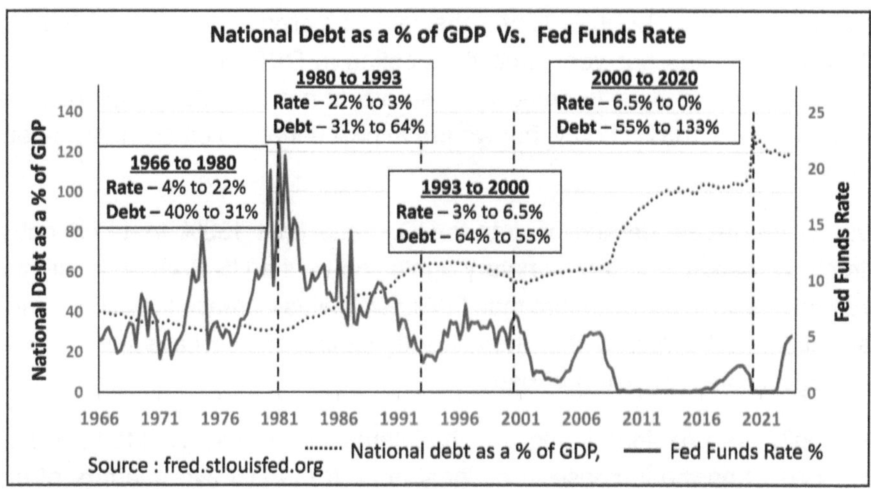

Fig 3.10 – Correlation between National debt as a % of GDP and the Fed Funds Rate

i.   1966 to 1980 saw a decline in the debt-to-GDP from 40 to 31% with a steep increase in the Fed Funds Rate

ii. Both 1980 - 1993 and 2000 - 2020 saw more than a doubling of the debt % as a consequence of the decline in interest rates.

In the post-WW-II period, there have been two periods in which National debt as a % of the GDP has witnessed a significant reduction. Between 1966 and 1980 when the Fed Funds rate was increased from 4% to 22%, the National debt declined from a little over 40% to 31%. The second and probably the last meaningful reduction happened between 1993 and 2000. The Fed Funds rate was increased from 3 to 6.5% and the National debt declined from 64% to 55%. Even this cyclical low of 55% is much higher than the starting point of the previous cycle at 40% during 1966.

Post the year 2000, National debt as a % of GDP has almost been a unidirectional trend with increases in Fed funds rate merely slowing down the rate of increase. For example, between 2004 and 2007 (Greenspan till 2005 and Bernanke for 2006 - 2007), the Fed effected a significant increase in the Fed Funds rate from 1.04% to 5.30% over nearly 3.5 years. But all this steep increase did was to slow down the rate of growth and we still witnessed a marginal increase from 60 to 62%.

We have witnessed a decline between 2020 and 2022 from nearly 133% and this probably bottomed at 117% during Q1 2023. At the end of Q3 2023, this ratio stood at 121.6%. Given the rate of increase in national debt (at close to $3 trillion per year) and the decline in GDP going forward (more in sections 4.B & 4.C) is going to ensure that not only do we exceed the all-time high of 133% shortly, but we are almost certain to cross 150% before the end of 2025.

Why is the recent decline of debt-to-GDP ratio from 133% to 117% not a structural response to the monetary tightening by the US Fed? After all, the US Fed has done a steep more than 500 basis points increase in the Fed funds rate during 2023. Surely that monetary tightening should have reduced the leverage in line with historical patterns.

Not really. As explained in Fig 3.4, the interest rate hikes seem to have had little impact on the increase in national debt. If the last two quarters of the calendar year 2023 are indicative, the national debt is growing at more than a 12% annualized rate. To hazard a guess, it could well be because very few people actually believe that the rate hikes are here to stay and that at the first sign of economic trouble, these would be rolled back. Powell's observations "I've said that we wouldn't wait to get to 2% (inflation) to cut (Fed funds) rates," also seem to confirm such perceptions.

So if it wasn't the interest rate hikes, then what caused the fall in the debt-to-GDP ratio between 2020 and Q1 of 2023? Readers should remember that the rate hikes did not commence till April of 2022. The year 2020 saw a combination of two factors

i.   An abnormal increase of more than 4.2 trillion in the national debt (an 18% increase in national debt from 22.72 trillion in 2019 to 26.94 trillion by 2020).

ii. A COVID induced decline in the GDP.

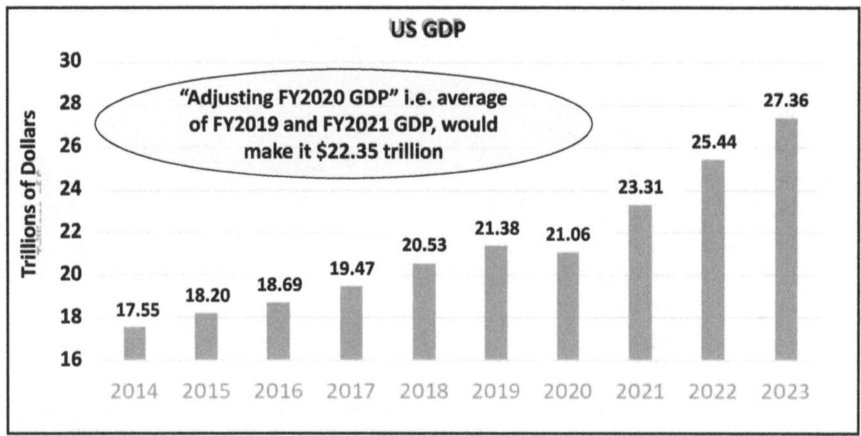

Fig 3.11 – Growth in US GDP from 2014 to 2023.

i.   The COVID dip during 2020 was normalized in the subsequent years. With the lower base of FY2020, GDP numbers for the subsequent years show an extraordinary growth.

It is this double whammy that pushed the debt-to-GDP ratio to the level of 133% by 2020 - a few years ahead of time. With or without the Fed Funds rate hikes by the US Fed starting 2022, the debt-to-GDP would have temporarily declined to its trend line of growth before resuming the upward trajectory. If we merely adjust the 2020 GDP for the "COVID dip" as shown in Fig 3.11, the peak debt-to-GDP ratio would drop to 125%. So it is this twin effect of a steep increase in national debt concurrently with a GDP decline that caused a temporary spike within an overall trend of increasing debt-to-GDP ratio.

What would push this debt-to-GDP ratio to 150%+ in the next couple of years? There are any number of factors that are screaming recession for the US economy and that will be expanded upon in sections 4.B and 4.C.

But just sticking to some historical pattern, also indicates the same. The Federal tax to GDP ratio has hovered between 16 and 18% for the last 50 years as shown in Fig 3.12. It has crossed the 18% mark twice - the first time in 1981 when it touched 18.7% and this was followed by the Volcker induced recession; the second time in 2000 it touched 19.75% and was followed by the dot-com recession. So a value of above 18% has always been followed by a recession within a 12 to 18 month time window. Even prior to GFC 2008, this ratio was fairly close to 18% as can be observed from Fig 3.12.

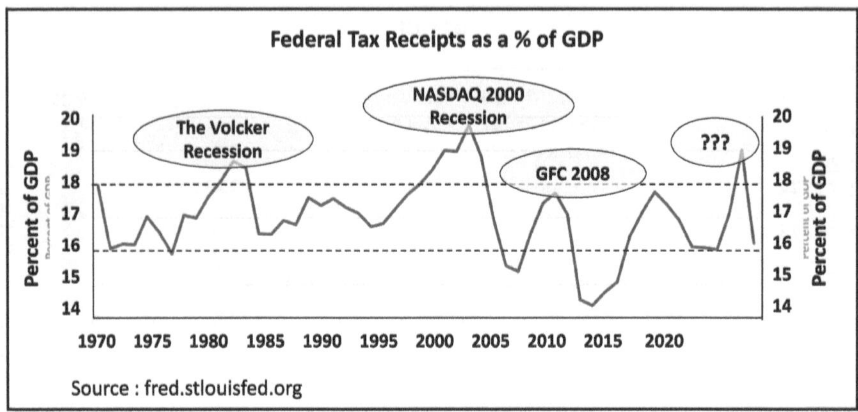

Fig 3.12 - Federal tax receipts have been between 16 to 18% of GDP. A reading in excess of 18% has been followed by a recession within the next 12 to 18 months.

What does it behold for the future? A high tax-to-GDP in excess of 18% seems to be a forerunner of an impending recession. This ratio peaked at 17.75% in 2007 just before the GFC of 2008. This ratio was 19.6% in 2022 and 18.3% in 2023. The cyclical artificial boom causes an upswing in speculative profits where the marginal rate of taxation is higher and hence a higher % of GDP comes through as tax collections. The higher taxes reduce the fiscal deficit while at the same the artificial boom also reduces certain expenditures such as unemployment benefits etc. When the current high wears off, it will result in a recession and soon we should see a substantive increase in the debt-to-GDP ratio.

Monetary Policy – Still Expansionary: Despite the recent unprecedented hikes in the Fed funds rate from 0 to 5.25%+ during 2022 and 2023, the monetary policy continues to be very accommodative. The national debt continues to expand at the rate of nearly $3T per year despite these measures indicating that the interest rate hikes have largely been ineffective. Seen in the context of an apparently booming economy, low unemployment and a near record tax-to-GDP ratio, one could see why this recent decrease in debt-to-GDP is set to reverse and skyrocket going ahead. In fact, the projection of 150% for 2025 could well be a very conservative estimate.

Even at the current rate of expansion in national debt, we should be having a 40 trillion debt by FY2025. Let us assume a very mild recession where the GDP is akin to what we had in FY2023 at $27.36 trillion. These are very conservative assumptions and even under these conditions, the debt-to-GDP touches 150% by FY2025.

Is it possible for this debt-to-GDP ratio to hit 200% by FY2025? In all probability, we will witness the bursting of the housing bubble later this year i.e. 2024. If there is any difference this time, it is that we have a bubble in the commercial real estate as well. So the bubble burst would be followed by a massive increase in national debt to at least $50 trillion and accounting for a contraction in the GDP, a 200% debt-to-GDP ratio is not an improbable outcome. If not by 2025, extending the timelines to 2026, would make it much more probable.

House Hold Debt - Effect of Low Interest Rates

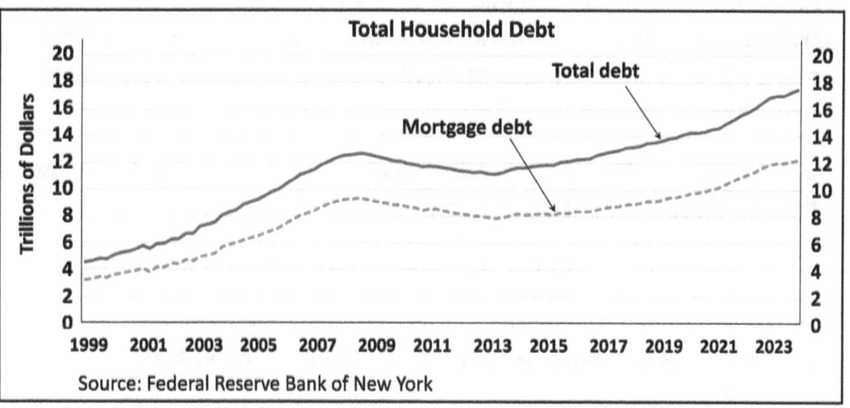

Fig 3.13 – Growth in total Household debt. Total debt includes mortgage debt + credit card, student loans, auto loans and others.

Much the same phenomenon as we saw with US National Debt, can be observed with the individual household debt as shown in Fig 3.13. From a little over 5T at the start of the year 2000, the household debt is now nearly 18T (out of which mortgage debt alone accounts for $12.5T). We will get into why the nearly 15 years of ZIRP have created a housing bubble that is far bigger than the one that burst in 2008 and triggered the GFC. This is explained in "Section 4.C - Housing Bubble 2.0"

The modest decline between 2008 and 2014 was on account of a decline in the mortgage debt. The non-mortgage related portion of the household debt went up during the above period, courtesy - ZIRP.

If there is any consolation, it is that the household debt has grown at a slower rate as compared to the national debt. Both national and household debt were at $5T each at the beginning of the century. So while the household has grown to nearly 17.5T at the start of 2024, the National Debt at the same point is almost twice the number at $34.5T.

3.D - Inflation 101

As the supply of money (of claims) increases relative to the supply of tangible assets in the economy, prices must eventually rise. Thus the earnings saved by the productive members of the society lose value in terms of goods. When the economy's books are finally balanced, one finds that this loss in value represents the goods purchased by the government for welfare or other purposes with the money proceeds of the government bonds financed by bank credit expansion.

In the absence of the gold standard, there is no way to protect savings from confiscation through inflation.

- Alan Greenspan, Gold and Economic Freedom

Inflation is always and everywhere a monetary phenomenon

- Milton Friedman

Of the three topics mentioned in the Preface as being misunderstood by economists and people alike - money, interest rates and inflation - the last one i.e., inflation, is the word whose meaning itself has changed over the centuries.

Inflation - 101 is therefore mandatory and we will start with the basics as we have done for money and interest rates.

The Inflation Basics

As said earlier, the definition of Inflation itself has morphed over time. When it was first used in the 19th century, Inflation referred to an increase in the money supply. It was quite common (AND CORRECT) to think of currency inflation causing an artificial expansion leading to an eventual implosion and depression.

The Webster's Dictionary in 1864 defined inflation as *"undue expansion or increase, from over-issue; - said of currency."*

Over time, this understanding was modified and during the early part of the 20th century, the generally accepted definition was "an increase in the supply of money and credit relative to the goods and services produced within an economy resulting in higher prices."

> *The first panacea for a mismanaged nation is inflation of the currency; the second is war. Both bring a temporary prosperity; both bring a permanent ruin. But both are the refuge of political and economic opportunists.*
>
> *– Ernest Hemingway*

The modern definition of inflation as a "general increase in the price levels of goods and services within an economy" did not come about till the 1960s. Perhaps, not coincidentally, this was also the period when macroeconomists started to take a more benign view about deficit spending.

But as Mises would point out, "this semantic innovation was by no means harmless." By separating the root causes and the effects, policy making becomes ineffective. This is especially so when the rationale for the price rise for an individual item is very different from that of the general price level for a basket of goods. For example, if there is a drought, there is a shortage in the production of food grains and this leads to a price rise for that particular item. But as long as the quantity of money circulating within an economy doesn't change, prices for other goods and services would decline to an extent to ensure that the price for a basket of items remains the same.

To make matters worse, when policy makers fight the consequences of inflation i.e., a rise in prices, they only make matters worse. This arises out

> *"As you cannot name the policy increasing the quantity of the circulating medium, it goes on luxuriantly,"*
>
> *– Von Mises, Planning for Freedom*

of a misunderstanding of *"the causal relation between the increase in money in circulation and credit expansion on the one hand and the rise in prices on another"* as Mises would elaborate.

What has happened on account of the "semantic innovation" of the word "inflation" is that Governments all over the world are today fighting an enemy they cannot recognize. So we should distinguish the cause and effect for our purpose:

Monetary Inflation: An increase in the supply of money and credit within an economy in relation to the goods and services produced.

Price Inflation: An increase in the general price level of goods and services.

So what should a government do to fight "inflation?" Defined correctly i.e., an expansion in the supply of money and credit, the solution would be obvious. To increase interest rates to a level that would reduce the additional demand for money / credit to well within the GDP growth rates. If "inflation" is defined as rising prices, then the solution would be wage/price controls and other such symptomatic measures that would do little to solve the problems; or indeed make them worse.

So how did the US handle the issue post the break out of price inflation after Nixon closed the Gold Window? When Inflation was around 6% in the US during 1971, then President Nixon in a televised address announced, *"I am today ordering a freeze on all prices and wages throughout the United States."* This was a temporary 90-day freeze that of course did not work. Nixon would reintroduce the temporary freeze in June 1973 but the economy ground to a halt. The market reaction to price controls was quite predictable and as written in the book *The Commanding Heights: The Battle for the World Economy*, *"**Ranchers stopped shipping their cattle to the market, farmers drowned their chickens, and consumers emptied the shelves of supermarkets.**"*

Richard Nixon was not the only US President to commit the folly of trying to control the effects while ignoring the cause. Gerald Ford when he assumed office in August 1974 had the twin problems of high unemployment and double-digit inflation at 12.3% to deal with. This was a conundrum unexplained under Keynesian economics - the Fed could not raise interest rates due to the high unemployment but could not cut interest rates either due to the high price inflation.

President Ford would continue to ignore the causative factors with his WIN (Whip Inflation Now) campaign in 1974. In a televised address, Ford declared inflation "public enemy number one" and proposals for citizens to participate in this Win initiative included carpooling, home gardens and turning down thermostats. The WIN form (Fig 3.14) was made available to members who were supposed to mail the same to the President and they would receive a WIN button as an acknowledgment of their participation. This would later be described as "one of the biggest government public relations blunders ever."

The WIN form was made available on the day of Ford's **Whip Inflation Now** speech during October 1974. It read

"Dear President Ford:

I enlist as an inflation fighter and Energy Saver for the duration. I will do the very best I can for America".

Fig 3.14 – <u>W</u>hip <u>I</u>nflation <u>N</u>ow (WIN) campaign. The form was mailed to the President and the sender would receive a WIN button.

With no focus on the monetary causative factors, the campaign would soon fall apart. People started wearing the WIN buttons upside down indicating NIM - "No Immediate Miracles," "Nonstop Inflation Merry-go-round" etc. Greenspan who was part of the Ford administration during the "Whip Inflation Now" campaign would later recall the same as *"This is unbelievably stupid."*

It would take a Paul Volcker and an interest rate of 22% to quell the price inflation of the 1970's. The price inflation was near 13% in 1981 and then

Volcker had to offer a real interest rate of 9% to vanquish the price inflation. It has been more than 40 years since the battle against stagflation was won and the lessons have been completely forgotten. Biden's "Inflation Reduction Act" of 2022 is going to worsen the causative factors i.e., it is going to result in an expansion of the deficits and consequently greater monetary inflation. The fiscal conditions today are worse than what led up to the 1970's inflation and the solutions proposed are much worse.

Given the debt levels, can the US Economy even afford the current 5.25% interest rate let alone 22%? Quite obviously not. So what gives? We should not get ahead of ourselves and we shall answer the above questions in Section 4.

What happens to Price Inflation under a Gold Standard? Generally speaking, prices tend to fall under a gold standard. The quantity of gold increases at a rate slower than the growth in GDP. So under a gold standard, the nominal GDP is lower than the real GDP. Historically, we have never used a "GDP inflator" and so the reported GDP growth rates under the gold standard have always been understated.

The concept of "GDP inflator / deflator" is worth expanding - GDP is the output of a country in a given period and is calculated using the nominal currency value of the products and services. However, due to the monetary inflation (under the current fiat monetary standard), prices of the basket of goods and services would have increased and this conveys a higher GDP than what is the case. So after calculating the "nominal GDP," we use a "GDP deflator" to reduce the same to get the "real GDP" to neutralize the impact of price inflation. Of course, under the classical gold standard, prices were falling and so the governments should have used a "GDP inflator" and not doing so actually understates the GDP growth achieved in the economy without the aegis of the Federal Reserve to manage the economy.

Fig 3.15 shows the annual price changes for the period 1800 to date. As readers would recall, the US was under the classical gold standard and did not have a central bank till the year 1913. During the above 113 year period, prices were almost continuously declining and by the end of the period, prices were down by more than 40% as compared to 1800. The purchasing power of the dollar had substantially increased and this was even without accounting for the tremendous improvement in the quality of the products. The quality of life of the citizens had vastly improved in almost every facet under conditions of falling prices. Electricity, mechanized transportation, modern medicine, telecommunications, computers, mass production - all of them happened during the 113 period under the classical gold standard.

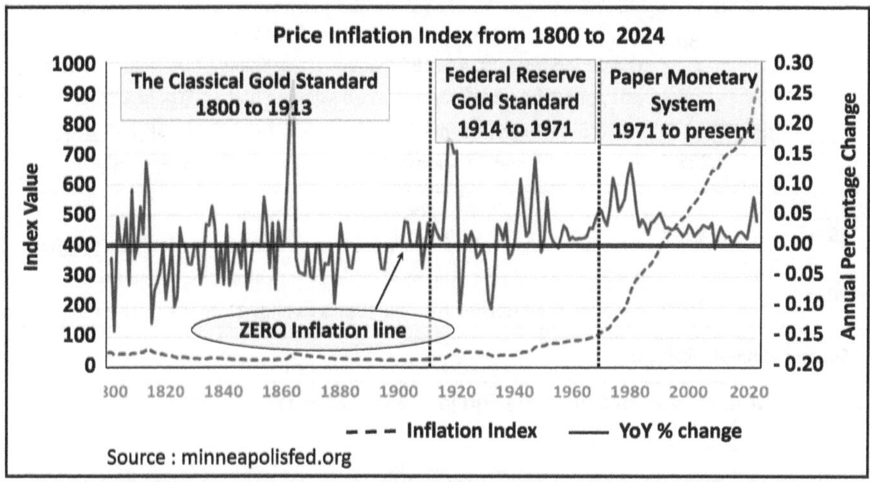

Fig 3.15 - History of Price Inflation over 225 years under three Monetary Standards.

i.   The Classical Gold Standard for a CAGR of -0.05% over 114 years

ii. Federal Reserve Gold Standard for a CAGR of 2.5% over 57 years

iii. Fiat / Paper Monetary System for a CAGR of 3.95% over 53 years

The term "Gold Standard" referring to a product / service in any industry indicating it's the pinnacle of quality is not without reason.

So what happens after the Federal Reserve gets introduced? The 224 years considered are split into different phases in Fig 3.16 to reflect the key monetary events in history and the impact on the price index levels on account of the same.

Time Period	Price Index	Comments
1800	50	**The Classical Gold Standard**
1913	29.7	A cumulative decline of more than 40% in prices over a 113 year period from 1800 to 1913 for a **CAGR of -0.05%** under the Classical Gold Standard and without a Central Bank.
1914	30.1	**The Federal Reserve Gold Standard**
1933	38.9	The period from 1914 to 1932 when convertibility of US Dollars to gold was permitted for US citizens, Price inflation had a **CAGR of 1.35%.**
1971	121.7	With convertibility banned, between 1933 and 1971 **CAGR was 3.05%** For the combined duration of 1914 to 1971, the **CAGR was 2.5%**
1971	121.7	**Fiat Currency Standard** A cumulative growth of nearly 650% over a 53 year period for a **CAGR of 3.95%.** This is despite the methodology for calculating the Index has
2024	910.4	been changed starting the mid-1980's to understate the price index.

Source: minneapolisfed.org

Fig 3.16 - A summary of Price Inflation in the US from 1800 to date.

An obvious conclusion from the above Fig 3.16 is that unless convertibility is allowed for the citizens, the central banks will figure out a way to inflate the currency even if the Gold Window for other central banks remain open. It will just be coordinated monetary inflation across global central banks and the citizens would be powerless to handle these conditions even assuming they understand what is happening.

The difference between post and pre-1971 price inflation rates of 3.95% and 3.05% does not appear very significant, except that we should remember that the "Price Inflation" put out by governments across the world carries all of the pitfalls of "self-appraisals." Additionally, the incentives to understate are magnified at higher levels of price inflation. A series of modifications (hedonic adjustments, substitutions, owner's equivalent rent etc.) were introduced by the US government starting from the early 1980's that has led to an understatement of the price inflation numbers.

Alternate calculations of the price inflation report a 2 to 5% understatement by the Government price inflation during the mid-1980s to early-1990s. This difference has subsequently increased to 5 - 10% since the mid-1990s. The point is that the average price inflation since the US closed the Gold window in 1971 is not 3.95% but substantially higher than that number.

Shadow Government Statistics produces alternate calculations for several Government reports on price inflation, unemployment, GDP etc. and these alternate numbers indicate the bias built into the government calculations. The comparison for price inflation is given in Fig 3.17 but similar data is available for the other macroeconomic statistics as well.

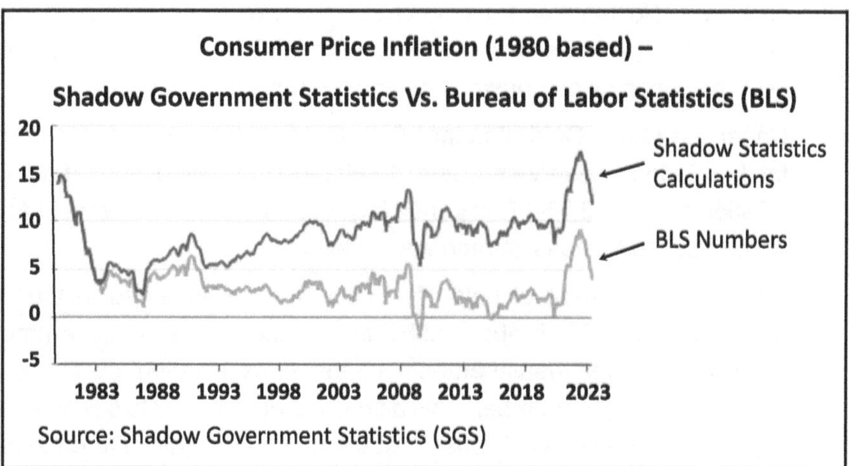

Fig 3.17 - A comparison of Consumer Price Inflation between official BLS reported numbers and SGS calculations using the 1980's methodology.

i.   **SGS calculations show a 5 to 10% points higher inflation as compared to BLS numbers starting the mid 1990's**

Monetary Inflation - Cui Bono?

If price inflation is a deliberate central bank created phenomenon as explained, then the question arises as to who benefits from this exercise.

Now the topic of Inflation (monetary inflation + price inflation) is complex enough that we could do well with an interim summary of what we have covered till now.

i.   Inflation is essentially an expansion in the supply of money and credit that causes an increase in the general price level of a basket of goods and services.

ii. Since the term is used to denote both the cause and the effects, we will use the term Monetary Inflation (i.e., increase in the supply of money) to refer to the cause; Price Inflation i.e., increase in price of a basket of goods and services, refers to the effects or the fall-out of Monetary Inflation.

iii. Under the classical gold standard, there is a general tendency for prices to decrease over the long-term. Readers might recollect that one of the properties desired of money is that it is a "store of value" over long periods. Gold maintains its purchasing power / intrinsic worth over hundreds of years as shown above in Fig 3.15 and Fig 3.16. In reality, gold maintains its purchasing power over thousands of years.

iv. Under the Quasi-Gold standard (i.e., Gold exchange standard under the US Federal Reserve between 1914 and 1971), we observed a price inflation of about 2.5%. This period included the two World Wars both of which had led to massive monetary inflation.

v. Without the restraint of gold, the price inflation observed in the US Economy since 1971 is about 3.95% as indicated by the US government statistics. Private measurements of the price inflation puts it at a substantially higher number. This difference was about 2 to 5% between the mid-1980s and mid-1990s. Post the mid-1990s this difference has increased to 5-10%.

We can now get to the all-important question of "Cui Bono" i.e., who benefits? After all, if monetary inflation a deliberate policy as we can make out, and we have been consistently getting high inflation for more than 50 years under the Federal Reserve, somebody ought to be gaining from it.

Having understood monetary inflation for what it is, we can now start with what causes an expansion in the supply of money / credit and who the primary beneficiary of that increase is.

Let us start with the basics once again on the need for monetary inflation. What are the sources of Government income?

i. **Taxes** - Direct and Indirect taxation. However, there is a relationship between the taxation rates and the amount collected as is demonstrated by Laffer's curve in Fig 3.18. At some levels of taxation rates, citizens start under-reporting their incomes or worse, just stop working. So taxation has its obvious limitations.

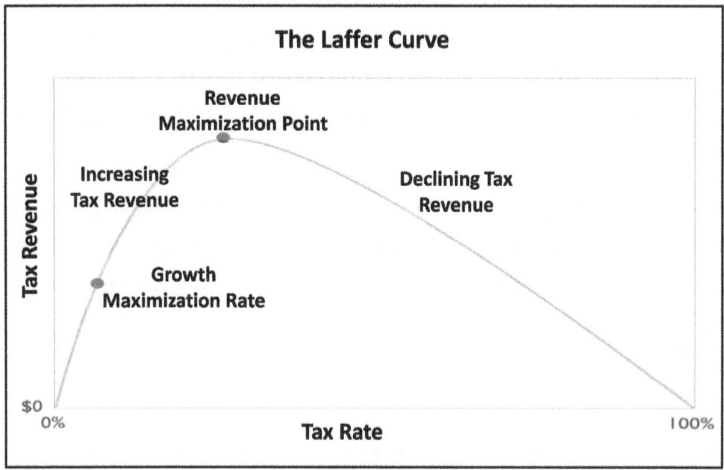

Fig 3.18 – The Laffer Curve indicating the relationship between Income Tax Rates and the Tax Revenues generated.

ii. **Borrowings** - Government can borrow from the market and through other sources. But this essentially would mean that the government has to pay regular interest and also repay this sum (and hence a decline in future net revenues to the government). These borrowings by the Government also tend to crowd out the productive private sector investments (required to grow the economy) as the quantum of savings to borrow against is fixed.

Though governments would like to spend as much as possible today, the entity realizes that it is the private sector that is the golden goose and there is little point in killing it by starving it for funds - either through increased taxation or excessive borrowings.

So what happens when the taxes and borrowings are not enough to meet the expenditures? Voila, the brilliant innovation of the printing press - just print pieces of paper (or just digital entries these days) and spend it. Of course, there needed to be a semblance of economic justification for doing the same. The ever willing Keynesian economists provided the perfect intellectual cover for deficit spending.

Debt Monetization is the practice of the government borrowing from their central banks to finance their deficits. This obviously increases the monetary base and this is the process of creating the "Monetary Inflation." The Federal

Reserve has tried to mask this monetary inflation by using phrases like "Quantitative Easing." In some other countries, phrases like "Economic Stimulus" would be utilized as a euphemism to mask what is really happening behind the scenes. In all these cases, the correct terminology to be utilized is "Monetary Inflation."

Incidentally, it is indeed very very rare for a non-Keynesian economist to be employed by the government. They share a symbiotic relationship where one class is employed to intellectually / morally justify an ever increasing role for their employer in economic activity. I am not talking about this relationship as a collusion between two independent entities - it's far more likely to be an incentive-caused subconscious bias.

So the entity that is a beneficiary of monetary inflation is the government. So let me redefine for what it really is - *Monetary Inflation is stealth taxation by the government where the purchasing power of the currency is reduced by an expansion of the monetary base through central banking.*

Having defined Inflation correctly, we can now answer the question of what causes the prices to fall under the classical Gold standard. And increase subsequently. Essentially, prices are a confluence of two factors

i. Markets, competition, technology and entrepreneurship working overtime to reduce prices and improve the quality for consumers.

ii. Governments living beyond the means and also inducing a demand for paper currency by the artificially low interest rates through the mechanism of central banking. Both these lead to monetary inflation which is the root causative factor for the price inflation.

Prices for a basket of goods & services are therefore a net result of (a) competition working overtime to reduce prices and (b) governments living beyond their means that causes prices to rise. Under the classical gold standard that prevailed before 1913, the governments practically had no role in the monetary system (despite the two limited attempts at central banking) and consequently, we witnessed a period of falling prices for the 113 years under the classical Gold standard as shown earlier.

Once the Federal Reserve was formally instituted in 1913 and given a monopoly over monetary policy, it was only a matter of time before it started corrupting the prevailing gold standard. Therefore, it was a given that some monetary inflation would happen through the Federal Reserve even though it functioned under the restraints of a modified version of the gold standard.

There are industry standard banking practices today that nobody even questions, such as the Fractional Reserve Banking system. This is just another form of monetary inflation and so after the formation of the Federal Reserve in 1913, the US witnessed moderate inflation over the next few decades till 1971 on account of the fractional reserves.

Of course, once the floodgates were opened by removing the shackles imposed by the Gold Window, the sky (i.e., hyperinflation) is the limit for how much monetary inflation would be created. It might take different timelines for different governments to reach that hyperinflationary zone, but reach there, they will. In the long history spanning thousands of years, governments / kings have never failed even once in doing so. **Given sufficient time, the probability of hyperinflation in unbacked currencies is 100%. The only question is the timelines.**

I will make one more observation before I conclude the discussion on monetary inflation. Is the reduction in purchasing power the only deleterious aspect of monetary inflation? Of course not, and in my individual opinion, price inflation, insidious as it is, is not even the most destructive one. Monetary inflation and the artificially low interest rate environment lead to what Von Mises refers as *malinvestments.* The boom-bust cycle caused by malinvestments has a far greater lasting and pernicious impact on the societal fabric as compared to even price inflation.

There are other consequences of monetary inflation as well e.g., Wealth Inequality. These two - malinvestments and Wealth Inequality - will be described as part of Section 4.D The NICE Conundrum & Cantillon Effects.

Given the monetary inflation since the late 1990s, we should not be surprised by the frequency of bubbles - the NASDAQ bubble of 2000 and the Housing bubble of 2008 are good examples. If the relatively small monetary inflation (compared to what we have witnessed post the 2008 GFC) could cause those two bubbles, what would nearly 15 years of ZIRP lead to? We are indeed living through the mother of all bubbles, the "stocks-bonds-housing bubble of 202X," the unraveling of which is going to destroy the dollar. It is not the bubble bursting that will destroy the dollar, but the solutions proposed by the US Government and the Federal Reserve as a response to the bubble bursting that will destroy the USD. *More in Chapter 4.*

We will conclude the discussion on Inflation-101 here. We will summarize the three basic concepts explained i.e., money, interest rates and inflation in Fig 3.19.

Summary of Key Economic Concepts	
Concept	**Explanation**
Money	A commodity that is used as a Reserve Asset and can be used to purchase other goods and services in the future. The 5 properties that are required to satisfy the criteria for being accepted as money are – Desirable, Durable, Divisible, Convenient and Consistent. Over thousands of years or experiments, markets have standardized on Gold and Silver as being the most suitable forms of money.
Interest Rates	Interest Rates is the "price of borrowing" money for a defined period of time. In a free market, this would be determined by the confluence of supply from savings and demand arising from borrowers.
Inflation	There are two versions – Monetary Inflation and Price Inflation. Monetary Inflation is the cause; Price Inflation is the effect. Monetary Inflation refers to the excess supply of money and credit relative to the goods and services produced within an economy. Price Inflation refers to an increase in the price level of a basket of goods and services.

Fig 3.19 – A summary explanation of the three basic concepts in Economics

There is one additional phenomenon that needs further elaboration before we start the discussions on the US Economy and the dollar and that is about "Markets." This is particularly important if you are a resident in the developing economies without much exposure to the developed countries.

3.E – The Virtue of "Markets"

Markets are a mechanism in which potential sellers of goods and services transact with interested buyers and transactions happen at mutually agreeable conditions. A transaction happens ONLY because both parties agree on the terms. Thus markets are a voluntary platform for conducting mutually beneficial transactions and there is no element of coercion involved. In every transaction, both the buyer and seller benefit or else the transaction would not occur in the first place.

Companies compete with each other in the marketplace to gain the support and loyalty of their clientele and to achieve the same, they have to constantly innovate and improve. Companies aim to differentiate their products to attract new customers and as a consequence, products become better and cheaper over time. As you can infer from the Fig 3.16, aggregate prices had fallen by more than 40% over 113 years under the classical gold standard. Not only had these become substantially cheaper, but the quality of these products had also vastly improved as well. The 40% reduction in prices is without any hedonic adjustments for quality.

Most major innovations (except perhaps the Internet) happened under the classical gold standard. All of these transformations happened with very little to no government interventions. But the whole point about "Markets" is that producers / companies engage in these innovations in their own interests and for maximizing their profits on a long-term basis. **In pursuing their self-interest, they end up benefitting the customers.** Or to put it differently, absent government granted monopolies and privileges, serving customers to the best of their abilities and in a better / cheaper way as compared to the competition is the ONLY way for companies to maximize their long-term profitability.

> *"It is not from the benevolence of the butcher, the brewer, or the baker that we expect our dinner, but from their regard to their own self-interest"*
>
> *– **Adam Smith, An Inquiry into the Nature & Causes of the Wealth of Nations.***

Aren't there "Bernie Madoffs" in the markets as well?

Bernie Madoff ran the largest Ponzi scheme in recorded history at an estimated $65 billion through his asset management business - Bernard L. Madoff Investment Securities. He was a one-time chairman of NASDAQ and ran his Ponzi scheme for nearly 4 decades till he was arrested in December 2008. His name is now synonymous with corruption in Wall Street.

Most companies and individuals care far more about their reputations than short-term profits. They understand that long-term sustainability and profitability are the consequence of the brand loyalty and the trust customers place in their goods / services. And companies would take extraordinary measures to build this trust - both with the customers as well as their employees.

Incidentally, we also have companies that are inefficient / incompetent in the marketplace. But once again, markets are the best to identify and wean out these companies. Competition easily ensures that the inefficient companies are unable to sustain themselves and go out of business very soon.

But the bigger issue is that there are outright crooks who also operate in the marketplace in disguise. Absent government support or inefficient handling by the government regulatory bodies, these companies are also usually spotted by other market participants who specialize in this. Even the celebrated case of Bernie Madoff was reported to the SEC (Securities and Exchange Commission - responsible for oversight and enforcement of regulations in the securities industry) with evidence on multiple occasions from the year 2000 onwards - a full 8 years before SEC was finally forced to act in 2008. These complaints were registered to the SEC by a private forensic accounting and fraud investigator Harry Markopolos.

Harry was a former executive in the US securities industry and a financial fraud investigator. He reported that the Madoff wealth management business was a Ponzi scheme repeatedly in 2000, 2001 and 2005 to the SEC with detailed supporting documentation. The SEC would ignore and treat the complaints of Harry with cursory investigations absolving Madoff of any wrong-doings.

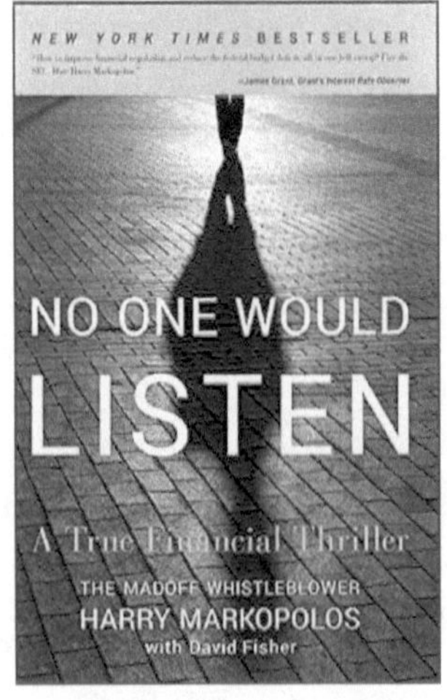

The Madoff Ponzi scheme finally unraveled only when the sons of Bernie Madoff contacted the Federal Bureau of Investigation in 2008. Harry would later author a book *"No One Would Listen"* explaining how the SEC failed in its regulatory duties despite repeated tips and their actions ended up protecting and growing the interests of the firm that it was supposed to investigate for fraud.

The point is, in markets, for every "Bernie Madoff" trying to swindle money, there will be a "Harry Markopolos" who will try to uncover these schemes in the hope of making a name (& profits) for themselves. There are even companies that specialize in identifying these types of short-selling opportunities. In the absence of government regulatory bodies like the SEC that have usurped/monopolized the task of oversight, markets would be far more efficient at identifying such opportunities before these companies become very big. In fact, forensic auditing would have been an industry by itself in the marketplace and customers would willingly pay for their reports.

Having said all of the above, developing economies suffer from the ability of the markets to evolve due to the extensive regulatory systems. This is worth understanding as in general, businesses and markets are looked down upon in developing countries. Quite unfortunately, governments are seen as the savior from predatory business practices through the mechanism of creating and enforcing regulations.

In the developing economies, the singularly important skill in building and running a large business is "to manage the regulatory environment." The control of the state and the approval systems are so extensive that the customer becomes the secondary factor in the determination of success. Also depending on the industry, this "managing the regulatory environment" could well be the only skill that is required and almost every other activity could be "outsourced."

This ability to "manage and influence regulatory systems" are very pervasive in some industries such as natural resources, infrastructure, real estate, higher education etc. The common-thread running amongst these industries would be that the customers do not have much a choice but to accept what is provided to them by the local firms. The competitive advantage of the companies in this space is to manage "the system" to create a monopoly for their goods and services or at least give themselves a significant cost advantage vis-à-vis their competitors.

In the industries that have to export for their survival e.g. software, manufacturing, textiles, pharmaceuticals etc. the regulatory influence is much less as these industries compete in the global marketplace and the inefficiencies introduced by the regulatory system makes them uncompetitive. So in cases where regulations are pervasive and companies need to export for survival, these industries get destroyed from within.

However, given that most customers are not aware of the background environment and have a rather benign view of "governments," they attribute the poor quality of goods and services to the market players. For example, the poor quality of roads in the developing economies is blamed on the road construction firms. Most users may not be aware that these are the very same individuals who build roads in the developed countries and they do an exceptional job in those markets. It is the regulatory constraints within the operating environment that give the developing countries substandard products and services and not the market players themselves.

Let me provide two examples from the developing economies to illustrate that it is not the regulatory systems but companies creating and enhancing their reputations that protect the customers and workers.

1. Retail gold jewelry has been a huge business in India for decades. An approximate 800 tons of gold is purchased by Indians every year out of the estimated world production of 3500 tons. However, till the late 1980s and 1990s, the quality of gold sold in the Indian retail market left much to be desired. Though government regulations existed, it was easy for these companies to circumvent the same and short-change customers.

    An established brand worldwide, Tata, got into this business towards the mid 1990's (the company's name is TANISHQ) and within a span of less than 10 years turned the focus of the entire industry and today most of the major retailers stick to quality specifications as promised. Incidentally, the Tata's charged a premium which the customers willingly paid for the guarantee that they are getting what they were promised.

    No amount of regulations would have delivered the quality to customers that the market competition ensures.

    If you see an industry that is dominated by poor quality of service, the reason invariably would be the barriers to entry created by government regulations that protect the inefficient and are lobbied for by companies that want to maintain the status quo.

2. The second, also an example from India, is the now world renowned Indian software industry. This was not always the case and even till the mid to late 1990's, Indian technology companies were looked down

upon primarily due to the lack of work ethics, poor working environment and lack of software engineering certifications. The change, as the reader would have guessed by now, happened with companies offering the best-in-class work atmosphere and HR practices (and in many cases, rivaling the best to even what the US had to offer) as a means of acquiring and retaining talent. There were many good companies in this space but the clear leader in setting the pace for the adoption of western management and corporate governance practices was Infosys Technologies Limited (NASDAQ:INFY).

Related to the Indian software industry, there is a joke that I think is a truism i.e. The Indian software industry did exceptionally well till the Indian government decided to form a "Ministry of Information Technology."

The subject of explaining why "Markets is the solution to our problems" is not easy especially if one comes from the perspective that businesses are bad / swindlers and government is the savior. What genuinely surprises me is that the average person experiences pervasive corruption in most government departments on a daily basis, and yet, he or she looks up to the government for protection from companies in the market.

That competition is the best solution to the issue of quality / pricing of goods and services in the marketplace is still a minuscule minority opinion in developing countries. The correct form of protest, if any, to the government should be to reduce the barriers to competition and allow the markets to decide the winners and losers.

Given below is a set of reading materials on this specific issue for readers to understand that solutions come from the marketplace and not through government regulations.

i.   *"In defense of Capitalism - Debunking the Myths"* by Rainer Zitelmann

ii. *"Defending the Undefendable"* by Walter Block

iii. *"Economics in One Lesson"* by Henry Hazlitt

iv. *"The Virtue of Selfishness"* by Ayn Rand

It was much easier to explain the misunderstandings about money, interest rates and inflation as the bias is not deep. Most readers would not have a subconscious opinion on these topics and so it is easier to dispel the wrong notions on those three issues.

I fully recognize that the topic of "Markets as the solution to our problems" could be a bridge too far to cross, especially if the reader has not been exposed to the western environment. For the skeptical reader, I would suggest that he or she keeps an open mind and observe how the regulations exist to protect existing players and prevent innovations in the market place. I will provide one example in the context of this book before concluding the discussions on "Markets."

How would "Free Markets in Money" work i.e., without a central bank to protect us?

Let us assume that a reader is reading this section first having skipped all of the preceding chapters and discussions. Can that reader imagine a private monetary and banking system without a central bank in place to print "money" and fix "interest rates?" The reader would naturally conclude that if the job of a central bank is privatized, then the arbitrage opportunity in creating new currency units (i.e., nominal value of the currency minus the cost of printing the same) would ensure that the private banking entities would print money "*ad nauseum*" till it becomes worthless. That we would need a "government / central bank" to protect us from the "greedy bankers" would be a corollary.

Can the reader conceive that without a central bank, the only private sector money that could circulate would have to be based on gold? Any other product would have little resonance in the marketplace. That any bank which prints more currency than the gold it has in its vaults would be subject to "bank runs" and that this is the free market mechanism of keeping the banks in check. The most trusted banks would be the ones that maintained a 100% reserve standard and customers would automatically gravitate towards these banks.

How would "interest rates" i.e., the price of borrowing, be set? In the same way that the price of tomatoes is set. A willing confluence between producers (savers) and consumers (borrowers). Interest rates automatically coordinate the investment - consumption patterns across timelines as per the needs of the markets.

> *Incidentally, central banks are doing exactly what the "greedy bankers" would have been expected to do i.e., printing the currency till it becomes confetti. That they are doing it with an "altruistic motive" & "for the greater good," if that's indeed really the case, is a small consolation.*

Hopefully, with the short few lines above, the contours of a free market system in banking appears plausible - or at the very least doesn't sound like an outlandish proposition anymore. For any reader interested in exploring this specific theme further, I would recommend the book "End the Fed" by Dr. Ron Paul.

Some Common Economic Misconceptions

There are a few more pervasive and widely believed myths in Economics that I will point out in this section. Interested readers can understand these issues further through the suggested reading materials included at the end of chapters 1 to 4. Some of the common themes for these misconceptions would include price inflation, causes of the Great Depression, how Governments should respond to recessions, the economic equation between US and China etc. Over the next 3 pages, these "Economic Myths" are listed against which the "Economic Truisms" are briefly explained.

I have also included a table that outlines the difference between Money and Currencies at the end of this Chapter. Given the pervasive banking system today, it is important to understand how the removal of the constraints of gold has created a system that gives the illusion of stability but has many intrinsic structural fractures underneath.

Common Economic Misconceptions

Economic Myths	Economic Truisms
Price Inflation	
"A little inflation," typically 2% is good;	Deflation - or falling prices - is great. Inflation - as defined correctly - is stealth taxation and even 0.1% Price Inflation is bad.
Deflation is bad for the economy.	As shown in Fig 3.15 and Fig 3.16, the 113 year period prior to 1913 was deflationary. The transition of the US to a Superpower happened under the classical gold standard.
Price Inflation is caused by GDP growth; As a corollary, recessions will cause prices to fall.	In the absence of Monetary Inflation, GDP growth will cause prices to fall as we have observed under the classical Gold standard of 1800 to 1913. Growth causes an increase in supply and this leads to falling prices. Recessions refer to a period of economic contraction (negative GDP growth). By definition, this is a reduction in supply and this causes prices to rise.
Natural calamities and Wars cause prices to rise	Price inflation refers to "a basket of goods" going up in price and not one or two items. Let us say we have a drought and price of food items goes up. In the absence of monetary inflation, price of other things (e.g. leisure services, labor etc) have to come down and so the basket of prices will remain stable.
The Great Depression was Caused by Deflation	
The falling prices under the gold standard made people postpone consumption and lead to the Great Depression	The Great Depression was deflationary and was not caused by it. It was caused by the monetary inflation of the "Roaring twenties (1920's) induced by the US Fed. The repeated interventions of Hoover / Roosevelt to prevent the market cleansing process of the bubbles post the 1929 stock market crash delayed the required liquidation of malinvestments.

Economic Myths	Economic Truisms
Response to Recessions	
The appropriate response to an recessions / economic downturn is deficit spending and monetary stimulus	The first recognition has to be that an economic downturn is caused by a bubble bursting; the recession is a cure to clear the malinvestments made during the artificial boom so that resources can be reallocated. The correct response is to cut back government expenditures (so as to make greater capital available for productive private investments) and deregulate to promote economic activity.
Philips Curve	
Employment Rate and Price Inflation are positively correlated. So to reduce prices, we should decrease the employment rate	Higher employment created by the market results in greater output and hence higher GDP. In the absence of Monetary inflation, this will lead to lower prices. Higher employment in the government sector is usually counter-productive. Employment mentioned in the context of the Philips Curve are market generated opportunities.
To Stimulate Supply or Demand?	
Recessions are caused by a "lack of demand". So an economy can be stimulated by increasing demand.	Jean-Baptiste Say wrote "A product is no sooner created, than it, from that instant, affords a market for other products to the full extent of its own value". Or in other words it is supply that is always the constraint. In fact, Economics could well be described as a study of "how we fulfill our unlimited wants / desires (i.e. demand) with our limited resources (i.e. supply).

Economic Myths	Economic Truisms
USA - China Economic Equation	
The US is a consumption driven economy. So the way to increase the GDP is for the citizens to increase their consumption.	There can NEVER be a "consumption based" economy. Production has to precede consumption. Somebody has to save before capital can be borrowed. Somebody has to produce before goods can be consumed. The key is savings and production. We can have a manufacturing or services oriented, tourism or agriculture dominated economies. An economy is defined by what it produces. Consumption is a consequence of production and imports a consequence of exports. The main export of the US has been the US Dollar and those days are numbered.
Chinese economy is dependent on exports to the US.	China is NOT selling to the US. It is vendor financing the US i.e., giving the goods to the US consumers and also purchasing the US treasuries that gives value to the US Dollar. China is better off stopping the exports to US and allowing its own citizens to consume the goods; or allowing industries to manufacture for the requirements of its own citizens. The *"invisible hand of the free markets"* can manage this entire transition with a revaluation of currencies i.e., allowing the RMB to gain against the USD.
China needs to keep the RMB undervalued to enable exports	The key to economic prosperity is production. It doesn't matter whether the manufactured goods are consumed locally or exported. We all recognize that as a planet, Earth doesn't have to export for growth. The only purpose of exports is to import, and if all that China can get is digital entries of US Dollar in lieu of exports, it would be much better off allowing the RMB to appreciate. This would allow the Chinese citizens to consumer the goods that are currently exported.

Money vs. Currencies

Money and Currencies are two different economic concepts and this distinction is largely lost on most people today. Money is any commodity that can satisfy the D3C2 properties as described in Chapter 1 and Fig 1.2. Currencies are receipts for money and are liabilities of the Central Banks. They are supposed to have value because these are backed by money.

A detailed comparison between Money and Currencies is given in the table below for a better understanding.

Money Vs. Currencies – An overview

Money	Currencies
FUNCTIONAL ATTRIBUTES	
Medium of Exchange – evolved from human exchange to facilitate voluntary market exchange.	**Medium of Exchange** – imposed by diktat and legal tender laws within a geographical setting.
Store of Value – Is an asset that appreciates in value over long periods of time.	**Store of Value** – guaranteed depreciation and even complete loss of value over long periods of time.
CATEGORICAL DIFFERENCES	
Convertibility - Paper Certificates are convertible into specie.	**Convertibility** - Paper Certificates NOT convertible.
Convertibility constraints Central Banks; limits creation of new supply and abjures centralized monetary planning.	Unlimited expansion or infinitely elastic supply allows for monetary central planning. Practically zero near-term restraints on Government expenditure.
Debt: Debt is self-liquidating on the part of the Issuer.	**Debt** – Debt is carried in perpetuity on the books of the Central bank and never extinguished.

Source: Prof.Lingle's Compilations

Money Vs. Currencies – An overview continued	
Money	**Currencies**
EFFECT ON PRODUCTION STRUCTURE	
System functions without "rules" and the invisible hand coordinates the supply-demand for money and hence less disruptive on economic activity and the production structure.	Debt created to exchange for real goods and services is not backed by actual savings. This disrupts and distorts the production structure.
Boom-Bust Cycles: smaller, infrequent and limited impact.	**Boom-Bust Cycles**: large and increasing magnitude with time; threatens stability of the economy.
BANKING PRACTICES	
Lending - Private and competitive issuance under "free banking" supports sound banking practices.	**Lending** - Central Bank's unlimited issuance leads to bad behavior and reckless lending by banks ignoring the risk of defaults.
Fractional Reserve Banking (FRB) – limited capacity to leverage money due to fear of bank runs.	**FRB** – greater capacity to leverage circulating medium as fear of bank runs is non-existent.
Accounting Logic - The notes are liability of the Issuer and this is covered by the asset (specie) held by the issuer.	**Accounting Logic** - Paper certificates are liabilities of the issuer but not offset by assets held by the issues.
Source: Prof.Lingle's Compilations	

Chapter 3 - Takeaways

1. An explanation of how the Classical Gold Standard operated and permitted free commerce amongst nations. A series of marginal changes starting 1913 leading to a dilution of the classical gold standard with gold being completely removed from the monetary system by 1971.

2. An introduction to the concept of interest rates and explaining the differences between interest rates falling naturally due to excess savings and the artificial low interest rates engineered by the Central Banks.

3. How the gold standard prevents deficit spending by the Governments. The following economic concepts have introduced and explained.

    a. **Fiscal deficit** - It is the excess of expenditures over revenues in a given fiscal year. Post 1971, fiscal deficits have become a permanent feature and an increasing number at that. We are at the stage of having $2+ trillion per year of deficits.

    b. **National Debt** - This is the accumulated fiscal deficit and the associated interest payments since the start of the Republic. While the US took nearly 200 years to touch $1 trillion in national debt, this is roughly the amount the US is adding on a quarterly basis. The US is on track to reach $40t of nation debt by FY2025 under normal conditions.

    c. **Inflation** - An introduction to the terms monetary inflation and price inflation to distinguish between the cause and the effect.

4. An introduction to the virtues of the marketplace and how solutions to our problems emerge in the marketplace and not on account of government regulations.

Chapter 3 - Suggested Reading

1. *"The Case for a 100% Gold Dollar"* by Murray Rothbard

2. *"America's Great Depression"* by Murray Rothbard

3. *"France and the Breakdown of the Bretton Woods International Monetary System"* ** by Dominique Simard et al, IMF Working Paper.

4. *"Theory of Money and Credit"* ** by Ludwig Von Mises

5. *"Man, Economy and the State"* ** by Murray Rothbard

6. Website for reference articles**

    a. *"Fallacy of the Equation of Exchange"* - By Murray Rothbard at www.mises.org

    b. *"Non-neutrality of money in Classical Monetary Thought"* - by Thomas Humphrey at www.richmondfed.org

** - For the scholars

The Road Ahead for the US Economy

As explained in Section 3, the monetary inflation after 2008 has created an unsustainable situation for the US Economy with massive malinvestments. The fundamental question as to why we are at the inflection point "right now" will be addressed in this section. This cycle of monetary inflation is not something new although the timelines for the causes and effects have been different historically. But the patterns have always been the same i.e., monetary inflation induced malinvestments (i.e., bubbles) followed by a crash in asset prices.

What happens is that the currency gets progressively devalued over the cycles. Though the monetary inflation is a near continuous process, the manifestation in terms of price inflation is not so unidirectional. There have been extended periods spanning decades where we have had monetary inflation, but commodity prices have fallen despite the tailwinds. A good example would be the period from 1981 to 2000 when gold prices fell from $850 to $250/oz. The period from 2008 to 2020 would be an even better example and this will be explained later in this chapter.

This lag effect of monetary inflation, especially on commodity prices, induces a false sense of optimism about the state of the economy. The artificial boom induced by the optimism is usually justified using various new theories by the government as well as the central banks. But the structural imbalances keep building over the years and eventually results in a crisis in the form of bubbles bursting e.g., NASDAQ 2000, GFC 2008 etc. Quite naturally, the greater the extent of the monetary inflation during the artificial boom, the worse would be the consequences of the bubble bursting.

The bubbles also tend to become progressively bigger as ever increasing doses of monetary inflation are required to induce the artificial boom within the economy. These cycles of monetary inflation continue till we reach the blow-out stage of the currency in which the monetary inflation required is so massive that it leads to a complete collapse in the purchasing power of the currency.

4.A - The Cycles of Monetary Inflation

The quote from the book *Dying of Money* by *Jens O. Parsson* is particularly apt for our current situation and is given below. The explanation of the full cycle of monetary inflation is split into two phases as he had explained.

Monetary Inflation in the US Economy from 2008 to 2021

Everyone loves an early inflation. The effects at the beginning of an inflation are all good. There is steepened money expansion, rising government spending, increased government budget deficits, booming stock markets, and spectacular general prosperity, all in the midst of temporarily stable prices. **Everyone benefits, and no one pays...**

Price Inflation in the US Economy from 2022 to 202X

In the terminal inflation, there is faltering prosperity, tightness of money, falling stock markets, rising taxes, still larger government deficits, and still roaring money expansion, now accompanied by soaring prices and ineffectiveness of all traditional remedies. **Everyone pays and no one benefits.**

4.A.I - An Explanation of the Monetary Inflation Cycles

Fig 4.1 is a representation of how the cycles of monetary inflations become bigger over time. This indicates a depreciation in the value of currencies till they become completely worthless and loses almost all of their purchasing power

> *The phrase "The Road to hell is paved with good intentions" is singularly most applicable for the program of "Deficit Spending" by governments.*

in the final cycle of monetary inflation. A brief description of the cycles of monetary inflation is given below.

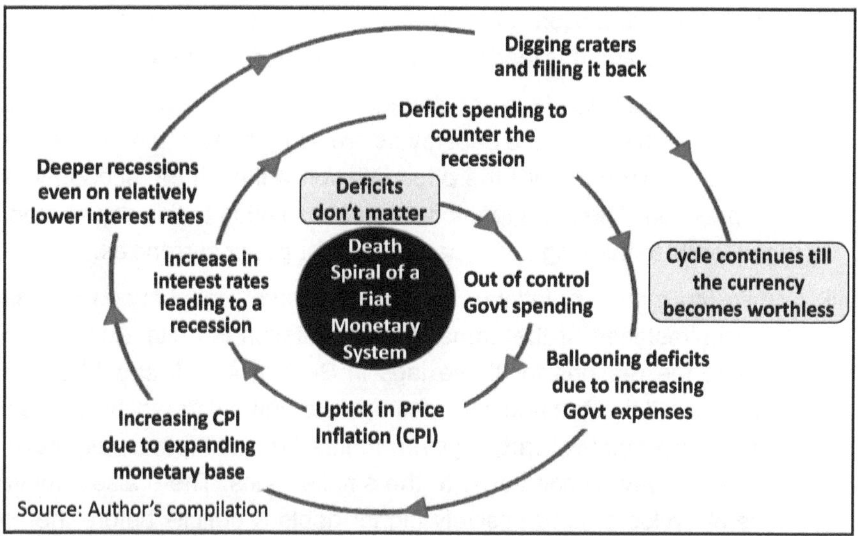

Fig 4.1 - Cycles of Monetary Inflation. Progressive devaluation of the currency eventually results in a collapse of the purchasing power.

i.   Government's deficit spending starts on a relatively small scale and usually with good intentions (misguided ones though) as well.

ii. The monetary inflation on account of the fiscal deficits leads to a gradual uptick in the consumer prices. The government/central banks main defense, and a very flawed one at that, is that falling prices cause an economic depression. So most individuals, especially economists, believe that "a little bit of price inflation" is good for the economy.

   a.   That the entire progression of the US economy to a super-power during the 100+ years before the formation of the Federal Reserve was deflationary doesn't seem to count for anything (Fig 3.15 & Fig 3.16).

iii. The report card on price inflation is published by the governments and like all self-appraisals, this leaves much to be desired (refer Fig 3.17).

iv. Once the price inflation is above the tolerable limits, then the central banks are forced to embark upon an interest rate-hiking cycle.

v.   This causes a temporary reduction in the price inflation numbers. Depending on the extent of the monetary inflation and the interest rate hikes, there could be an overall reduction in the debt-to-GDP debt ratio as well.

vi. The above reduction in price inflation relieves the pressure on governments and this leads to another round of monetary inflation.

vii. The cycles can continue for decades till the end stage of monetary inflation. At this point, the debt levels are so high that interest rate hikes that are required to curb the price inflation will push the economy into a depression. The monetary inflation as a solution to this depression is what leads to the stage of hyperinflation for paper currencies.

viii. While the monetary inflation is almost always a continuous process, the manifestation of the same in price inflation is quite episodic. We will see the reasons for these lags in Section 4.D. It should also be remembered that the above cycles operate under different timelines for different economies. Larger governments / economies usually have a greater leeway as compared to the smaller ones. There also could be several cycles of progressively higher debts & deficits before the end stage of a currency.

The premise of the book is that we are NOT in one of the intermediate inflation cycles that can be cured with the traditional fiscal & monetary policy tools; We are at the end stage wherein the dollar can become worthless within a few short years through hyperinflation. Or what Mises refers to as the condition of a "Crack-Up Boom."

There could be several questions on the above described cycles of monetary inflation and we will address some of the more common issues here.

Q.1 - Do these cycles not operate under a gold standard as well? - The answer to this question should be obvious to the reader by now. We had seen in sections 3.B and 3.C how it's almost impossible for governments to run deficits and debts under the Gold standard - particularly the classical gold standard that had prevailed till the formation of the Federal Reserve in 1913. A summary is provided below for a better understanding.

i. The accumulated national debt from 1789 to 1914 - a period of 125 years - was less than $3 billion. All of the liabilities / debts before the formation of the Federal Reserve were self-liquidating and so there was no build-up of debt at the federal level.

a. Adjusting for the monetary inflation, and using gold price movements as a proxy, this $3 billion would be $300 billion today (gold has moved from $20 to $2000/oz. during the same period).

This $300 billion is roughly the addition to the national debt in a calendar month these days. **What took 125 years (1789-1914) under the gold standard, the government now does in 30 days.**

b.   It was not that the US government did not fight wars or there were no recessions during the 1800's. There were at least 4 national wars including a civil war. There were also a several economic recessions in addition to the *Long Depression* from 1873 to 1879. But as mentioned earlier, it was the formation of a Federal Reserve in 1913 that allowed for accumulation of debt in perpetuity by the federal government.

ii.   Even after the formation of the Federal Reserve, the debt accumulation was nominal till the early 1960s. Balanced budgets and limited government were the accepted norm. Besides, 85% of the debt accumulated between 1914 and 1960 happened during the two World Wars.

iii.   The 1960s was the period when the economic ideology of "a little deficit spending is good" started gaining ground. Commencing from that "little deficit spending," we have now come a long way when 2 trillion dollar annual additions to national debt are unquestioned even during times of "economic prosperity" and "record low unemployment" e.g. FY 2022 and FY 2023 during which the additions to national debt were $2.5 and $2.24 trillion respectively.

Q.2 - How does the US government finances stack up today after 50 years of deficit financing and how has it led to the formation of bubbles?

The headline numbers of FY2023 for the US federal government is shown in the table below. The federal deficit for the year FY2023 is $1.69 trillion.

US Government Finances Summary

Federal Revenues (FY 2023)	: $ 4.44 trillion
Federal Expenses (FY 2023)	: $ 6.13 trillion
National Debt	: $ 34+ trillion
Unaccounted liabilities*	: $ 175+ trillion

* Financial Report of the US Government, 2023

If a smaller country had finances similar to the US government, the currency would have been categorized as "JUNK" according to the rating agencies. The fact that the dollar has been the reserve currency of the world has given the US government an extended rope to continue their experimentation with monetary inflation. Predictably, the US government has used the opportunity to create a noose around the dollar.

The national debt and unaccounted liabilities shown are the outcome of decades of the inflation cycles operating under both governments i.e., Republicans and Democrats. The problem today has been a truly bipartisan outcome of the fiat monetary system.

Talking of bipartisan US governments, the Republicans and Democrats are in remarkable agreement on the most relevant and important issues. Both agree to central banking based on fiat monetary standard, both believe in large deficits and ever increasing debts, both have interventionist foreign policies and support the military-industrial complex, both perpetuate the bankrupt Medicare and Social Security schemes, both subscribe to the concept of an ever-increasing role of governments in the life of citizens etc. The perceived differences that the elections are based on are indeed trivial compared to the consensus on the issues that matter.

Just to make it abundantly clear, I am not suggesting a grand conspiracy between the two political parties to bring the US to the brink of an economic disaster through deficit spending. What I am saying is that the short-term incentives of the government (and this is especially true for democracies) is are not aligned with the overall long-term interests of the society.

> *It is not a political gridlock between Republicans and Democrats that has created this situation for the US. It's the exact opposite -* ***complete consensus between the two political parties*** *on major economic policies.*

Governments can always find problems to fix and justify the monetary inflation - especially when even the well-meaning (read as liberal / Keynesian) economists do not seem to connect the dots. In the short-term, this monetary inflation even appears beneficial on account of the way we measure GDP (e.g., government programs that do the task of digging holes and filling it them back would mean an addition to the GDP). It is the gold standard that prevents these misadventures of government by limiting deficit spending.

It is also not that the political parties are alone in initiating these reckless spending programs. The *"public choice"* is equally in favor of these fiscal misadventures as they do not bear the consequences immediately. While almost everybody understands that "there is no free lunch," the public is quite content to pass the tab on to the next generation.

We can now see how the monetary inflation cycles depicted in Fig 4.1 worked in the context of the US Economy.

i. **The first cycle** - As a result of the monetary inflation of the 1960s there was the price inflation during the 1970's. Under Arthur Burns who was the Federal Reserve chairman from 1970 to 1978, the Fed was not decisive and did not increase the interest rates high enough to tame the surge in price inflation. That said, by today's standards of central banking, Arthur Burns might be called an "Alpha Hawk." It would eventually take the combination of Reagan and Volcker to put the inflation genie back in the bottle.

ii. **The second cycle** - The NASDAQ recession was triggered by the Fed funds rate of 6.5% by Q2 2000. Rates had been around 5%+ for the previous 5 years and this monetary tightening brought about the NASDAQ bubble burst. A Fed funds rate of 3% caused the monetary inflation during the early to mid-1990s.

iii. **The Third cycle** - The GFC 2008 was triggered by the Fed funds of 5.25% for just 1 year. A Fed funds rate between 1 and 2% during the 2002-04 caused the monetary inflation that resulted in the housing bubble of 2008 (HB1.0).

iv. **The Fourth (current and probably final) cycle** - The current bubble was stimulated by ZIRP & QE for nearly 15 years. The interest rate hike started in 2022 and the current rate is 5.25%.

The role of monetary inflation in the formation of the last 3 bubbles (including the current one) is depicted in Fig 4.2. Mises had drawn the comparison between a fiat currency induced bubbles and a drug addict getting artificial highs on heroin.

Role of Monetary Inflation in Bubble Formation and Bursting		
Bubble	Monetary Easing causing the Bubble Formation	Monetary Tightening causing the Bubble Bursting
Patterns	Greater and longer durations of monetary inflation required to stimulate the bubble	Lower and shorter durations of monetary tightening leads to bursting of the bubble
NASDAQ 2000	From 8% in Sep 1990, the interest rates were reduced to 3% by Jan 1994.	From 3% in Jan 1994 the interest rates were increased to 6.5% by Jun 2000
	Starting Interest Rate – 8 % Ending Interest Rate – 3 % Duration – 40 months	Starting Interest Rate – 3 % Ending Interest Rate – 6.5 % Duration – 78 months
GFC 2008	From 6.5% in Nov 2000, the interest rates were reduced to 1% by Jun 2004	From 1% in Jun 2004, the rates were increased to 5.25% by Jul 2007
	Starting Interest Rate – 6.5 % Ending Interest Rate – 1 % Duration – 44 months	Starting Interest Rate – 1 % Ending Interest Rate – 5.25 % Duration – 37 months
Current "Unnamed" Bubble	From 5.25% in Jul 2007, the interest rates were reduced to 0% by Dec 2008 and stayed at near zero till Feb 2022	From 0% in Feb 2022, the rates were increased to 5.25% by Mar 2024
	Starting Interest Rate – 5.25 % Ending Interest Rate – 0 % Duration – 188 months	Starting Interest Rate – 0 % Ending Interest Rate – 5.25 % Duration – 26 months and counting...

Source: Author's compilation

Fig 4.2 – The monetary easing that caused the bubbles and the subsequent tightening that caused the burst. The role of QE is not included in the above and that is discussed in a comparison of HB2.0 with HB1.0 that lead to the GFC 2008 as part of Sec 4.C.

The patterns that Mises had predicted can be observed as explained below.

i. A higher quantity of the drug is required to induce each subsequent high. Similar to that we can see that the monetary easing required is substantially higher (through much lower interest rates for a longer duration) to induce the subsequent bubbles.

ii. Withdrawal symptoms occur with even moderate reductions of the drug in successive cycles. We can observe that the extent of monetary tightening required in the successive cycles is lower. A much lower interest rate and monetary tightening for a lesser duration is sufficient for the bubbles to burst.

A more detailed explanation of the above is done in Sec 4.C where a comparison of the current HB2.0 is done to HB1.0. A pictorial representation of how we have the boom-bust cycles operating in the US economy is shown in Fig 4.3. This shows how the boom-bust patterns are repeated with each successive bubble requiring greater monetary inflation.

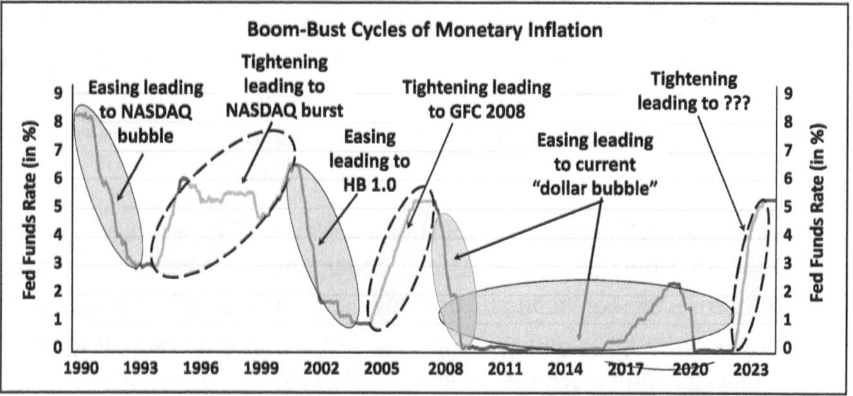

Fig 4.3 – How monetary inflation leads to the formation of bubbles followed by a burst.

i.   Nasdaq bubble formation followed by the burst during the period 1990 to 2000. This was followed by HB1.0 formation followed by the burst that lead to GFC 2008 during the period 2000 to 2008

ii. Current "dollar bubble" formation from 2008 to 2021. Tightening that will lead to the inevitable burst started in 2022.

Q.3 - Why would the current cycle lead to the "Crack-Up Boom?"

What is clear from the trends is that progressively lower interest rates for greater durations are required for the monetary inflation to work. Also, the bursting of the bubble occurs at lower interest rates (compared to the previous cycle) given the increasing size of the bubble.

The one exception to the above is that the current bubble that has not burst as yet despite the steep rate hikes. The primary reason is the enormous additions to the national debt ($2+ trillion for each of the previous 2 years and almost $1 trillion for each of the last 2 quarters) which has softened the impact of the interest rates hike on the economy. But it also means that the Fed funds rate hikes have had little impact on the borrowings by the government and the build-up of the national debt (in absolute as well as debt-to-GDP terms) is accelerating on the unsustainable trajectory.

However when the bubble bursts, the required additional monetary inflation (similar to the solutions adopted after NASDAQ 2000 and GFC 2008) has to be so enormous that the dollar would become the victim. The only way to prevent the dollar from collapsing would be to maintain the interest rates at a high enough level that would result in a reduction in the debt-to-GDP levels. But this could virtually send the US economy into a depression overnight. It should be remembered that the current 5.25% in the Fed funds rate has only resulted in an acceleration of the national debt (refer Fig 3.10 and discussions on debt-to-GDP as part of that) and so this is well below what could be considered as the interest rate that would result in monetary tightening.

In summation, the US economy would need a very low interest rate to prevent the bubbles from bursting; however, the dollar needs a high interest rate to maintain a semblance of its purchasing power. It's a Hobson's choice in some sense. An (Austrian) economist will choose the higher interest rate to protect the US dollar for tomorrow; the politician will favor the lower interest rate to (temporarily) protect the economy for today. It's not too difficult to guess as to what the eventual decision would be.

Having understood the cycles of monetary inflation and the choices to be made, we can now get into the details of why we are indeed at the breaking point and also why the current bubble is substantially bigger than the one that resulted in the GFC 2008.

4.B - IT IS DIFFERENT THIS TIME - Why we are at the breaking point.

None of the issues that have been pointed out in Chapter 3 - fiscal deficits, national debt, interest rate manipulations and monetary inflation are recent issues. They have been issues for at least the last 2 to 3 decades though these problems have become acute over the last 15 years since the GFC 2008. Through all of this the US dollar has only gained in strength relative to most other currencies and the US economy also seems to be on a reasonable growth path.

So what are the factors in the current cycle that makes the US economy and the dollar vulnerable to a catastrophic decline in the years ahead?

There are four factors indicating why *this time is indeed different* as far as the impact of the monetary inflation on the dollar is concerned.

I.   Increase in interest payments on national debt as a % of tax receipts

II.   Precedence of monetary inflation to handle downturns

III.   Flow through of monetary inflation into price inflation

IV.   Profligate increase in national debt

4.B.I - Increase in Interest Payments on National Debt as a % of Tax Receipts

i.   The US government has to pay interest on the national debt and this has become a significant fraction of the Federal revenues in the last few years. From an annualized interest payment of around $520B during Q4 2020, interest payments have increased steadily to $612B during Q4 2021, $830B during Q4 2022 and $980 by Q3 2023. This is shown in Fig 4.4 along with the increase in interest rates on National debt.

This near doubling in interest payments over the 3 years 2020 to 2023 has been caused by the movement in the interest rate on national debt from 1.7% during Dec 2020 to 3.11% in Dec 2023. The National debt also increased from $27 trillion to $33 trillion during this period contributing to an increase in the interest payments.

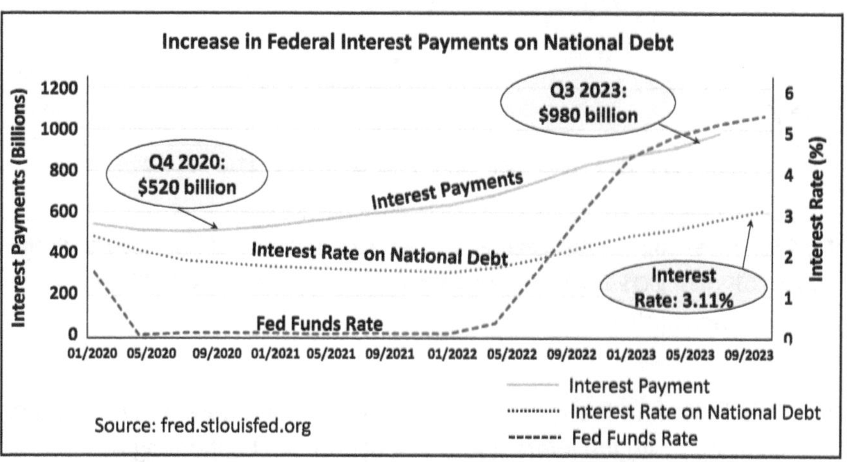

Fig 4.4 - Increase in Federal interest payments due to increasing interest rates and ballooning National debt

i.   Interest payments on National Debt has doubled in the last 3 years primarily on account of increasing interest rates on National Debt that even now is at a low 3.11%.

ii.   The interest rate of 1.7% on the national debt was caused by 15 years of ZIRP on the Fed funds rate that has lowered the long-term bond yields of all categories to hitherto unseen levels.

iii. The current interest rate of 3.11% on national debt is well below the prevailing Fed funds rate of 5.25%+ and so interest rates on national debt are set to rise further even assuming constant or marginally declining Fed funds rate. This is on account of the addition to national debt (at approximately $3 - 4 trillion/year) and about $7 trillion of existing debt maturing in 2024 and 2025. So approximately $10+ trillion of new financing at rates substantially higher than the current 3.11% has to be done for 2024 and 2025.

iv.   Interest payments as a % of Federal tax receipts bottomed at just above 20% during Q1 2022 as shown in Fig 4.5. This is even lower than the 23% recorded during Q1 1970 when the national debt was just a little more than 1% of the debt today ($370 billion in 1970 vs $34 trillion today).

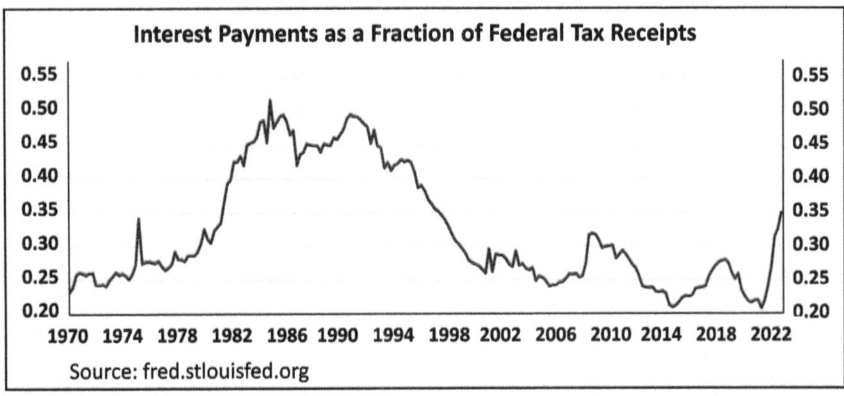

Fig 4.5 – Increasing interest payments as a fraction of Federal Tax receipts. From about 20% during Q1 2022, interest payments are 35% during Q3 2023 and is set to increase further.

v.   This bottom in the interest payments as % of federal tax receipts also coincides with the interest rate on national debt bottoming at 1.7%. The interest payments as a % of Federal tax receipts stand at 35% as of Q3 2023 and are set to increase even further in the years ahead.

vi.   Though this 35% during Q3 2023 is well below the 50% that prevailed during the mid to late 1980s, it is a bigger problem today for reasons below

a.   The Fed funds rates during the 1980s peaked in 1981 at 22% and witnessed a steady decline subsequently. The rates today at 5.25%, despite the series of hikes during 2022 and 2023 are closer to the historical lows. The last 15 years of ZIRP have foisted a misaligned set of expectations with governments, companies and the public.

b.   The governments largely ran balanced budgets (excluding interest payments) during the 1980's. Today, the federal govt runs trillion dollar deficits excluding interest payments.

c.   The 1980s was the starting point of a period of an economic boom; we are near the starting point of an unprecedented economic bust at this juncture.

So essentially, the US government cannot afford even the prevailing 3.11% interest rate on the national debt. But a more pressing issue, as will be explained, is that the dollar cannot afford a lower interest rate. In fact, the current Fed funds rate of 5.25% is far too low to arrest the growth in national debt. It is this unfettered growth in national debt that will bring about the demise of the dollar as it exists today.

4.B.II - Precedence of Monetary Inflation

Since 1980, only for a brief couple of years (just before the NASDAQ 2000 crash) did the US government run a budget surplus. Since then, the US government has had 23 years without having come close to running a budget surplus. The SOP (Standard Operating Procedure) for every recent downturn has been QE a.k.a monetary inflation. The size of deficits is only getting bigger and trillion-dollar-deficits are the norm these days even with a supposedly "strong economy" e.g., FY2022 had a deficit of $1.45 trillion and for FY2023 it was $1.56 trillion.

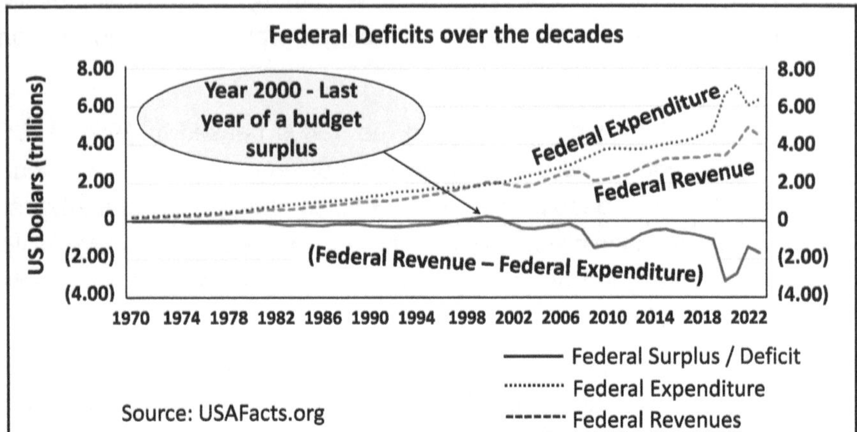

Fig 4.6 – Federal Government finances, adjusted for inflation (FY2022 dollars)

i. **Federal Deficits – the excess of Federal Expenditure over Federal Revenue has been in "the trillions" for more 4 years now.**

Fig 4.6 shows the federal deficits since 1970. Though deficits started becoming a near-permanent feature of the budgets after 1971, it was not until the NASDAQ 2000 induced recession, that the scale of the deficits started becoming significant. The first trillion dollar deficit happened after the GFC 2008 recession i.e., FY 2009 had a federal deficit of $1.4 trillion. Though subsequent deficits were lower, it was only a temporary respite. FY 2019 was the last year during which the US had a sub-trillion dollar deficit.

Concomitant with the monetary inflation, the size of the balance sheet of the Federal Reserve has seen an unprecedented growth since the GFC 2008 as can be seen from Fig 4.7. The US Federal Reserve's balance sheet was less than $1T before the burst and today it stands at $8T. The growth happened in spurts as shown with the steepest increase happening during the COVID years. An interesting question would be what would the Fed balance sheet look like by 2026?

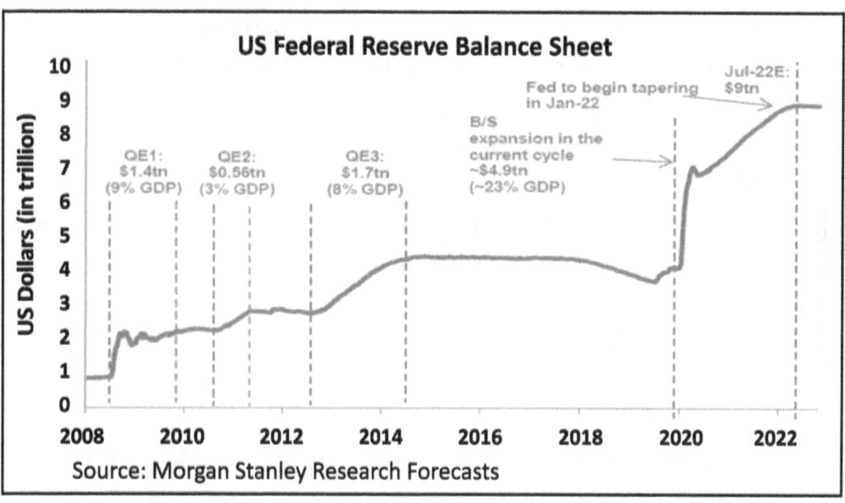

Fig 4.7 – 8-fold growth in the Federal Reserve's balance sheet to $9 trillion since the GFC 2008. The first trillion took 95 years since the formation of the Federal Reserve in 1913

There are two parts to the above question - (i) what would the organic growth in the Fed balance sheet be and (ii) what would the size of the QE be when the housing bubble 2.0 bursts during 2024/25?

i. The Federal Reserve's balance sheet is set to grow significantly even if there is no economic crisis in the form of a HB2.0 burst during 2024.

An estimated $7.6 trillion of the current debt of $34+ trillion matures in the current year 2024. Add to this the expected addition to the national debt of at least $3T and we are looking at new buyers for at least $10T of treasuries during 2024. The estimate for 2025 is another $10+ T to be financed. It is hard to envisage an external buyer for this quantum of debt in the current environment and most of it might have to be purchased by the Federal Reserve i.e., buyer of the last resort.

Since the GFC 2008, the % of the national debt held by the US Fed has tripled from less than 5% to 15% indicating the decrease in appetite for US treasuries with foreign investors as shown in Fig 4.8. With almost all countries suffering from their own price inflation malaise, the appetite to support the US dollar is waning with the foreign central banks. Today, the Federal Reserve is the single largest holder of the national debt. The rationale is not too difficult to fathom - Why will any investor buy long-term bonds given the financials of the US government and at rates that guarantee loss of purchasing power due to price inflation?

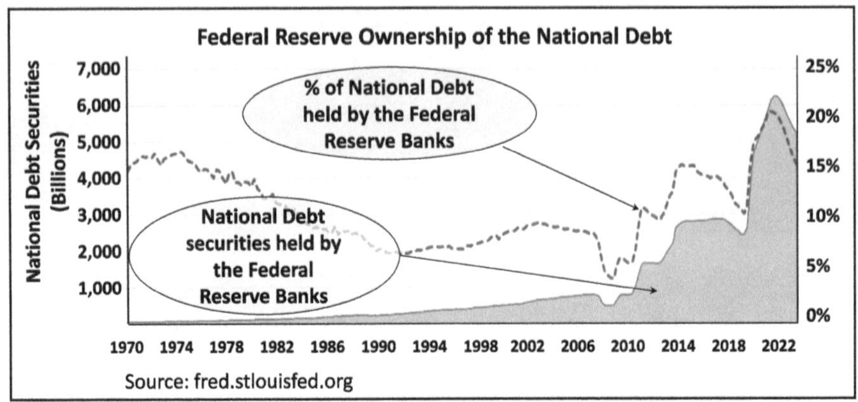

Fig 4.8 – Holdings of National Debt Securities by the Federal Reserve banks; by face value and as a share of the National Debt.

i.   From less than 5% during the GFC 2008, today the Federal Reserve holdings are at 15%.

ii. The Fed has to purchase an even greater share of the debt issuances in 2024 & 2025.

At the minimum, the US Fed would have to monetize at least 50% of these treasuries to be issued in 2024 and so we should witness the Federal Reserve's balance sheet growing by about $5T each year for 2024 and 2025. This of course is assuming normal operating conditions.

ii. 2024 / 25 is anything but going to be normal. We will witness the bursting of the HB2.0 (as will be explained in sec 4.C) and this is going to necessitate monetary inflation the quantum of which will dwarf what we witnessed post the GFC 2008 or even during the COVID years.

QE 1, 2 and 3 was merely stabilizing the effects of the HB1.0 burst and this necessitated a quadrupling of the US Fed balance sheet from $1T to $5T.

Even without a housing bubble, the banks are in much bigger trouble today because of the asset-liability mismatch (more in section 4.C). Add to it, the reality that the HB2.0 is much bigger than the one that led to the GFC 2008 crisis.

So how big will the next round of monetary inflation be as a response to the collapse of HB2.0? Linear extrapolations will always be erroneous under these circumstances and it's best we answer this question after we understand the HB2.0 as explained later in section 4.C. Suffice to state at this juncture that we are at the very least looking at a Fed balance sheet of $20 to $25T within 18 to 24 months of the HB2.0 burst.

If this is going to be the extent of the monetary inflation in the years ahead, what is going to be the effect in terms of price inflation?

4.B.III - Flow Through of Monetary Inflation into Price Inflation

There were 4 factors listed in the early part of section 4.B as to why the US dollar is at a breaking point right now. Of the 4 factors, the most important one is the "flow through of monetary inflation into price inflation." While it is well acknowledged that there is a lag between monetary inflation and price inflation, what is not well understood is that this lag could span a decade or longer; even less understood is what happens to all of the monetary inflation created in the interim.

Does this imply that if this "flow through" had not happened now, we would not have had this crisis? Not at all. As was explained in the first section of Chapter 4, these inflation cycles are inevitable in a fiat currency system and it is only a matter of time. If the flow through had not happened now but say by 2030, all it would imply is that we would have gained time but we will a much bigger problem on our hands down the line. For example, confronting this issue of the national debt would have been easier in 2008 when it was $10T than today when it is at $34T. If for some reason the Federal Reserve is able to maintain ZIRP and "kick the can" to 2030, then we would have to confront a national debt that would be $60 trillion at the barest minimum. And a much bigger HB2.0 to contend with as well.

After the GFC 2008, the US had witnessed a hitherto unprecedented monetary inflation - QE's that would result in an 8-fold increase in the Fed balance sheet from less than $1T to more than $9T and a tripling in national debt from $10T to more than $34T. While we had some price inflationary pressures, especially after 2020, the US dollar has largely maintained its purchasing power vis-à-vis other foreign currencies as well as commodities over these 15 years period despite the massive monetary inflation.

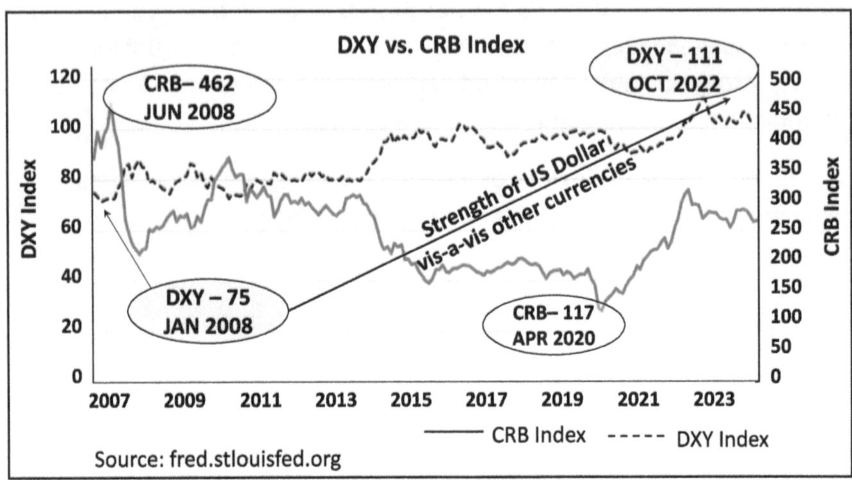

Fig 4.9 – Comparison of DXY and the CRB Indices since the 2008 GFC

DXY: The Dollar Index is an index of the value of the US Dollar relative to a basket of foreign currencies. These currencies are the Euro, Japanese Yen, Pound Sterling, Canadian Dollar, Swedish Krona and Swiss Franc.

CRB Index (Commodity Research Bureau): Renamed as the FTSE / Core Commodity CRB Index and consists of a basket of 19 commodities in 4 categories – Energy, Agriculture, Precious metals and metals.

What is obvious from Fig 4.9 is that the dollar has strengthened despite the monetary inflation. The DXY that shows the relative strength of the dollar vis-à-vis other currencies has increased from a value of 75 during January 2008 to 102 by January 2024. The CRB - which is an index of commodity prices - had reached a peak of 462 by June 2008 and had declined almost 75% to 117 by April 2020. As of Apr 2024, it trades at 340 which is still 25% below the peak of 2008 despite the massive monetary inflation during the intervening period.

The movement in both DXY as well as the CRB indices over the last 15 years since the GFC 2008 is the exact opposite of what ought to have happened as was explained under "Inflation-101" (Section 3.D). How do we explain this?

The increase in the DXY could reflect the even greater extent of monetary inflation in other currencies worldwide: Eurozone had negative interest rates from 2014 to 2019 and the real interest rates in these regions continue to be negative even using the official numbers for consumer price inflation. Japan continues to have negative nominal interest rates even today. Japan was on ZIRP from 2010 to 2016 and if that was not enough, had shifted to a negative interest rate of -0.1% and has remained at that level ever since. So on a relative basis, there is a case to be made as to why the US dollar has strengthened against other currencies over the last 15 years.

This particular issue / conundrum is a fatal flaw of the current monetary system of the "fluctuating fiat currency standard." There is no standard basis for comparison of a currency and as long as other currencies "inflate" at about the same rate, there would be no obvious impact in the currency markets. All currencies would be losing purchasing power and the imbalances could continue to build up for an extended period of time as has been the case for nearly 15 years now.

How about the CRB Index? How does one explain the decline of the CRB Index in the face of massive monetary inflation witnessed from 2008 to date?

As mentioned earlier, the translation of monetary inflation into price inflation does not happen in a linear fashion. When a central bank creates additional money supply and credit within the economy, it does not directly flow into commodities that largely reflects in what we measure as consumer prices.

Fig 4.10 shows the possible destination for the monetary inflation created by the central banks. The new money created could flow into the financial assets of stocks and bonds, real estate (e.g., housing, farmlands etc), or commodities. **When the new money created flows into the first two asset classes, i.e., financial assets and real estate, these are viewed favorably by the markets and the false similarity of booming stock indices and real estate to economic prosperity deceives the markets.** It is only when the money starts flowing into the asset class of "commodities" does it starts reflecting in what we measure as consumer price inflation numbers.

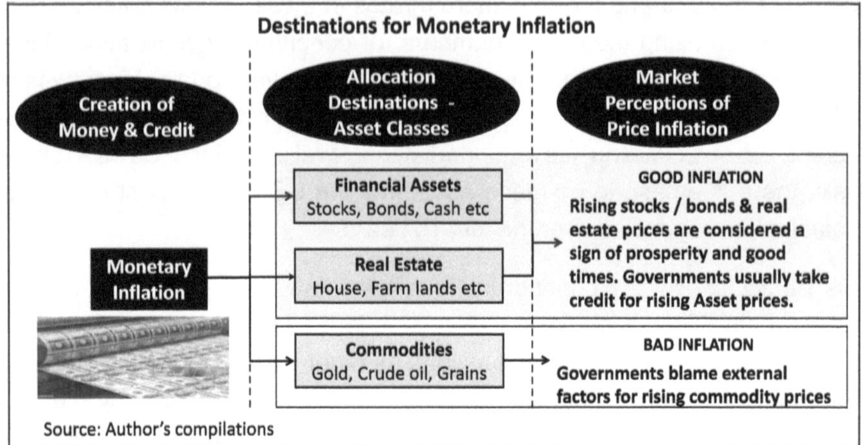

Fig 4.10 – The monetary inflation created by Central Banks can flow into Financial Assets, Real Estate and Commodities. An appreciation in the price of the first two Asset classes are viewed favorably by market participants and the government.

In what must be a truly bizarre economic phenomenon, governments have even started taking credit for this. Successive US Presidents have used the stock market high as a barometer of their performance. Trump claimed in January 2024 "This is the Trump Stock Market. Because my polls against Biden are so good that investors are projecting that I will win, and that will drive the Market up."

In reality, the stock markets going up is entirely the work of the Federal Reserve. Paraphrasing the famous quote of James Carville, **"It's the monetary inflation, stupid."**

But the final destination for all monetary inflation is commodities. While individuals might keep their earnings in stocks and other financial assets, this is merely a form of investment for consumption

Does it now stand to reason as to why price inflation is a given in any monetary system other than the Gold Standard?

Inflation is a form of taxation without consent or even explicit payments from the citizens to the government.

When the times are good, governments can take credit for the effects of monetary inflation; and when times are bad, external factors can be blamed. It is not an accident that we have had deflation or falling prices for the 113 years before the formation of the Federal Reserve; and rising prices for the 110+ years after the event.

to happen in the future. When individuals divest their investments in favor of consumption, the same money flows into commodities. Of course, governments usually blame the weather, greedy businesses, geopolitics and all other factors for the rise in prices of the commodity basket. All factors other than the one true reason i.e. monetary inflation created by central banks, would be offered as the reason for the rising prices of the basket of commodities.

So how do we determine into which asset class the monetary inflation will flow into over the next few years? In some sense, this is the trillion-dollar question; fortunately, there are historical patterns to guide us.

Fig 4.11 shows the relative valuation of commodities as compared to stocks. This ratio compares the Goldman Sachs Commodity Index Returns to the S&P 500. A high number indicates that the commodities are expensive relative to stocks and vice-versa. Not only is this ratio well below the "bottom trend line" of the last 50 years, it has stayed below that level for the last 7 years indicating the extreme undervaluation's of commodities for an extended period of time. That this trend has persisted, indeed worsened, in the face of unprecedented monetary inflation makes it an even more bizarre situation from a theoretical perspective. Some key observations that we can draw from Fig 4.11 are given below:

i. The median valuation is around 4 at which point both stocks and commodities seem to be reasonably valued on a relative basis.

ii. The ratio of above 6 makes commodities relatively expensive and puts it in the region of "bubble valuations." Gold at $850/oz during the early eighties and nearly $2000/oz after the GFC 2008 are good examples of the bubble in commodities.

iii. A valuation of below 2 makes commodities relatively cheap and stocks in the region of "bubble valuations." The early 1970s when gold was at $35/oz and the year 2000 when gold was at $250/oz are good examples of when commodity valuations were depressed.

iv. The current valuations are even lower than what prevailed during the early 1970's which has been the historical bottom for this ratio till the current cycle.

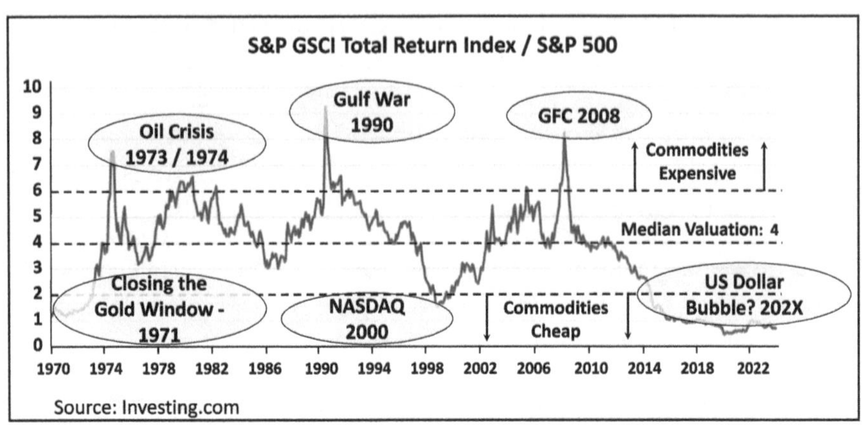

Fig 4.11 – Ratio of Goldman Sachs Commodity Index Total Returns Vs. S&P 500

i.   The Median Valuation of the last 50 years is 4

ii. The last two bottoms historically was at 1.17 in April 1971 and at 1.52 in February 1999. For the last 7+ years, this ratio has been below 1 with the reading of 0.46 during April 2020

So though the CRB Index has moved up significantly (as shown in Fig 4.9) since the bottom of April 2020, in terms of relative valuations, we are still hovering well below the bottoms of 1971 and 2000. Notwithstanding the current all-time high price of gold, investors could well be justified in concluding that we are still in the starting phase of a "supercycle in commodities." Adjusting for the monetary inflation, it is easy to see why commodities are cheaper than what they were during 1971 as Fig 4.11 indicates.

Historically, a major event has caused the upturn from the commodity cycle bottoms. In the year 1971 it was the closure of the gold window and in the year 2000 it was the bursting of the dot-com bubble. Possible triggers could be the bursting of HB2.0 later in 2024. Or it could well be the anticipated "Powell Pivot" during H2 of 2024.

4.B.IV - Profligate Increase in National Debt - Pushing on Strings?

The growth in national debt from less than $1T during 1980 to more than $34T by Q1 2024 has been discussed earlier in section 3.B. The "debt limit" that was envisaged for very legitimate reasons is now just a political tool for *quid pro quo* deals between the two political parties. Since 1960, the Congress had 78 raises to this debt limit and not once has this increase in limit been refused on grounds of principle.

Even on the rare occasions where there has been a delay in increasing the limits on the national debt and we have had a "Government Shutdown," it has been a case of disagreement on where to spend and never has it been an issue of "IF." These increases have been a truly bi-partisan affair with 49 increases under Republican Presidents and 29 times under Democrat Presidents.

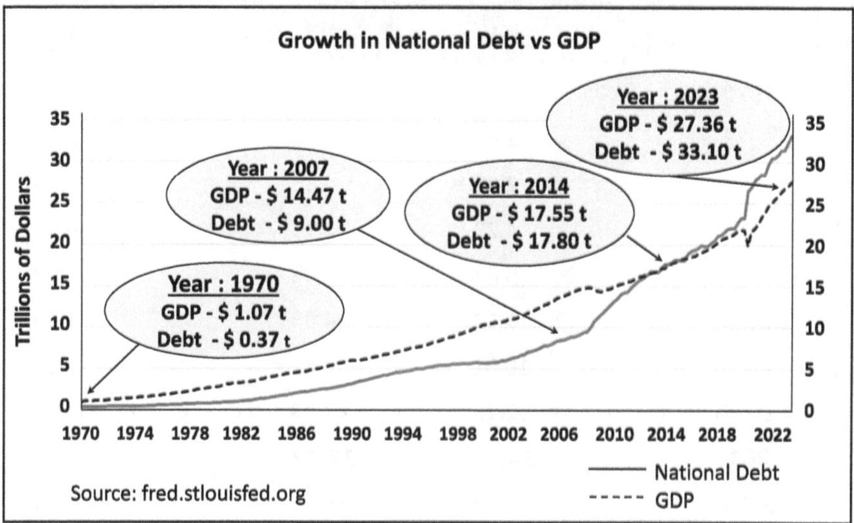

Fig 4.12 – Growth in National Debt has outpaced GDP from 1970. This has accelerated since the 2008 GFC

The trend of the national debt increasing at a faster pace than the GDP can be seen in Fig 4.12. In absolute terms, the national debt was just 1/3rd of the GDP in 1970. However the US has increasingly relied on debt and by FY 2014, the national debt was greater than the GDP.

This indicates that the utilization of debt has become less effective over the decades as shown in Fig 4.13. The last column measures the ratio of growth in debt to the growth in GDP over the previous 5 year period. This ratio has had an increasing trend indicating that the US has required a progressively greater amount of debt to generate a unit of GDP.

This diminishing returns on the usage of debt has been stark post the GFC 2008 crisis and since then we have required more than $1 addition to debt for every additional $1 generated in GDP. Notwithstanding the diminishing returns and despite a series of interest rate hikes since 2022, there seems to be no respite in the growth of debt. We are now perilously close to the point where the growth in debt causes an increase in the annual fiscal deficit as the taxes generated from the marginal GDP generated are lower than the interest payments on the marginal debt added.

Diminishing Marginal Utility of National Debt			
Period	Real GDP ($ Trillion)	National Debt ($ Trillion)	$ growth in Debt for $1 growth in GDP
Q1 1970	1.01	0.37	
Q1 1975	1.61	0.51	0.23
Q1 1980	2.79	0.86	0.30
Q1 1985	4.23	1.71	0.59
Q1 1990	5.87	3.05	0.82
Q1 1995	7.52	4.86	1.10
Q1 2000	10.02	5.77	0.36
Q1 2005	12.76	7.77	0.73
Q1 2010	**14.76**	**12.77**	**2.50**
Q1 2015	18.06	18.15	1.63
Q1 2020	21.7	23.22	1.39
Q3 2023	27.06	33.26	1.85
Q1 2026**	**28.43**	**42**	**2.79**

Source: fred.stlouisfed.org

Fig 4.13 – Growth in National Debt Vs. the Growth in GDP since 2010

i. The last column is the Ration of "growth in debt" to "growth in GDP" since previous time period.

ii. The 1st inflection point is as shown in 2010 when the more than >$1 of Debt is required for $1 of GDP growth.

iii. ** - The 2nd inflection point is a projection wherein the marginal taxes generated is not covering the interest on the marginal debt. This is expected to happen by 2026.

What is the basis for the projections of Q1 2026 which is the last line in Fig 4.13? The GDP growth has been assumed at a CAGR of 2% and a growth in debt of about $1T/quarter. Both are conservative assumptions given the imminent bursting of the HB2.0.

We had seen in section 3.C as to how the federal tax revenues as a % of GDP have remained constant between 16 and 18% (Fig 3.12) over the last 50+ years. What this shows is that every $1 of GDP results in 16 to 18 cents in tax revenues. When the ratio of "growth in debt / growth in GDP" crosses 2.8 times, then at a 6% net interest rate on government debt, the additional tax generated would equal the interest cost to be paid on the marginal debt. We could probably reach the 2nd inflection point even earlier than Q1 2026 indicated. The soon-to-burst HB2.0 will ensure that the growth in national debt breaks the linear assumptions made.

The 2nd inflection point would be the situation in which an increase in national debt leads to greater fiscal deficits. This would have the same effect as "pushing on strings" as the government would have to borrow to pay the interest. This is the classical definition of a Ponzi scheme and the US is perilously close to one at this point.

We have had several signposts indicating the looming disaster that the debt situation was leading the US economy to.

i.   The 1st inflection point in 2010 should have been a wake-up call when more than $1 in debt was required to generate $1 in additional GDP.

ii. The 2nd warning signal should have come in 2014 when the national debt exceeded the GDP. The trends were in the making for decades and yet not only did the politicians ignore the signs, but even the economic advisors were asleep at the wheels.

iii. 2017 was the last year in which the addition to national debt was less than a trillion. 2021 was the last year in which this addition was less than $2 trillion. For the year ending FY2022, the national debt increased by $2.5 trillion and for FY2023, the increase was $2.2 trillion. Both these years recorded GDP growth in excess of 2% with record low unemployment numbers. What was the rationale for the $2+ trillion addition to the national debt?

iv. For the year FY2024, we are set to easily surpass the $2 trillion addition once again. The addition to debt could well be more than $3 trillion for the current fiscal year. In the first 6 months of FY2024, the addition to the national debt has been $1.45 trillion.

To say that these trends are alarming would be an understatement. Yet, Treasury Secretary Janet Yellen recently made the following observation when the national debt crossed $33 trillion. Instead of expressing deep concerns at the unsustainability of current trends, she remarked *"The statistic or metric that I look at most often to judge our fiscal course is net interest as a share of GDP, and even with the rise we have seen in interest rates that remains at a very reasonable level."*

So it is not that the signs were not there or that this was an overnight situation. The crisis had been developing for decades and we are now very close to the tipping point.

4.C - The Bursting of Housing Bubble 2.0 (HB 2.0)

The term "GFC 2008" has been referred to several times and it's a recent event in comparison to the other historical economic crises described i.e. 1929 Great Depression, Stagflation of the 1970s etc. Even so, we will start this section with a brief description of how the collapse of the housing bubble 1.0 caused the GFC 2008.

4.C.I - The "Wh" Questions of Housing Bubble 1.0 (HB1.0)

The monetary inflation following the NASDAQ 2000 bubble burst (details in Fig 4.17 and Fig 4.18) led to the formation of the HB1.0. To control the consequent price inflation, the Federal Reserve started hiking rates during 2004 and this eventually led to the bursting of the bubble by 2008. Several studies have done a post-facto analysis of GFC 2008 and have listed multiple causes of the housing bubble - risky mortgage products and lax lending standards by the banks, housing tax policy, deregulation including repeal of the Glass-Steagall Act, mandates to promote affordable housing, historically low interest rates including the usage of Adjustable Rate Mortgages (ARM's) that offered loans at 1%, speculative behavior on the part of buyers etc. These are listed in Fig 4.14

However, all of these reports fail to distinguish the primary causative factor from the secondary factors. There is one and only one primary factor which is the monetary inflation caused by the Federal Reserve. In the absence of that, even if all of the secondary factors had worked overtime, we would not have had a housing bubble. Paraphrasing Friedman, we can state that **"All bubbles are a phenomenon caused by central banks through monetary inflation."**

<table>
<tr><td colspan="3" align="center">What Caused the Housing Bubble 1.0?</td></tr>
<tr><td>Primary Causative Factor</td><td align="center">Secondary Factors</td><td rowspan="8">When a post-facto analysis of the causal factors for HB2.0 is conducted a couple of years down the line, the secondary factors listed could be different from the ones listed for HB1.0

The "unlisted" Primary Causative Factor would continue to be the monetary inflation during the preceding years.</td></tr>
<tr><td rowspan="7">Monetary Inflation caused by the Federal Reserve after the crash of NASDAQ 2000.</td><td>Lax lending standards</td></tr>
<tr><td>Deregulation – Repeal of Glass - Steagall Act</td></tr>
<tr><td>Promotion of affordable housing</td></tr>
<tr><td>......</td></tr>
<tr><td>......</td></tr>
<tr><td>Predatory lending practices</td></tr>
<tr><td>Speculative behavior of home buyers</td></tr>
<tr><td>Risky mortgage practices</td></tr>
<tr><td colspan="3">Source: Author's compilations</td></tr>
</table>

Fig 4.14 – The Primary & Secondary Causative Factors for HB1.0

i.   A few Secondary Factors are shown as "…..". This is because, in the larger scheme of things, these are not-so-important. Once the monetary inflation was created and this started flowing into the housing market, each of secondary factors merely played a minor accretive role.

ii.   These secondary factors did not cause the bubble; they just made it bigger.

Also, if the monetary inflation was a given, then even if all the mentioned secondary factors had been eliminated, we would still have had a housing bubble back in 2008. New secondary factors would have emerged to take the place of the original ones. **The secondary factors have the effect of making the bubble bigger; they do not cause the bubble.**

The situation today is a good example where the banks are heavily regulated with no ARM's or an explicit "subprime" category of borrowers. Yet, today we have an even bigger HB2.0 as will be explained in this section.

All bubbles eventually find a pin and it was no different for the HB1.0. The collapse threatened the entire financial system with even talks of martial law being put in place. Several movies were made about the events leading up to the collapse of the mortgage industry which brought the banking system to the brink of a systemic collapse. Some of the more educative movies are shown in Fig 4.15 though all of them deal with only the secondary factors listed in Fig 4.14.

Fig 4.15 – GFC 2008 was the biggest economic crisis since the Great Depression of 1929 to 1946. Several movies were made describing the events leading up to the near collapse of the banking system.

Another interesting aspect of the HB1.0 was the denial of its very existence till the inevitable burst. The then Federal Reserve Chairperson Bernanke when questioned about the existence of a housing bubble during the formative period would offer the following explanation.

The peak of housing prices as part of HB1.0 would happen during Q1 of 2007. The declines immediately after Q1 2007 were relatively modest and were treated as a cyclical downturn in an otherwise structural bull market. However, housing prices would continue their decline during the subsequent months and the weakest link in the housing chain, the subprime housing segment would be the first to collapse. Even after the collapse of the subprime housing market, Bernanke would continue to offer optimism about the housing market and the strength of the overall economy.

The decline in housing prices would soon spread to all segments of the housing industry and it was pretty clear soon afterward that

> *"Well, I guess I don't buy your premise. It's a pretty unlikely possibility. We've never had a decline in house prices on a nationwide basis. So, what I think what is more likely is that house prices will slow, maybe stabilize, might slow consumption spending a bit. I don't think it's going to drive the economy too far from its full employment path, though."*
>
> **– Ben Bernanke, July 2005**

> *"At this juncture, however, the impact on the broader economy and financial markets of the problems in the subprime market seems likely to be contained"*
>
> **– Ben Bernanke, May 2007**

the housing bubble 1.0 had burst. The definitive moment that signaled the GFC 2008 was the bankruptcy of Lehman Brothers in September 2008. The subsequent consequences were a severe recession, rising unemployment and a fall in net worth as indicated in Fig 4.16

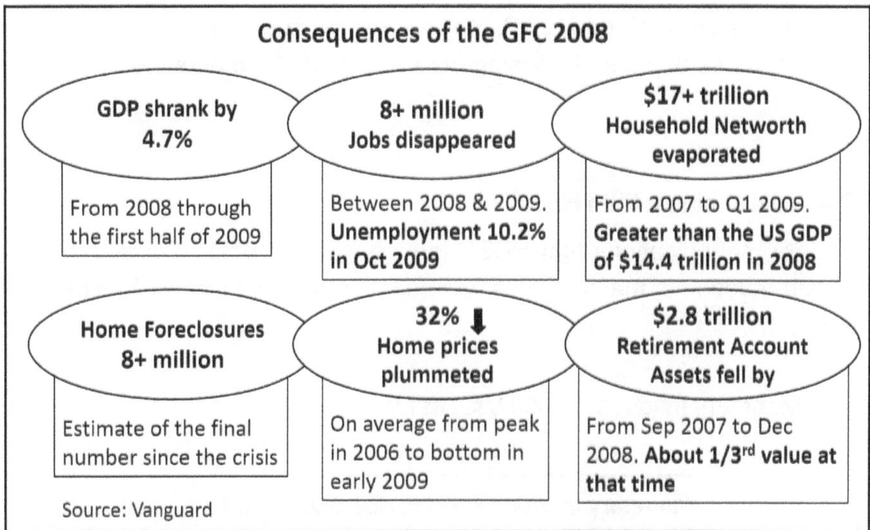

Fig 4.16 – Consequences of Housing Bubble 1.0 bursting went well beyond foreclosures and collapse of housing prices. GDP, Unemployment and Household Networth were significantly impacted.

The above discussed HB1.0 that burst during 2008 and led to the GFC should be a good comparison as we are dealing with very similar conditions currently. As mentioned earlier, the GFC 2008 is going to look like the proverbial Sunday school picnic compared to what lies ahead. Therefore, it would be useful to explain the current HB2.0 in the context of what happened back then along the following themes.

i.   HB2.0 is far bigger than HB1.0 - This is true in every possible way such as prices, affordability, no. of units etc.

ii. The banks are in far greater trouble even if HB2.0 is to be of the same size as HB1.0. This is account of the differences in the nature of mortgages (predominantly floating rates during HB1.0 as compared to 30-year fixed now) and the movement in the 30-year mortgage rates between then and now. Even if HB2.0 doesn't burst for another couple of years (a very remote possibility), the banks would be in serious trouble on account of the above reasons.

During the years leading up to the HB1.0 burst, there used to several discussions in the media about the issue. The majority opinion denied the existence of a bubble back then and it is not a surprise that it indeed was the case. The markets witnessed a similar "bubble denial" phenomenon before the crash of NASDAQ 2000 as well. The odd phenomenon today is that there is no discussion at all on HB2.0. Yet, as we will see in this section, we are well past the peak price of housing in this cycle and the bursting of HB2.0 is imminent.

4.C.II - HB2.0 bigger than HB1.0

What are the indications that HB2.0 is bigger than HB1.0? For starters, the size and duration of the causative factors i.e. monetary inflation, has been far greater.

i.   **Monetary Inflation: HB2.0 Vs. HB1.0**

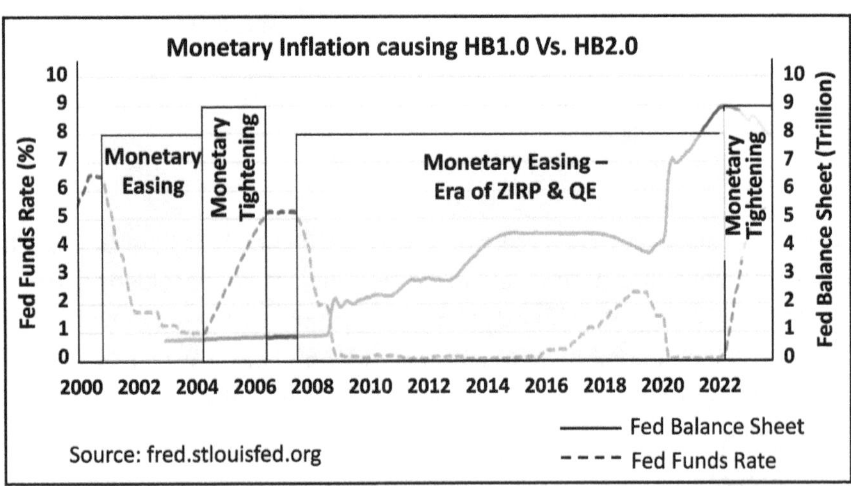

Fig 4.17 – A comparison of Monetary Inflation causing HB1.0 and HB2.0

i.   **HB2.0 had 15 years of ZIRP / low single digit rates Vs. a few years of low single digit rates for HB1.0.**

ii.   **The Fed balance sheet grew nearly 9 times for HB2.0 as compared to almost a flat-line for HB1.0**

As can be seen from Fig 4.17, both the interest rate regime (interest rates and the duration) as well as the expansion of the Fed Balance sheet were an order of magnitude more stimulative for HB2.0 as compared to HB1.0. Interest rates were practically at zero for most parts of the 15 years leading up to HB2.0. If a few years of low single-digit rates could cause the GFC 2008 what would more than a decade of ZIRP lead to? Combine that with a nearly 10-fold expansion in the Fed balance sheet and this was a non-existent factor for HB1.0. The monetary inflation leading up to HB2.0 is anything but the typical "stimulus" that the market has become accustomed to.

Money Supply (M2) growth, expansion of the Federal Reserve's balance sheet, growth in national debt - all of these have been substantially higher for HB2.0 as compared to the previous bubble as can be inferred from Fig 4.18.

Comparison of Monetary Inflation - HB1.0 and HB2.0		
Monetary Inflation	**Nasdaq 2000 to HB1.0 Q4 2000 to Q1 2007**	**HB1.0 to HB2.0 Q1 2007 to Q4 2022**
Interest Rates	Interest rates reduced from 6.5% during Q4 2000 to 1% by Q3 2003. Rates raised from 1% Q3 2004 to 5.25% by Q3 2006 where it stayed till Q2 2007.	ZIRP from Q1 2009 to Q1 2022 excepting for an intermission from Q1 2016 to Q1 2020 where it was increased to 2.5% and brought back to ZIRP again. Rates raised from ZIRP during Q1 2022 to 5.25% during Q1 2023.
Money Supply (M2)	From 4.9T to 7.16T for a total growth in M2 of 2.26T Cumulative growth of 46% in M2 during this period.	From 7.16T to 21.36T for a total growth in M2 of 14.2T Cumulative growth of 187% in M2 during this period.
US Fed Balance Sheet	From 0.7T to 0.87T for a cumulative growth in the Balance sheet of 0.17T	From 0.87T to 8.55T for a cumulative growth in the Balance sheet of 7.68T
National Debt	From $5.66T to $8.85T for a growth in debt of $3.21T	$8.85T to $31.42T for a growth in debt of $22.57T

Fig 4.18 – The quantum of monetary inflation that had lead to the current HB2.0 is far higher as compared to the one that caused HB1.0.

For all of the evidence of monetary inflation provided in Fig 4.18, it is easier to prove the existence of the bubble showing the price inflation in the housing markets. This is easily demonstrable using a few statistics such as (i) housing prices: today vis-à-vis 2008 (ii) housing prices relative to income and (iii) affordability of the US consumer given the current interest rate environment.

ii. Housing Prices: HB2.0 Vs. HB 1.0

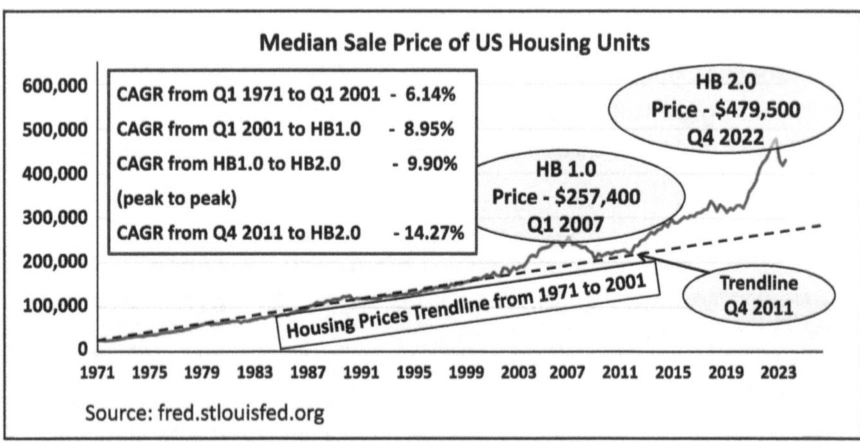

Fig 4.19 – Growth in median sale price of US housing units

i. **Houses at the peak of the current HB2.0 during Q4 2022 are 86% more expensive as compared to the peak of the HB1.0 during Q1 2007**

The movement of housing prices as part of HB2.0 has been far in excess of the historical norms as indicated in Fig 4.19. Housing prices corrected by almost 40% after the GFC 2008 and prices had returned to the long-term trend line of housing price growth by Q4 2011. Starting from this level, housing prices have a CAGR of 14.27% growth till the peak during Q2 2022. Assuming a return to this trend line over the next few years would imply a nearly 40% reduction from the peak prices recorded during Q4 2022 for the median housing unit in the US.

Even when starting from the peak pricing during HB1.0, housing prices have increased at an annualized 9.9% to the peak of HB2.0. Seen in the context of the abnormal monetary inflation that preceded HB2.0, we should not be surprised at the extent of price inflation in the US housing markets.

> *Objectively, and if we use the deviation from the trend line as the starting point of a bubble,* **HB1.0 witnessed a CAGR of 8.95% over 6+ years and HB2.0 had a CAGR of 14.27% over 11+ years.** *If 2008 is accepted as a housing bubble, there is no rationale to describe HB2.0 as anything other than as a* **"housing bubble on steroids."**

iii.   Housing Prices relative to Income: HB2.0 Vs. HB 1.0

Can the higher housing prices be justified using some fundamental factors such as a rise in the incomes of the buyers? As we shall soon see, this is hardly the case and even after accounting for the higher incomes, HB2.0 is substantially larger than HB1.0

What is noticeable in studying the inflation adjusted income and house price movements in the US is that house prices have outpaced household incomes for the last 50 years. Since 1965, house prices have increased by more than 120% while household incomes have increased by about only 15% as shown in Fig 4.20.

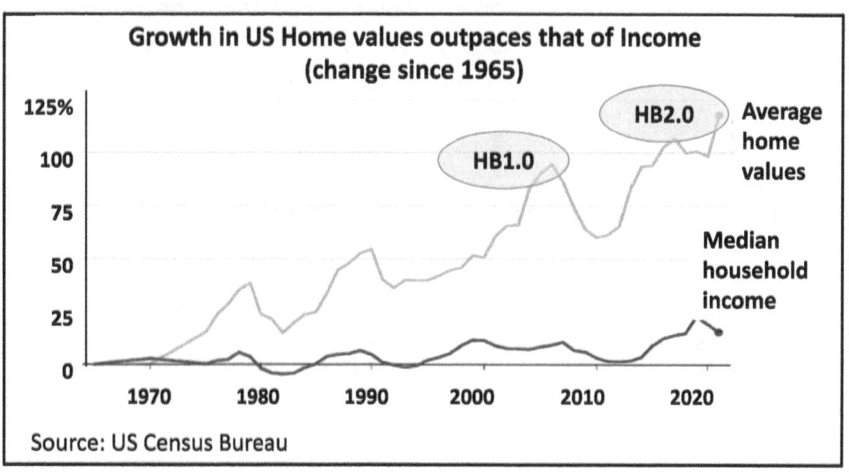

Fig 4.20 - Inflation adjusted increase in home prices and household income

Is there a reason for the phenomenon of house prices outpacing household incomes over such an extended period? The answer is the same as to how the US government has managed a much higher debt-to-GDP ratio over the decades i.e., the magic of falling interest rates. The 30-year fixed rate mortgage in the US has declined from a high of 18.28% during Oct 1981 to a bottom of

2.67% during Dec 2020 in a near linear trend over 4 decades. This ensured a much lower monthly mortgage for a given amount and hence these lower rates automatically raised the affordability (and hence the housing prices) for the US consumer. This rate is at 7.31% as of April 2024.

Can this trend of house prices increasing at a rate much faster than household incomes continue into the future as well?

Most certainly not. For one, the trend of interest rates falling is over for the foreseeable future. Even if the Fed funds rates are decreased, the 30-year mortgage rates are likely to go up in the years and decades ahead. But even ignoring the trend in interest rates, the above phenomenon depicted in Fig 4.20 is unlikely to continue for another critical constraint i.e. the limits of leverage.

What is the maximum leverage that would be financially prudent for a home buyer? Most lenders use a "*rule of 28%*" of an individual's gross income (before taxes) towards housing payments. This includes not only the home mortgage payments of principal and interest but also related property taxes and home insurance. For individuals with other loans such as car loans, student loans etc. this 28% can be extended to 36%. This is the pre-tax income and so net of taxes is what is available to the individuals for their monthly expenses and savings.

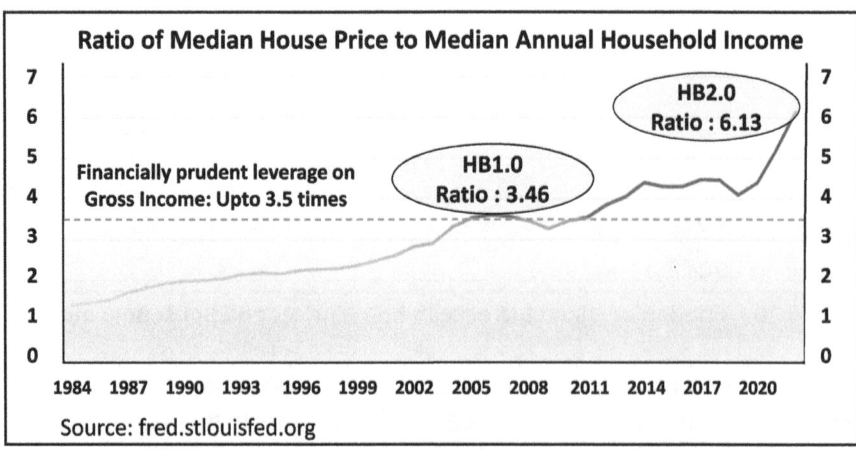

Fig 4.21 – Leverage on median household income for purchasing houses.

i.   **From an Annual household income perspective, houses are more expensive by 77% today as compared to the peak of the HB1.0 during 2008**

There is a similar metric to the "rule of 28%" that could be used and this is depicted in the Fig 4.21. This indicates the leverage on the gross income that could be considered for the purchase of a housing unit and it is generally accepted thumb-rule that the house price should not exceed 3 to 4 times the gross annual income. While this is generally used as a thumb-rule, this measure suffers from the disadvantage that it does not take into account the interest rate on the mortgage.

So while this ratio would have been a good indicator a few years ago when the 30-year fixed rate was less than 3% during 2020, this is no longer a good indicator when the 30-year fixed crossed 8% during 2023.

The 28% rule indicated earlier which takes into account the mortgage interest rate is a better guide than the "home price to income ratio." Fig 4.21 is shown primarily to indicate how much more skewed this ratio has become today as compared to the HB1.0. This is even before taking into account the interest rate movement scenario that is likely to be far more unfavorable today as compared to what happened during HB1.0. If 3.5 was the breaking point for HB1.0, the ratio today should be lower today given the prevailing higher interest rate environment.

iv.   **Housing Affordability for the US Consumer – HB2.0 Vs. HB1.0**

As we have seen in the earlier two points (i) house price increases and (ii) house prices relative to income, multiple factors determine the affordability of housing. There is one number, the Housing Affordability Index, which combines all these factors to define one number that indicates the strength of the housing market. The first two points have been included for the readers to gain a better understanding as to why the housing affordability numbers today, despite the apparent stability of housing prices, are substantially worse than even the depths of the HB1.0 crisis.

The Goldman Sachs Housing Affordability Index (GS-HAI) is one of the more commonly used Indices to indicate housing affordability. An Index level of 100 is considered the equilibrium level wherein the house prices are at a level that makes it just about affordable for the buyer. A level above 100 indicates that housing prices are comfortably affordable for the buyer and conversely, a level below 100 indicates the risky leverage required on the buyer's income to accommodate the purchase at prevailing prices.

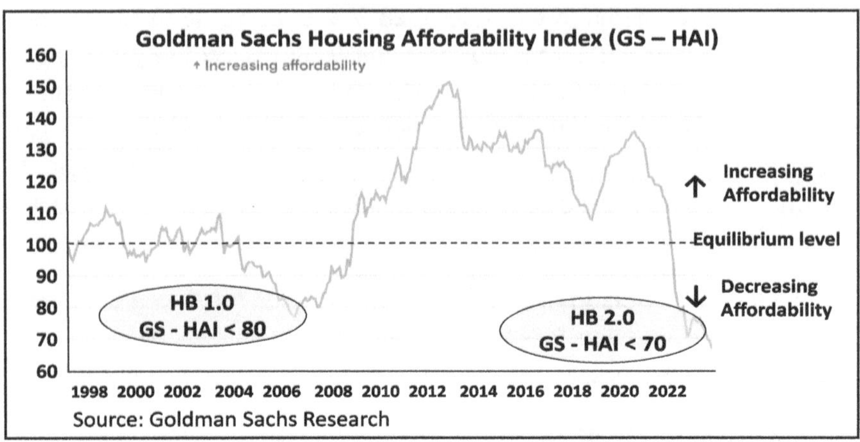

Fig 4.22 - GS-HAI indicating affordability is lower today as compared to HB1.0

The GS-HAI fell below the level of 100 during mid-2004 and would stay below 100 till 2009. However, the house prices would continue to increase for another nearly 3 years (as part of HB1.0) post-2004 to peak during Q1 2007. The definitive event that signaled the GFC was however the collapse of the investment Lehman Brothers that would happen by Sep 2008 - nearly 18 months after the peak in house prices. The current cycle of HB2.0 is a bit different. Both the fall of the GS-HAI below 100 and the peak of housing prices (as part of HB2.0) would happen during 2022 - with a gap of just a few months.

This GS-HAI chart in Fig 4.22 indicates what has been consistently seen in the first two points made regarding the comparisons between HB1.0 and HB2.0 i.e., HB2.0 is bigger and worse as compared to HB1.0 though the bubble is yet to burst.

Will the bursting of HB2.0 reverse the trend of declining GS-HAI as happened with the bursting of HB1.0?

Not necessarily. While many factors determine the GS-HAI, the two most important ones are the housing prices and the 30-year mortgage rates.

While the housing prices will decline with the bursting of HB2.0, the 30-year mortgage rates are set to move substantially higher quite independent of the short-term movement in the Fed funds rate. This coupled with increasing insurance and property taxes might cause the GS-HAI to dip even further. Perhaps with a breather during the period immediately post the HB2.0 burst.

There are several other fundamental factors – No. of housing units, No. of housing units as a ratio of the working age population, No. of units under construction, marginal addition to population for new housing units – all of these indicate not only a housing bubble today, but one that is substantially bigger than HB1.0.

v. **Timing the Housing Bubble 2.0 Burst**

It is but obvious that we are in HB2.0 and past the peak of housing price in this cycle as well. The bubble bursting is just a question of time and that's just the nature of bubbles and markets. As we will see in the next part, but for the actions of the US Fed in forestalling a mortgage crisis during March 2023, we would already be in a crisis similar to the GFC 2008 (or worse).

When will the HB2.0 burst? It is hard to define the exact timelines given the visible hand of the Federal Reserve in forestalling the burst. However, we can make some extrapolations from the HB1.0 burst timelines as below

i. Fig 4.17 shows that there was a 36 month lag between the end of monetary easing and bursting of HB1.0. The monetary easing of the current HB2.0 cycle ended in Q1 2022.

ii. Fig 4.17 also indicates that it took 12 months after the end of monetary tightening (i.e., end of the Fed funds rate hike) for HB1.0 to burst. The current monetary tightening ended in July 2023.

iii. Fig 4.19 indicates that there was an 18 month lag between the peak of housing prices and the bubble bursting. The peak in the current cycle happened during Q4 2022.

Other factors could alter these timelines as well – for one, HB2.0 is much bigger and so should take less time as compared to HB1.0 to burst; the Fed's actions in backstopping the losses on mortgage securities (more in the next section 4.B.2) could delay the inevitable. All taken together, there is better than a good probability of HB2.0 bursting during H2 2024.

Of course, I have to emphasize at this juncture that the bursting of HB2.0 is not going to lead us to a GFC 2.0 but a GCC 1.0 (Global Currency Crisis). More on that in Section 4.D

4.C.III - Banks in bigger trouble today than HB1.0

It must be a very obvious corollary to the above section "*4.C.II - HB2.0 bigger than HB1.0*" that the consequences of the bubble bursting must be more severe as well. That is a given and so we will focus on the differences in the bank lending practices between HB1.0 and HB2.0 in this section.

Banks have a very different issue to deal with this time around and that has to do with the nature of mortgages and the specific problem caused by the differences in directional movement of the 30-year fixed mortgage rates between HB1.0 and HB2.0. The outcomes on account of the above are the following:

    i.   Unwillingness of underwater Homeowners to sell

    ii.   Losses in "All" housing transactions

    iii.   Losses in Bank Treasury bond portfolios

    iv.   2023 - Worse for Banks than 2008 / 2009

All of the above mentioned issues have been caused by one and one reason alone i.e. increasing interest rate scenario. The Fed Funds rate and consequently the 30-year fixed mortgage rates have been continuously declining from 1981 till 2021. This is the first time in 40 years in which the US Economy is facing a crisis while being in a *rising interest rates regimen*. The last time the US faced this situation was during the stagflationary 1970s.

Before explaining the above mentioned 4 points, we should look at the structural difference in the lending environment between HB1.0 and HB2.0. This has been missed even amongst the handful of analysts talking about the HB2.0

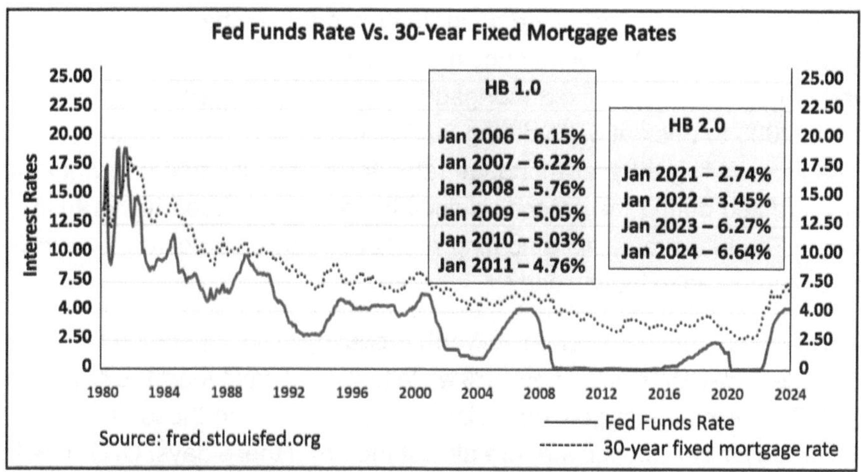

Fig 4.23 - The 30-year Fixed mortgage rate had 40 years of decline from 1981 to 2021

i.   The years leading upto HB1.0 and subsequent to the bust also had a declining 30-year Fixed Mortgage rate as part of the trend mentioned above.

ii. The 30-year Fixed Mortgage rate is now on an increasing rate and is at the highest level in the last 25 years.

As can be observed from Fig 4.23, the 30-year fixed mortgage rate was continuously declining from 1980 till the bottom in 2022. This made housing more affordable, or more realistically, caused the increase in housing prices.

There is also a very subtle, overlooked but a key issue associated with the 30-year mortgage rates. **The 30-year fixed mortgage rates in the decade (i.e., 2012 to 2022) leading up to the current HB2.0 were at substantially lower rates as compared to the current fed funds rate. This was not the case with HB1.0 as shown in Fig 4.23.**

The 30-year fixed has been quoting below 5% from 2012 onwards and was almost as low as 2.5% during a couple of years leading up to 2022 when the fed funds rate hikes were effected. This was not the case during the previous episodes of the Fed funds rate increases i.e.,1986 to 1990, 2003 to 2007 etc. Besides the reliance on the 30-year fixed rate mortgage as a form of financing house purchases today is overwhelming at more than 95%.

This might appear to be a normal event for the average person. After all, banks are expected to handle these interest rate movements as part of normal business operations. Besides, there have been "reasonable" increases in the

Fed funds rate even recently e.g., in 2003 and 2007 when it was increased from 1% to 5.25%. But even during that period of a steep increase in the Fed funds rate, the 30-year fixed mortgage rates hardly moved i.e., from 6.15% during 2003 to peak at 6.7% during 2007. So for the banking system used to a stable or falling 30-year mortgage rates for 4 decades and one where the 30-year fixed during the preceding decade has always been higher than the current Fed funds rate, this is nothing short of a "CAT 5 hurricane." How well is the US prepared to handle one?

This is a point made earlier but is worth repeating. The US started the 1970's with a debt-to-GDP of less than 40% while today it is more than 120%. Besides the US government largely ran balanced budgets during those days while 2 Trillion-dollar deficits per year are almost the norm these days. Of course the problem today is substantially bigger than what the US faced during the 1970s, but the point is that the US economy is in a structurally weak foundation today as compared to back then. Not to make it too dramatic, the debt situation of the US makes it ill-equipped to handle a "CAT 1 hurricane."

Of course the correct solution even today is to raise interest rates to a level that will curtail the monetary inflation and force the government to live within its means. That was what Paul Volcker did as can be inferred from Fig 4.23 when he had put the Fed funds rate at 22% by 1981. It is easier said than done today with the National debt at 34+ trillion. Even at the current 3.11% net rate on national debt, the outgo on account of interest costs is more than a trillion dollars. Over the next few years, when this 3.11% rate on national debt moves closer towards the fed funds rate of 5.25 to 5.5%, the US government would be staring at an economic crisis that cannot be "kicked down the road" any longer. So forget Volcker's 22%, the US government cannot handle even the current 5.25% Fed funds rate for a period of a few years.

Can the US postpone handling these problems caused by monetary inflation with more monetary inflation as they managed post the GFC 2008 with ZIRP and QE? Let us for a moment imagine that they repeat the monetary inflation solution to the GFC 2008 on a more grandiose scale today. The problems as outlined in the section 4.C.II are bigger and hence the monetary inflation has to be substantially larger as well. Even if possible, all that it would mean is that we would have successfully kicked the can down the road one more time.

While it is not good economics to postpone, assuming it's even possible, it will only lead to a situation where the national debt becomes 100T and the debt-to-GDP is well north of 250% a few years down the line. How does one handle an economic downturn then?

Thankfully that option is not even workable today (although it will probably be the default solution attempted) given the early stages of the flow through of decades of monetary inflation into price inflation as described in section 4.B.III

Having explained the structural differences in the 30-year fixed rates between 2008 and today, we can now look into the 4 factors mentioned earlier.

i.   **Unwillingness of the Underwater Homeowners to sell**

One of the differences in the current environment is the interest rate movement as compared to the previous 40 years. During HB1.0, the 30-year mortgage rates were relatively stable with a declining trend and this made the decision to sell a house an easy one for the homeowner. Apart from the transaction costs, it was relatively inexpensive to sell a house and buy another one at a later point. The falling mortgage rates ensured that it was even profitable to do so.

The existing 30-Year Fixed Mortgage is a Hand-cuff			
	Current Situation	**Scenario – I (Equivalent Home)**	**Scenario – II (Equivalent Mortgage)**
Home Value	$ 400,000	$ 400,000	$ 280,000
Down Payment	20 %	20 %	20 %
30-Year Fixed Mortgage Rate	3.25 %	7.00 %	7.00 %
Monthly Mortgage Payment	$ 1,721	$ 2,457	$ 1,740
Source: bankrate.com			

Fig 4.24 - Increasing interest rates makes selling houses units with low 30-year fixed mortgage rates an "expensive" proposition for owners.

Today, the biggest asset of a homeowner is the 30-year fixed mortgage and not the house itself. As shown in Fig 4.24, to sell a house and buy another unit of the same price would mean more than a 40% increase in the monthly mortgage fee purely on account of the increase in the 30-year fixed mortgage rates. Or put differently, to have the same monthly mortgage payment, the homeowner should be willing to accept a unit that is 30% cheaper (lower quality, size, location etc.). So the 30-year fixed rate is essentially a handcuff today on the homeowners and prevents a sale even when required for a change in their living circumstances.

Therefore, the homeowners would much rather prefer to make the payment than default on the mortgage. The incentive to default is substantially lower on the part of the homeowner today as compared to HB1.0. Surely, shouldn't the scenario be good news for the banks? Counter-intuitively, the answer is a "No." Once again, the specter of raising interest rates on the 30-year mortgage is going to haunt the banking system in multiple ways.

ii. **Banks - Losses in "All" Housing Transactions**

As explained in the introduction to section 4.C.II, apart from HB2.0 being substantially bigger than HB1.0, it also has one crucial qualitative difference of being in a situation of increasing 30-year mortgage rates. The consequences of this difference have been completely missed by the media; but then in one sense, it could be legitimately argued that HB2.0 itself has been missed by the media and so this is just part of a larger miss.

The Shift to 30-year Fixed Rates from ARM's: Before we go on to explain the implications of the raising 30-year mortgage rates, it is important to understand one more change in the mortgage type between HB1.0 and HB2.0. During the years leading up to HB1.0, ARMs (Adjustable Rate Mortgages) were a reasonably common feature. More than 60% of all mortgages up to $1M were on ARM's during 2004. Though the share of ARMs was declining steadily it was still more than 30% by 2008. In comparison, the share of ARMs by 2022 was much less than 10%.

Just to make it abundantly clear, in an ARM loan, the individual borrower carried the risk of raising interest rates. In a fixed rate environment, it is up to the lender (i.e., the banks) to protect themselves from this scenario. While it has been pointed out that more than 90% of the homeowners are insulated from the problem of raising rates, the issue of who pays for the differential rates remains. Today, even the Fed funds rate is at 5.25% while the 30-year mortgage rates are well past 7% while most purchases before 2022 were at around 3%. How does this affect the mortgage industry?

We can categorize the problems into 2 distinct categories due to the above.

✓ **Banks borrowing short-term and lending 30-year fixed**: For the 40 years leading up to HB2.0, the 30-year fixed mortgage rate was continuously declining and so banks always had a positive carry by adopting the above practice of borrowing short-term and lending long-term. Though there was a risk of raising rates, given that for 40 years the scenario had not been observed, the banks had a free ride in adopting this risky practice.

There is an inherent Asset-Liability mismatch in the above, but banks were reaping the benefits as long as the Fed Funds rate stayed below the rates of the 30-year fixed mortgages issued during the decade earlier. This is not the case anymore today even with the Fed funds rate of 5.25% while the 30-year fixed has been well below 5% right from 2010 till 2022. So for the portion of the mortgages that banks made using the above practice of borrowing short and lending long, the banks would be losing money on every mortgage issued before 2023. The situation is so bizarre today that it is better for the banks if the homeowner chooses to default today where the banks can take possession and re-issue the mortgage at an interest rate that makes it a viable transaction.

✓ **Mortgage Backed Securities (MBS) losing value due to raising rates**: During HB1.0, though banks were losing money on the defaulting loans, the MBS they were holding were rising in value due to falling interest rates. Today, the banks are losing money on their bond holdings of MBS even if there are no defaults.

The collapse of Signature Bank and Silicon Valley Bank happened for these very reasons. Most US banks would have faced a similar ordeal but in a preemptive move, the US Fed stepped in and offered a Bank Term Funding Program (BTFP) wherein Banks could get a loan for up to 1 year on the face value of the MBS holdings. As of Mar 2024, Banks had borrowed a whopping $163 billion against this program.

Though the US Fed has officially closed this program as of Mar 11, 2024, Banks can continue to borrow against their MBS holdings at rates that are slightly higher than the interest rates on reserve balances. The key is that the US Fed continues to provide liquidity to the overvalued MBS holdings of these banks to prevent a repeat of GFC 2008.

iii.   Losses in Bank Treasury Bond Portfolios

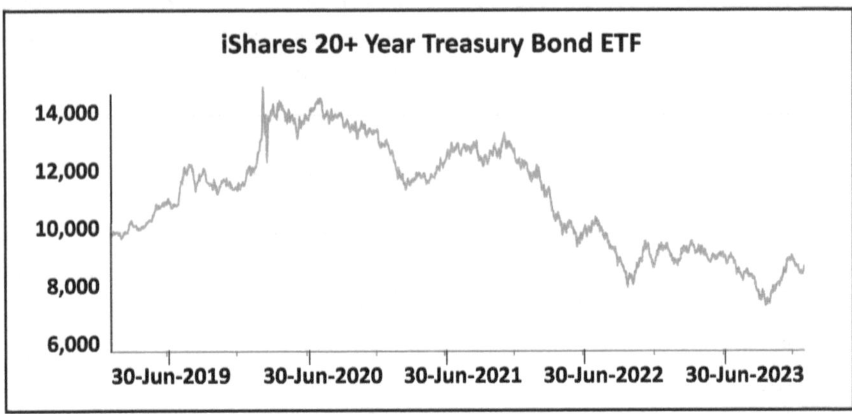

Fig 4.25 - Investment results of a hypothetical $10,000 in an index of US Treasury bonds with remaining maturities > than 20 years

Even if the banks somehow magically escape the housing debacle, they face an even greater loss in their Treasury bond portfolios. The reasons being the same i.e., raising interest rates across all maturities. Treasury bonds which are considered the safest of all asset classes, have reported more than 40% loss on their NAVs over the last 4 years as can be seen from the Fig 4.25

How big are the losses for the banks? Estimates vary and particularly depend on the prevailing interest rates at that specific point in time. In the last 12 months, estimates ranging from $600 billion to $1.7 trillion have been made for Treasury bond losses.

These losses are very likely to grow manifold going forward. Decades of monetary inflation is going to ensure that interest rates are likely to go northwards i.e. well in excess of 10% at the long end. Quite independent of where the US Fed keeps the short-term rates, the 30-year rates are very likely to explode to compensate investors for the risk of price inflation in the decades ahead.

iv.   2023 - Worse for banks than 2008 / 2009

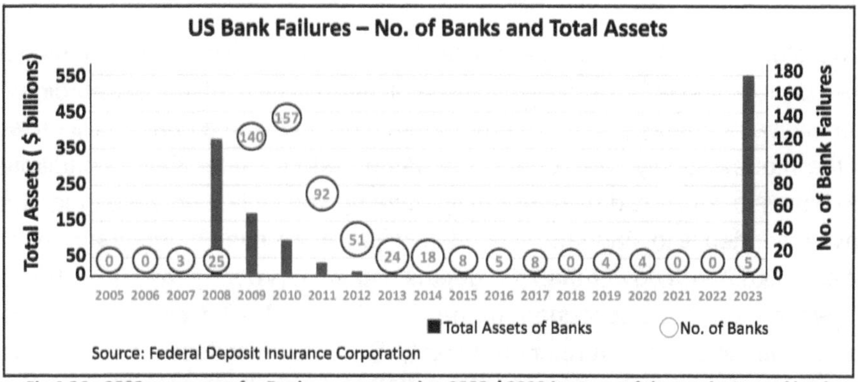

Fig 4.26 - 2023 was worse for Banks as compared to 2008 / 2009 in terms of the total assets of banks.

It will probably be a surprise to most readers, but 2023 was worse for the banks in terms of the total assets of banks that failed as compared to even 2008 and 2009. As shown in the Fig 4.26 and explained further in Fig 4.27 the 5 banks that failed during 2023, had almost the same size of assets as the 322 banks that failed during HB1.0 between 2008 and 2010.

It should be obvious from Fig 4.27 that the banks are in a structural trouble. But for the BTFP emergency bail-out, many more banks would have collapsed in 2023. The factors mentioned are not that complex to understand and once the housing bubble is recognized, the toppling of the dominoes can't be much behind.

2023 – The Worst Year in History		
Year	Number of Bank Failures	Total Assets (in $ billions)
2008	25	373
2009	140	171
2010	157	96
2011 to 2022	214	< 70
2023	5	548

A combined $640 billion in total Assets

ZIRP induced lull

Source: Federal Deposit Insurance Corporation

Fig 4.27 - Year 2023: Start of the Banking Crisis.

i.   The 5 banks that failed during 2023 had total assets that are comparable to the combined assets of the 322 banks that failed during 2008 – 2010

ii.   It was the BTFP (Bank Term Funding Program) and a complete bail-out of all depositors that prevented a spread of the bank failures during 2023.

Does the market not realize the fundamental predicament the banks are in?
Yes and No.

If we study the relative market valuation of banks, these are at a historical 80-year low vis-à-vis the S&P. This is in the context of an extraordinarily stimulative monetary policy - nearly 15 years of ZIRP and a near 200% growth in the money supply (M2) during the same period. Under these conditions, the bank stocks should have normally gone up vertically, and yet all that they have managed is to stagnate. The relative valuations even before the Fed rate hikes in 2022 were lower than the depths of the crisis during the GFC 2008 as shown in Fig 4.28. Subsequent to the rate hikes in 2022 & early 2023, these valuations have dipped further predictably. So the market does indeed seem to sense that there is something fundamentally wrong with the banking system. This is the explanation for the "Yes" part of the answer.

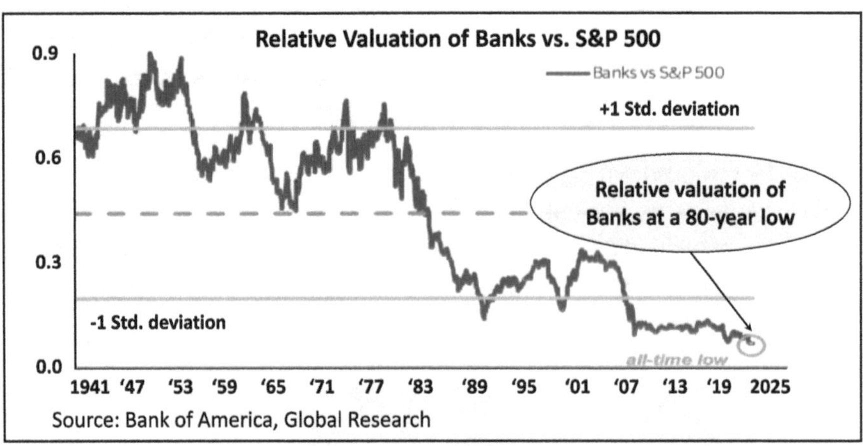

Fig 4.28 – Relative Valuations of Banks at a historic low

i.   **15 years of near ZIRP post the 2008 GFC has done little to lift the bank stocks.**

ii. **Are the recent collapse of banks – globally and in the US – indicative of a crisis ahead?**

Incidentally, the Fig 4.28 was used by BofA global research to indicate as to why the bank shares might be in for a cyclical upswing due to a pause in rate hikes by the US Fed. Even if the rationale for a temporary bump up in share prices were to be correct, this would be the equivalent of "picking up pennies in front of a steamroller."

The answer to the above question of the predicament of banks today is also a "No" because the markets are nowhere close to understanding the extent of losses that the banking sector faces in the years ahead. Again, just to remind the readers, the US banks have never witnessed a sustained increase in interest rates in the last 40 years. So even these historically depressed valuations do not account for the risks explained earlier. The losses the banks are going to lose on the housing mortgage loans, their MBS and treasury portfolios are going to dwarf the 2008 losses. Not to mention their derivatives positions.

Remember that the US Fed was able to reduce the interest rates to zero during 2008 and this along with QE saved the banks from a complete collapse. Given the current price inflation, ZIRP is probably no longer an option and the US Fed, much against its preferences, would be forced to keep the rates nominally higher.

It should be obvious to all readers by now that it was the rate hikes in 2022 and 2023 that has started this banking crisis. If one understood Austrian Economics, even at a basic level as explained in Chapters 2 and 3, the current crisis should have been obvious from a mile. While it was almost impossible to predict as to when the US Fed would try a semblance of normalizing monetary policy, it was inevitable that they would.

15 years of extraordinary monetary stimulus was longer than almost anybody could have anticipated, but "the attempt to normalize" was never a question of "IF," but rather always "WHEN." Once the Fed initiated the steps, it was just a matter of a few years before the burst of HB2.0 triggered the economic crisis described i.e. the depression. The US Fed's hand was forced by rising pressures of price inflation and they had no choice but to act during 2022.

Balance Sheet Normalization – An Impossibility

The US Fed had attempted to normalize monetary policy several times post the GFC 2008. In 2017, Janet Yellen, the then Chair of the US Fed announced the QT program (Quantitative Tightening i.e. shrinking of the Federal Reserve's balance sheet) and commented that the process would be **"like watching paint dry."**

The following year i.e. 2018, Wall Street had its biggest fall since the GFC 2008 and the normalization process had to be abruptly halted.

Now whether the depression is inflationary / hyperinflationary or deflationary is a matter of monetary policy. The 1930s Great Depression was deflationary ONLY because the US Fed still operated under the quasi-gold standard. Given that we operate under a fiat monetary system, it is almost guaranteed that the depression ahead of us will be inflationary. And possibly a hyperinflationary one at that!!!

Theoretically, there are four possible scenarios or ways in which the depression could play out as explained in Fig 4.29.

The Four Possible Economic Depression Scenarios!!!		
Fiscal / Regulatory Approach ⟶	Leaning Towards Lassiez Faire / Limited Government	Interventionist Government
TIGHT Monetary Policy	A. Short Deflationary Depression e.g. US during 1920 – 1921	B. Extended Deflationary Depression e.g. The Great Depression of 1929 to 1946 in the US
EASY Monetary Policy	C. Inflationary Depression Common in banana republics. Srilanka and Argentina are current examples.	D. The Crack-Up Boom – Hyperinflationary Depression e.g. Weimar Republic, Germany

Source: Author's compilations

Fig 4.29 – The policy combination that will determine the type of Depression ahead for US.

i.   The one pre-condition to all the 4 scenarios is a period of monetary inflation prior to the depression that creates the malinvestments that need to be liquidated.

ii. Options A & C deal with a condition where the government either consciously adopts a "free markets" policy as happened during 1920-21 in the US OR is powerless to intervene in the markets and prolong the malinvestments.

The one question that should crop up in studying the above Fig 4.29 is "Why did the combination of massive monetary inflation and very interventionist governments as the US has had, did not result in the outcomes indicated above after the GFC 2008?

4.D - NICE and Cantillon Effect

Till this point, we have avoided discussing complex economic concepts in detail - or at the very least using the jargon of economists. The endeavor has been to explain the fundamentals in a way that a reader without a background in economics can understand. We need to make an exception at this stage regarding the usage of economists jargon, but the attempt is to still explain in a way that the average reader understands the spirit of the economic concepts involved.

The above is required to answer what ought to be an overriding question in the mind of readers at this stage and that is - "if monetary inflation (i.e. expansion in the supply of money and credit) is the cause, and price inflation (i.e. an increase in the general price levels of goods and services) is the result, what explains the disconnect between 15 years of the massive increase in debt / money supply and a rather a muted increase in the consumer price inflation during this period?"

This was pointed out in two data points earlier and these are reproduced below for easy reference - "the CRB Index" in Fig 4.30 and the "GSCI Total Return / S&P 500 ratio" in Fig 4.31.

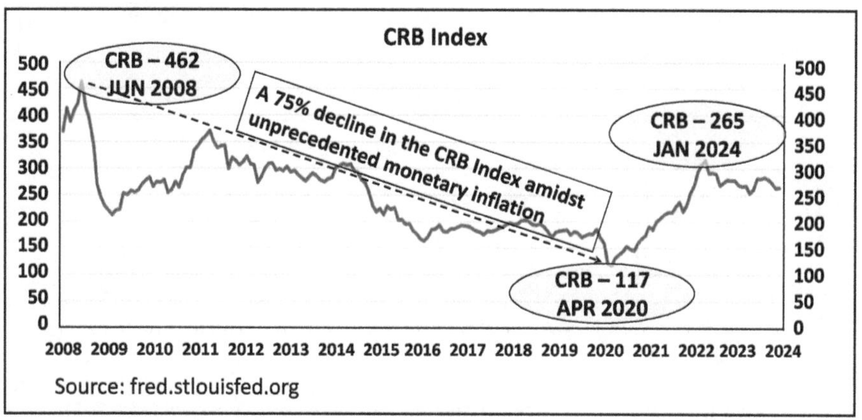

Fig 4.30 – Chart of the CRB Index from 2008 to 2024.

i.   A decline of more than 40% in the CRB from the June 2008 peak to Jan 2024.

ii.   At the bottom of the CRB index in this cycle during Apr 2020, the decline was 75%

The CRB index was trading at 460 during June 2008 before the bursting of the HB1.0. Consider the monetary stimulus between then and January 2024

i.   Near ZIRP for most of the period between June 2008 and now

ii.   A near tripling of the money supply (M2) from $7.7 trillion to nearly $21 trillion.

iii. More than a tripling of the National debt from $9.5 trillion to more than $34 trillion

iv. An eight-fold expansion in the US Fed balance sheet from $0.9 trillion to $7.7 trillion

What explains the extraordinary monetary stimulus outlined above and a near 75% decline (from peak to trough i.e., June 2008 to April 2020) in the CRB index during the same period? A naïve reader might be tempted into concluding that the more US dollars that the Federal Reserve prints (or digitally creates), the cheaper commodities get on an absolute basis.

4.D.I - The Extended Interlude between Monetary Inflation and Price Inflation

A part of the answer is explained in the Fig 4.31. What this shows is the relative valuation of Goldman Sachs Commodity Index to S&P 500 and this shows that all of the above mentioned monetary inflation has flowed into stocks making them relatively very expensive. Commodities today are substantially cheaper than they were in 1971 on a relative basis.

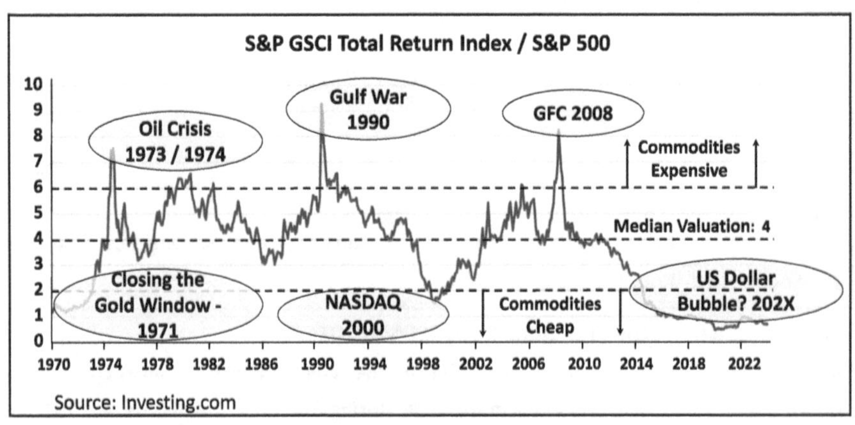

Fig 4.31 – The Ratio of Goldman Sachs Commodity Index to S&P 500

i. A ratio of "4" has been the median value and > 6 indicates that commodities are expensive.

ii. This ratio was 1.17 during 1971 when gold was $35 an ounce and oil was less than $3/barrel.

This ratio was less than 0.5 during Apr 2020 & even today trades well below the 1971 value

What this implies is that we are living in an all-good-assets bubble and this has indeed been the case for almost a decade now. Stocks, bonds and real estate are all in a bubble of varying proportions. The other asset class, i.e. commodities, has been at the receiving end and the relative valuations are cheaper than what it was during 1971.

While this is not a discussion about which of the 3 mentioned assets amongst stocks, bonds and real estate is a bigger bubble, it should be pointed out that bonds, especially long-term bonds are still in a hyperbubble despite the steep decline in valuations during the last 4 years. Even with a near 40% decline as pointed out in Fig 4.25, bonds continue to be a hyperbubble. While the risks are manifold, the primary risk in the current scenario is that bonds, at the end of the day, represent a claim on pieces of paper that could be rightfully valued at "0" at some point in this cycle.

But even if the forecast of hyperinflation turns out to be incorrect, bonds could lose another 90% from the current valuations over this cycle of increasing long-term interest rates.

So the answer to the question "Why did the CRB index as shown in Fig 4.30 not go up in conjunction with the monetary inflation?" is reasonably explained with the above figure. But that still begs the question "Why should money flow this way into only certain asset classes at certain points in time?" Is there an explanation for Fig 4.31 that shows asset valuations swinging between extremes for decades? Why do the asset valuations not move within a small band around the equilibrium (i.e., around the median value of 4)?

The title of this section "NICE and Cantillon Effect," is a condensed statement of the above question and includes the answer as well i.e., NICE - *Non-Inflationary Credit Expansion* refers to the lack of manifestation of the massive increase in credit on consumer prices. The answer or the explanation to the NICE phenomenon is the "Cantillon Effect."

But before the Q&A can be elaborated upon, some basics of economics need to be introduced and in particular the concept of *"Neutrality of Money."* Or really, the lack thereof.

4.D.II - Neutrality of Money

Neutrality of money suggests that changes in the supply of money affect only nominal economic variables like exchange rates, prices and wages. Such changes in the supply of money do not alter the real variables like production / GDP, employment, consumption etc.

There are many types of neutrality of money such as static neutrality, dynamic neutrality, institutional neutrality, super neutrality etc. and these distinctions are not relevant to our purpose. It is just for the reader to be aware that there are multiple versions of the definition of "Neutrality of Money." But even amongst the differing versions, the following two principles are generally agreed upon by most economists.

i.   It is accepted that neutrality of money is valid in the long run, but not so in the short run as real variables like production get impacted due to rising prices.

ii. It is also accepted that in the long run, changes in the money supply affect the producers and consumers of all goods and services proportionately.

While many have disagreed with the concept of *Neutrality of Money*, Mises has offered the most comprehensive explanations against the very concept of Neutrality of Money in stating "For, even in the quite impossible case (i.e. money balances of all members were to increase in the same proportion), every increase in the quantity of money would necessarily cause an alteration in the conditions of demand, which would lead to a disparate increase in the prices of the individual economic goods. Not all commodities would be demanded more intensively, and not all of those that were demanded more intensively would be affected in the same degree."

Suffice to say at this juncture, that prices of all goods and services do not go up to the same extent as the change in the supply of money. It is indeed conceivable that the prices for some goods and services decline while others go up.

The question again is "Why is money not neutral?" The answer is the Cantillon Effect.

4.D.III - Cantillon Effect

Murray Rothbard, my favorite Economist and whose books have shaped my thinking the most referred to Richard Cantillon as the "Father of Modern Economics," a title usually bestowed upon Adam Smith.

Cantillon's most important contribution is to discuss "the distribution effects resulting from the uneven changes in the money supply" published in his book

"Essay on the Nature of Trade in General." It is now referred to as the "Cantillon Effect" and describes the mechanism in which new money enters the system and the first recipient acquires goods from the market and the receivers will then use the money to acquire goods and services subsequently. This process cascades out into the economy and the money trickles down the economy providing greater benefits to those closer to the origin than further away. The late recipients are disadvantaged in this process.

What Cantillon advanced through his theory was the Non-neutrality of Money for three reasons:

i.   New money enters through specific channels to specific participants and is not evenly distributed throughout the entire economy.

ii. The above unevenness of changes in money supply means that it affects different businesses in very different ways.

iii. Changes in the distribution of income and wealth lead to a change in relative prices and hence alter the investments and the production scenario.

While we do not want to get into a detailed technical discussion in this book, it is the non-neutrality of money and money supply changes under the current monetary system that is the very reason for the amplified business cycles and leads to changes in the distribution of wealth within a society. I have provided references at the end of this chapter for interested readers to understand this phenomenon better.

The one conclusion that is easy for the readers to see is that money supply changes do not affect all the goods and services proportionately even in the long run. Fig 4.27 illustrates the same as very rarely do the relative valuations trade around the mean valuation band but keep moving to extreme valuations as the "Cantillon Effect" would suggest.

The other conclusion that is easily verifiable is the effect on income inequality as a result of the increases in money supply. As Newman's quote suggests, all of the monetary inflation has only resulted in greater concentration of wealth within the elite.

> Money printing creates winners and losers, and perpetual money printing creates *big winners* and *big losers*.
>
> *– **Jonathan Newman, Mises Institute***

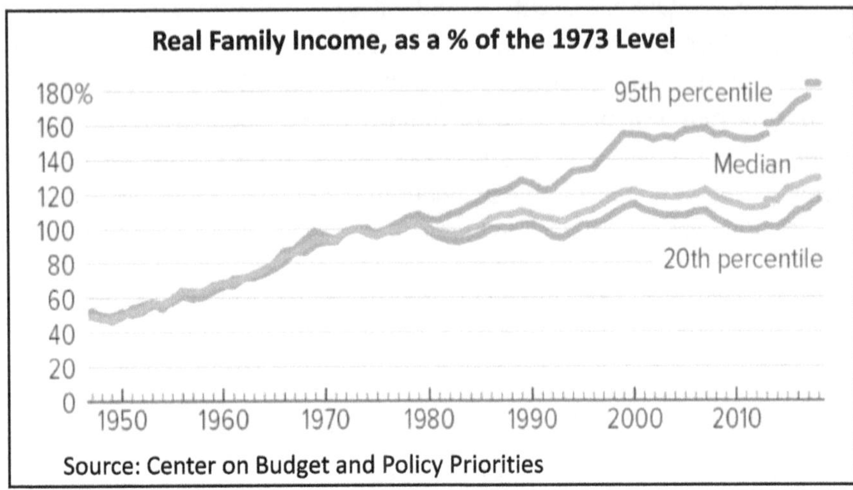

Fig 4.32 – Income Gains evenly shared across the population during the decades leading upto the 1970s.

i.   **Beginning in the 1970s, income growth for households in the middle and lower parts of the distribution slowed sharply, while incomes at the top continued to grow strongly.**

ii. **For the bottom 20%, income is up less than 20% as compared to 1973**

Fig 4.32 shows the increase in family incomes having a significant lead in the top percentile after the 1970's. Till that point in time, the % income increases were similar across the entire segment of the population. In the bottom 20 percentile, real family income has gone up just 20% in the last 50 years while it has almost doubled in the top 5 percentile. The median family income is closer to the bottom 20 percentile with real gains at less than 30%.

Many other parameters will show a similar outcome i.e., a greater concentration of wealth amongst the top since the 1970's. Some of the easily verifiable statistics could be - Net worth held by the top percentile (0.1, 1 or 5 etc.), Gini coefficient, relationship between credit expansion and wealth inequality, share of total wealth held by the top percentile etc. What is shown in Fig 4.32 is an easily understandable measure of the inequality created by the fiat monetary system. References are provided at the end of the chapter for interested readers to understand this better.

The objective of including the above is to show that monetary inflation has consequences other than price inflation alone. The two other almost equally important effects of monetary inflation are

i.   The boom-bust cycles that are created by artificially low interest rates that result in speculative bubbles.

ii.   Greater wealth and income inequality within the society.

4.E - Debt Default – Bankruptcy / Repudiation OR Monetary Inflation?

By this stage, it should be fairly obvious that the US government is in no position to pay back its debt. With a national debt of $34+ trillion, unaccounted liabilities well in excess of $200 trillion and additions to the national debt to the tune of nearly $3 trillion/year, the financials of the US government ought to be rated worse than "Junk." The reason it is not is because of a very peculiar form of default that is available to governments in general, and to the government that owns the reserve currency of the world in particular.

Several quotations of Greenspan have been used earlier to explain how the gold standard prevents deficit spending and creation of excessive debt by governments. Most of these statements were written as part of his article "Gold and Economic Freedom" which is reprinted in Appendix-I. While Greenspan's writings before his role as the Federal Reserve Chairman reflected his commitment to the free markets ideology and the gold standard, most of his observations during and post demitting office have been a far cry from his earlier thought process. Consider his following observation on the US debt default discussions that have been ongoing for a few decades now:

> **"The United States can pay any debt it has because we can always print money to do that. So there is zero probability of default"**
>
> **- Alan Greenspan, 2011**

Is the above statement "true?" If so, we don't need to bother about the issue of "excessive debt" at all. All that needs to happen is a lifting of the debt ceiling by the US Congress, and we already know from history that the ceiling is ALWAYS lifted. So why even bother about the debt at all?

As I will explain in this section, the above observation by Greenspan while being technically true is a very misleading one. The probability of default by the US government is 100% as will be explained. Though few anticipate the nature of default that the US government is going to embark upon. In hindsight, it will be clear to most as that's what the US government has been doing ever since 1971 and so the logical culmination of "closing the gold window" should not be surprising at all.

4.E.I - History of US Defaults

A frequent observation that is made is that "The US government always pays its bills." Recently, Treasury Secretary Janet Yellen made the observation **"The US has never defaulted. Not once."**

The observations are certainly not true and there have been 3 instances of defaults by the US government in the last 100 years and all related to the Federal Reserve operating under the quasi gold standard. Given below is short description of these events

i.   **Default on Sovereign Gold Bonds in 1933**: In April 1933, the then US President FD Roosevelt made holding of gold by US citizens illegal. This was effected through Executive Order 6102 "forbidding the hoarding of gold coin, gold bullion and gold certificates." This was followed by abolishing convertibility of US dollars to gold for the US citizens and unilateral rewriting of contracts with retroactive effect and the eventual devaluation of the US dollar from $20.67/ounce to $35/ounce. Citizens who had been promised that the bonds would be redeemed in gold coins were instead paid with depreciated dollars.

   This issue was referred to the Supreme Court and in a 5-4 majority the Supreme Court upheld the sovereign power of refusing to fulfill the solemn promise on gold bonds.

ii. **Default on Silver Certificates in 1964**: In March 1964, the then Treasury Secretary Douglas Dillon halted the redemption of silver certificates for silver dollar coins. For the next 4 years, redemption was permitted in the form of "uncoined silver granules" but even this was completely suspended in 1968.

Fig 4.33 – A One Dollar Silver Certificate signed by Secretary of Treasury Robert Anderson (1957 – 1961) payable in Silver.

The reason for the suspension of redemption should be obvious by now to the reader. Though the silver certificate (Fig 4.33) stated in unambiguous terms - "*This certifies that there has been deposited in the Treasury of the United States of America one silver dollar, payable to the bearer on demand.*," by now the all familiar monetary inflation wherein far greater certificates were issued as compared to the available silver coins meant that this convertibility had to be suspended.

iii.   **Default by Closing the Gold Window in 1971**: The August 1971 closure of the gold window by Richard Nixon has been explained earlier as well and will not be expanded here. The only difference between the first two and the third by Nixon is that the 1971 default affected only the foreign Central banks as the convertibility option was available only for them.

> **The observation that the "US government always pays its bills" is just rhetoric and history invalidates these claims. The US government has defaulted on multiple occasions – at least twice to its own citizens (1933 and 1968) and once to the foreign central banks (1971) that were holding the US dollar.**

There was another instance of default, though this happened before the adoption of the US Constitution in 1789. This had to do with the Continental dollar between 1776 and 1781. The readers must understand the default that happened with the Continental Dollar as it is similar in many ways to the current US dollar i.e., issued by fiat and not backed by gold or silver.

Not Worth a Continental: The monetary inflation happened on account of the Revolutionary War wherein recourse to paper money was adopted as a means to fund the war. In 1775, the Continental Congress authorized the issue of $2 Million in paper money which was increased in a series of steps to nearly $200 Million by 1779. The monetary inflation essentially made the Continental Dollar worthless and hence the phrase "Not worth a Continental."

Fig 4.34 – The monetary inflation of the Continental Dollars resulted in a rapid depreciation and the market prices reflected the quantity issued.

Fig 4.34 indicates the exchange rate between the continental dollar and $1 silver. Though the market stopped accepting these dollars, a few states accepted the continental dollar in lieu of taxes at varying exchange rates. Though there was no explicit default by the government, the loss of purchasing power ensured that the result was the same for the holders of these Continental dollars.

The default that lies ahead is going to follow a pattern similar to what happened with the Continental and not the first three instances where the promised convertibility to gold / silver which was repudiated.

What was the nature of the default with the Continental Dollar?

The first question to ask is did the Continental Congress default with the Continental Dollars? They did not promise convertibility to gold / silver to begin with and so there was no explicit default as happened in the three defaults that happened during 1933, 1968 and 1971 as explained earlier.

The three events of 1933, 1968 & 1971 are a case of default through bankruptcy or repudiation of earlier guarantees given. The US government / Federal Reserve had promised that the dollars could be converted to a fixed quantity of gold / silver and these claims were subsequently not honored.

No convertibility guarantees were made with the Continental Dollar and no explicit promises were broken. Yet, for the holders of the Continental Dollars, the losses were almost 100% in terms of the loss in purchasing power. These losses were near lock-in-step with the monetary inflation during the period as shown by the records maintained by Thomas Jefferson.

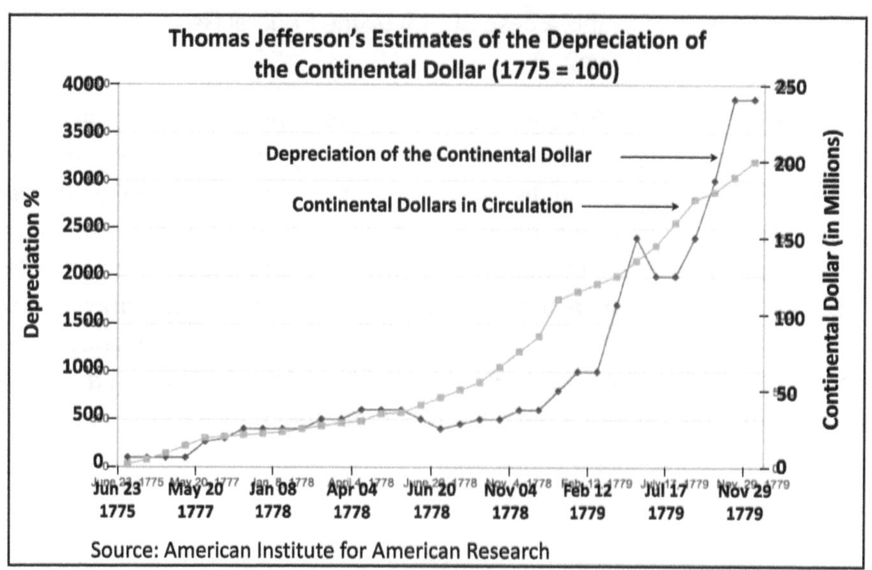

Fig 4.35 – Depreciation of the Continental Dollar during the Revolutionary War

i.   In 1780, the Continental Congress repudiated its paper money. The outstanding bills was accepted in tax payments at the rate of $40 in Continental Dollars to $1 in Silver.

ii. The State issued Continentals were accepted by different states in varying ratios for payment of taxes. In New York it was $128 for $1 in silver, in Pennsylvania it was $175 and in Georgia & Virginia it was $1000 to $1 in silver.

The loss with the Continental Dollar as shown in Fig 4.35 was even higher as compared to the earlier 3 cases of an explicit default on the delivery of specie by the US government. Due to lack of an established phrase to describe this phenomenon of loss of purchasing power of the currency due to excessive new supplies, we shall call the same **"Default through Monetary Inflation (DMI)"**

The one difference between DMI and Default through Bankruptcy / Repudiation is that in the former no explicit promise is broken or repudiated by the government. However, the loss to the holders of the currency is usually far greater and close to 100% in the terminal stages of an inflationary cycle on account of DMI.

4.E.II - Default through Monetary Inflation (DMI)

The price of gold has moved from $35 in 1971 to more than $2000/oz. during Q1 2024. This is more than a 98% decline in the purchasing power of the US Dollar vis-à-vis Gold. Is this a case of DMI by the Federal Reserve over the 50 years under consideration?

Of course, it is. The US Federal Reserve has continuously increased the Money Supply (M2) and this is reflected in the price of gold. In monetary terms, this is similar to the depreciation that happened to the Continental Dollar. Though these gold price movements are not anywhere close to what happened with the Continental where the depreciation was near lock-in-step with the issuance of new currency units as can be inferred from Fig 4.35. The price of gold, despite its current all-time high price when measured in US Dollars, is cheaper than what it was in 1971 on a relative basis (using the monetary base M0 for comparison) as shown in Fig 4.36.

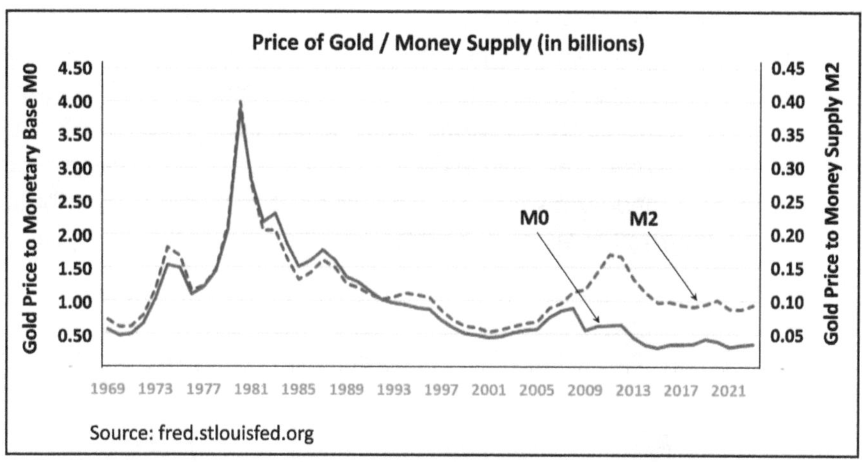

Fig 4.36 – Ratio of the Price of Gold to Money Supply (M0 and M2) in billions

i.   Gold price today is cheaper today on a relative basis to 1971 when compared against the growth in the Monetary base M0 over the decades.

Fig 4.36 is a graph that is often used to show how the gold price today at $2000/oz. is cheaper than it was in 1971 at $35/oz. when accounted for the monetary inflation created in the interim. While the above rationale is correct, it is hard to draw too many conclusions from the above analysis. For example, what does the peak value of 4 during 1980 indicate? Is there a sanctity to these peak values observed during the 1970's cycle of monetary tightening? Also, this ratio ignores the quantum of gold held by the US Federal Reserve and so this is not very meaningful for analysis other than to show that gold is cheaper today when compared to 1971.

What is more useful is to analyze and see the % of money supply that is covered by the value of the Federal Reserve's gold holdings. What this indicates is the gap between the monetary inflation of the Federal Reserve

> **"Gold – Simultaneous All Time High and All Time Low Prices"**
>
> The nominal gold price at $2000/oz. during Q1 2024 is at an all-time high.
>
> However, on a monetary inflation adjusted basis, the price of gold is at an all-time low. The 1971 price of $35/oz. when adjusted for the monetary inflation would mean a price of $2500+/oz.

and the market price of gold when a transition to the gold standard becomes imminent.

What Fig 4.37 indicates is that the markets indeed priced gold at the height of the 1970's bull market at a value that would have permitted the US government to put the US dollar back on the pre-Bretton Woods format of Gold standard i.e., allowing for convertibility to citizens at a price of around $650/oz. While the peak value of gold was more than $850/oz., Fig 4.37 uses a monthly average price of $ 615/oz. and so it was very much within the realms of possibilities to return to a pre-Bretton Woods gold standard that allowed convertibility for citizens.

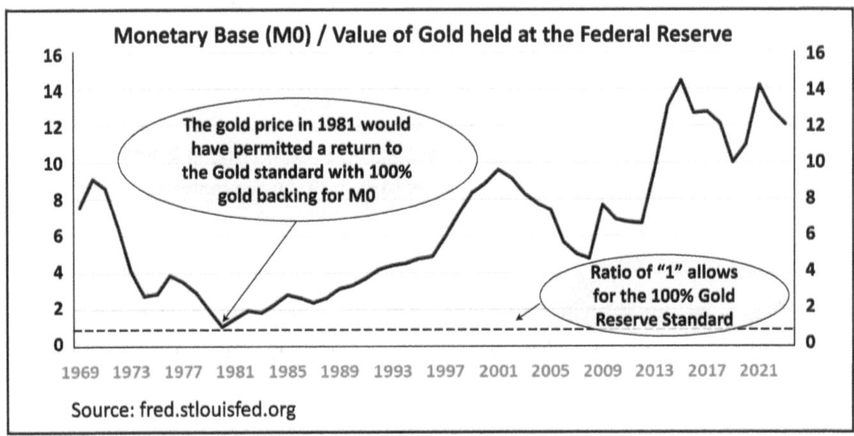

Fig 4.37 – Ratio of the Monetary base M0 to the value of Gold (at a price of $2000/oz)
i.   A 100% gold backed standard can be implemented when this ratio is 1. The markets in
    1981 had priced gold at a level that would have permitted a return to the Gold Standard.

An interesting question at this stage would be, given that I started the Preface with the supposition that a return to "some form of a gold standard" is inevitable, what would the price of Gold be that would allow for such a monetary standard to be implemented? That is another conclusion from Fig 4.37 and the answer is 12 times the current price as that's the current ratio between M0 and the value of the Federal Reserve's gold holdings. So at a price of $24,000/oz., the US government can indeed go back to the gold standard today (Q1 2024).

But there are many queries to be answered as part of the above number - Is the correct component of the money supply to be used M0, M1 or M2? What's the % of the money supply that should be covered by the gold holdings as traditionally most Central Banks have operated with a 40% gold reserve backing? The United States itself operated with a 25% reserve standard before the formation of the Federal Reserve.

But the biggest determinant is not which component of Money Supply or the % backing, but the tsunami of monetary inflation that lies ahead. Suffice it to say at this juncture that when the world transitions back to the gold standard, it is going to be at a price that is higher than $24,000/oz.

While the above forecast might seem outlandish today, the readers should remember that during the 1970s gold prices went up almost 25 times - from $35 to nearly $850/oz. A similar increase this time would put the price at $50,000/oz. We have also seen that on a relative basis, gold is cheaper than it was in 1971 and that the monetary inflation ahead is likely to be supportive of higher gold prices as compared to the rate hikes that happened through the 1970s.

So to answer the question we started this section with - Is the history of the last 50 years under the Federal Reserve a case of DMI? The answer obviously is yes but the bulk of the loss in purchasing power of the US Dollar as reflected in the consumer price inflation due to the historical monetary inflation (let alone what is there in the pipeline as a consequence of the soon-to-burst HB2.0) lies in the years ahead. So even in the absence of fresh monetary inflation, we are indeed headed for an environment of substantive consumer price inflation.

What is described above - the DMI of the last 50+ years - is "a case of death through a thousand cuts" or "slowly boiling a frog to death." The DMI has been one continuous near unidirectional process as can be witnessed in the growth of Money Supply over the decades since 1971 from Fig 4.38.

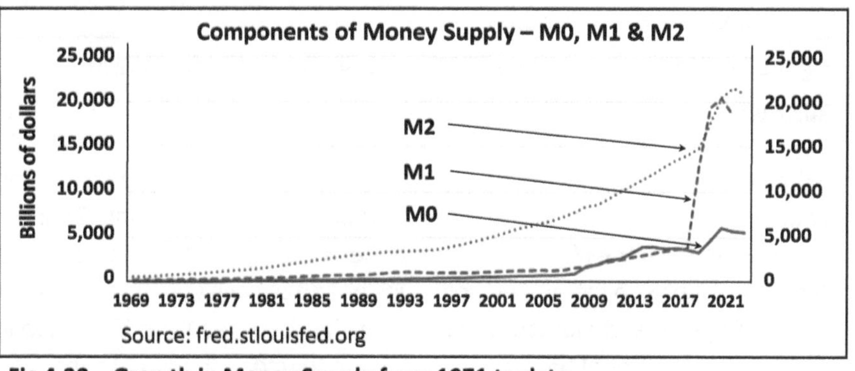

Fig 4.38 – Growth in Money Supply from 1971 to date

The Consumer Price Inflation (CPI) has however been subdued and has been under 5% post the inflation shock of the 1970s and early 1980s. In fact, for the period between 1983 and 2021, there was only one year in which CPI was more than 5% i.e., 1990 recorded a CPI of 5.39%. So though in terms of the direction, the CPI has tracked the monetary inflation, the magnitude has been substantially lower. This is quite unlike the scenario with the Continental Dollar where the depreciation of the currency happened concomitantly with the issuance of new currency units.

So why has the price inflation not tracked the monetary inflation over this long period? The two-part explanation has been elaborated upon earlier but it is worth repeating (i) under-reporting of the actual price inflation by the government methodology as shown in Fig 3.17 and (ii) Cantillon effects due to the Non-neutrality of money.

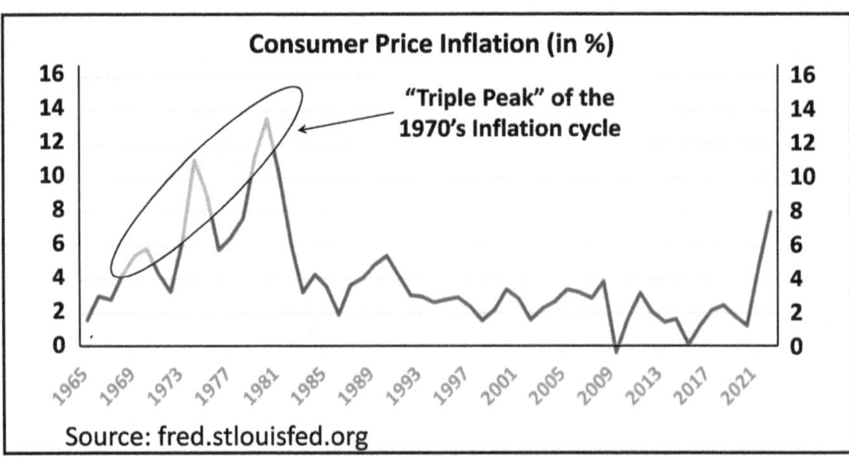

Fig 4.39 – "Official" CPI measured well below 5% during 1982 and 2022 with a > 5% reading only once in the 40 year period.

The gold price movements would appear even more perplexing to the average individual - perhaps even to the sophisticated market participant. That gold prices have to track the changes to the monetary base would sound as like an outlandish proposition today. The gold price changes have occurred in episodic patterns of spurts and slumps as shown in Fig 4.40, resulting in a situation where even most central bankers do not seem to understand gold's monetary role. Consider the following observations and actions from the central bankers of the US and UK on this issue:

✓ Reported below is an exchange between Ron Paul and Bernanke as part of a Congress testimony during 2011:

Ron Paul: Is gold money?
Bernanke: No. It's a precious metal
Ron Paul: Why do central banks hold it?
Bernanke: Tradition

Unless Bernanke was lying, it was fairly clear that he did not understand Gold's monetary role.

✓ Towards the end of gold's bear market that ended in 2001, the then Chancellor of the UK Exchequer, Gordon Brown sold nearly half of the UK's gold reserves. That event which marked the bottom of the gold prices at $256/oz. is now infamously referred to as the "Brown Bottom."

Periodic spurts / slump in Gold prices from 1971 to date			
S.No	Time Period	Gold Price Movements ($/oz)	Comments
1	1971 to 1980	$35 to $843	A 2300% increase over 10 years
2	1980 to 2001	$843 to $256	A 70% decline over 21 years
3	2001 to 2011	$256 to $1896	A 640% increase over 10 years
4	2011 to 2015	$1896 to $1049	A 45% decline over 4 years
5	2015 to Q1 2024	$1049 to $2064	A 97% increase over 9 years

Source: MacroTrends.net

Fig 4.40 – The episodic movement in gold prices.

The loss in purchasing power of the US Dollar through price inflation has not been consistent with the monetary inflation over the last 40 year period. So for those who believe that the worst of the inflation is behind us with the 5% interest rate hike, we have to say that the inflation monster is still in its infancy and all that we have had is a pause. If we are to draw a comparison with the 1970's, what we had is similar to the first peak from 1971-1973 as shown in Fig 4.39. The monetary inflation leading up to the current situation is greater by an order of magnitude and so we should not be surprised with double-digit inflation (even according to government numbers) for several years to come.

But the DMI we are talking about on account of the monetary inflation to be created in the years ahead is of a different kind. It could either be a worse form of the stagflationary seventies or something akin to what happened at the Weimar Republic from 1919 to 1923. Possibly the latter. We are in the blow-out stage of the inflation cycle and the currency could possibly become worthless in a short span of time.

Before we expand on the nature of the DMI that lies ahead, the reader needs to understand the role of a "Recession" within an economic cycle.

4.E.III - The Role of Recessions in an Economy

In a free market economy without any centralized capital allocation or mispricing of interest rates by Central banks, business failures occur at the margins. Failures and bankruptcies are part of a capitalistic system and any firm that does not deploy its resources efficiently goes out of business and the invisible hand of the free markets ensures that capital ends up where it is most efficiently allocated. So failures / bankruptcies lead to better utilization of scarce resources and the society is better off as a consequence.

These failures would not be a widespread or an industry-wide mispricing problem that leads to the formation of bubbles (Japanese stocks during the early 1990's, Nasdaq in 2000, HB1.0 of 2008, the current HB2.0) in the absence of artificial creation of credit. Von Mises referred to these as "malinvestments" and the recession as the cure to clear the malinvestments. The savings required to facilitate this artificial boom would have necessitated a higher interest rate and the artificial stimulus induced by central banking creates an investment bubble that is not justified by fundamental investment-consumption decision patterns within an economy.

This is the essence of the Austrian Business Cycle Theory (ABCT) and liquidation of debt / assets is the solution to the malinvestments made during the artificial boom. The Treasury Secretary during the Great Depression Andrew Mellow offered similar advice - "liquidate labor, liquidate stocks, liquidate the farmers, and liquidate real estate." However, President Hoover ignored and went on with an interventionist approach to handle the stock market crash of 1929 that had been fuelled by the speculative boom of the "Roaring Twenties (i.e. 1920's)."

So we see this pattern repeating in an economy:

i.   An artificial boom created by the central bank's mispricing of interest rates and creation of artificial credit within an economy that is not mandated by real savings.

ii. This boom leads to widespread speculative asset valuations e.g., high P/E for stocks, high housing prices leading to unaffordability etc.

iii. When asset valuations are not supported by fundamental factors, a correction is forced upon by the markets which results in a recession.

iv. There are two possible scenarios of for handling the recession as outlined below

a.   When the recession is not resisted by the Governments and the Central Banks, it runs its course to clear out the malinvestments made during the speculative boom. The symptoms of the non-interventionist approach would be higher interest rates and a reduction in government debt. This lays the foundations of a real savings-led investment cycle within an economy.

b.   When a Central Bank decides to lower interest rates to fight a recession, this creates the foundations of a larger bubble. The malinvestments continue to remain and perhaps continue to grow larger over a period of time resulting in an even greater bubble. The symptoms of this approach are lower interest rates and a much greater level of debt within an economy. So the asset bubble is replaced with an even bigger asset bubble to temporarily ward off the collapse of asset valuations.

How long can this cycle of propping up bubbles with a bigger bubble continue? This can go-on till we reach the condition of what Mises refers to as the "Crack-Up Boom." The Crack-up Boom has two characteristics

1. Expansionary monetary policy leading to out-of-control price inflation.

2. Mistrust or abandonment of a currency leading to hyperinflation coupled with a recession / depression.

The Crack-Up Boom is an outcome of the fiat monetary system. Under a gold standard, and howsoever loose a definition that a central bank chooses, deficit spending and inflation are severely constrained. This is exactly the reason why the Great Depression was deflationary.

Having described the ABCT in brief and the possible ways to handle a recession, we can now study the history of what has been happening in the US Economy after 1971. We have had three major episodes of recession since 1971 and this was briefly discussed as part of Fig 4.1. We can look at how these have been handled a little more closely from a monetary perspective.

i. **The Recession of the late 1970's and early 1980's - The Volcker Era:** Raising interest rates from 4 to 22% and reducing Debt-to-GDP from 40 to 31%. This is shown in Fig 3.10. The interest rates continued to be in double-digits for 4 years from Q4-1978 to Q3-1982. In particular from Nov '81 to Mar'82, rates were increased from 12.5% to 17% though the US was deep in a recession during this period.

   This monetary tightening laid the foundations for one of the longest economic booms in post WW-II history of the US.

ii. **The NASDAQ bubble burst Recession of 2000:** This was handled through monetary easing and interest rates were reduced from 6.5% during Q4 2000 to 1% by Q1 2004. Due to the rising housing prices, rates were increased to 5.25% by Q3 2006. But the Debt to GDP still went up during this period from 55 to 60%.

   The monetary inflation solution to the NASDAQ bubble burst created the Housing Bubble 1.0 the bursting of which was precipitated by the pin of rising rates from 2004 to 2006.

iii. **The housing bubble 1.0 burst recession of 2008 (GFC):** Reducing interest rates to zero and holding it there for nearly 15 years coupled with Quantitative Easing. This has increased the Debt to GDP from 60% during 2008 to 133% by 2020. The resulting price inflation necessitated an increase in rates from nearly zero during Q1 2022 to 5.25% by Q1 2024.

   Again, the monetary inflation as a solution to the HB1.0 has laid the foundations for an all-good-assets bubble that is in the process of bursting - again precipitated by the pin of rising rates and Quantitative Tightening from 2022 to 2024.

The last two recessions - NASDAQ 2000 and GFC 2008 - have been handled through a stimulative monetary policy. The NASDAQ bubble was replaced with a Housing Bubble 1.0 and this was in turn replaced with all-good-assets-bubble. Quite obviously the quantum of stimulus in the latter scenario has been substantially bigger and we now have a massive bubble on our hands.

So how will the bursting of this bubble be handled? While theoretically the options are still open, I think the die-is-cast in favor of monetary inflation as a solution.

Bernanke was awarded the Nobel Prize for Economics in 2022. While no explicit connection was made to his handling of the 2008 GFC and the Nobel Prize, it is obvious that the Nobel Prize was an affirmation of his *"Monetary Inflation-as-a-solution"* blueprint.

Oct 10th, 2022 – Nobel Prize in

Economics to Ben Bernanke

Statement of Nobel Prize Committee

Bernanke analyzed the Great Depression of the 1930s, the worst economic crisis in modern history. Among other things, he showed how bank runs were a decisive factor in the crisis becoming so deep and prolonged. This research has been of great importance in regulating financial markets and dealing with financial crises.

A good antidote to Bernanke's theory on the Great Depression would be to read the book "America's Great Depression" by Murray Rothbard.

So when we have the all-good-assets-bubble bursting later in 2024 (or 2025 - though hard to see what could prolong the bursting to 2025 at this point), is the world going to follow the footsteps of a Nobel Prize winner who "successfully" handled the previous burst OR some renegade Austrian economists who have never been part of the mainstream line of thinking?

It is indeed a rhetorical question and I have very little doubt that we will have QE's that dwarf the ones we had post the 2008 GFC. In other words, a Crack-Up Boom is a given even if the hyperinflation does not happen to the extent as happened in the Weimar Republic.

Just to remind the readers, hyperinflation is not the result of the bursting of the current bubble, but is indeed an outcome of the monetary solution to be adopted by the Federal Reserve to the bursting of the bubble. The US Dollar's inevitable demise in its current unbacked form is going to come as a result of the cure to the bursting of HB2.0.

4.F - The Nature & Quantum of Monetary Inflation Ahead

Hyperinflations are not linear progressions as far as the currency depreciation is concerned and so extrapolations do not necessarily work. What we can do is use the template of HB1.0 and project the subsequent monetary inflation to see what the numbers would look like by 2030. What we are not going to give is some specific targets / projections for the various numbers, but merely indicate the various factors that need to be considered in making these projections. Some of these are "wildcards" and it's almost impossible to make specific nominal projections.

There were several people who had forecasted the Weimar hyperinflation before 1919 but any projections on how these numbers would look like by 1923 would have been a near impossible task. The situation today is not very different.

But before considering those factors, there are some crucial differences in the interest rate movements between 2008 and now. These compound the worry for the US dollar as can be understood from the observations below.

i. The Federal Reserve was able to reduce the interest rates to ZIRP in the aftermath of the GFC 2008 and stay at that level for nearly 15 years. The benign / falling commodity prices supported such a move. We are at the opposite end of the spectrum today in terms of where commodity prices are likely to move in the years ahead.

   Much as the Federal Reserve might like to reduce the rates to zero once again, the price inflation would not support such a move. The very motives of the Fed would be questioned if they try to reduce the rates in the face of increasing price inflation.

ii. The 30-year fixed mortgage rates followed the path of the Fed funds rate and have indeed done that for almost the last 40+ years (Fig 4.19). We are likely to see a break in the above pattern, and quite independent of the move in the Fed funds rate, the 30-year fixed interest rates are likely to increase. The spread between the two rates will increase substantially and so even if the Fed holds the rates down, the transmission of the same to the end consumers would almost certainly not happen.

> ***Given the above issues, the primary mode of monetary inflation is likely to be QE than interest rate cuts. It would not be a very surprising outcome to see the Federal Reserve indulge in rate hikes and QE concurrently at some point in the future.***
>
> ***Paraphrasing Jim Grant, this would be the equivalent of the Fed playing the dual mandate of the arsonist and the fireman at the same time. Unquestionably, the fireman doesn't have the ghost of a chance of extinguishing the inferno.***

So what happened on this front in the aftermath of the 2008 GFC? This was elaborated in Fig 4.14 and is summarized below once again

i.   Money Supply (M2): A growth of nearly 200% between 2007 and 2023. The component M0, or what is known as base money, showed a much higher % increase, but for very technical reasons, M2 is a better indicator for our purpose.

ii. The Federal Reserve's balance sheet had a nearly 10-fold jump during the above period.

iii. The national debt nearly quadrupled during the same period.

These are ominous signs. Even without accounting for the fact that the current bubble is much bigger, the economy more fragile and the primary monetary inflation mechanism would be QE and not ZIRP.

Consider the following scenarios and one can see the case for hyperinflation becoming a probable one.

1. Can the national debt triple from the current levels and grow to $100 trillion over the next 5 years?

2. Is there a possibility of a larger geopolitical conflict just to divert the attention of the general population from the price inflation? Readers should know that what eventually triggered the Vietnam War, i.e., the Gulf of Tonkin incident, was indeed a false-flag attack. At the very least, the incentives for indulging in a war is always higher during periods of higher price inflation.

3. Could the Petro-dollar's days be numbered? China has indeed set up a gold-for-oil exchange. Henry Kissinger who set up the Petro-Dollar system in 1973 did not have to contend with a combative OPEC. Saudi Arabia today, completely understands the need to move away from pricing crude oil in US dollars.

4. Could the BRICS gold-backed currency move from a conceptual idea to implementation? For sure, China and Russia are solidly behind the idea and it is only a matter of time before other countries understand the rationale. Given the expansion of BRICS to include Saudi Arabia, Iran and the UAE, it would be very logically extension to start trading crude oil in terms of the BRICS currency than the US dollar.

    a. While the form of the gold standard remains to be unveiled, it is my supposition that they will start with a Bretton Woods like system. For all of its flaws, it is indeed a vastly superior alternative to the fiat monetary system that we have today.

So even if the US avoids a Weimar-style hyperinflation, substantially higher rates of price inflation (at the very least in double-digits where the first digit is not a "1") are guaranteed for years and years to come. Decades of the sins of monetary inflation cannot be wished with a few years of 5% interest rates.

4.G – What if we get "a Paul Volcker as the Fed Chairman?"

Paul Volcker had to offer a real yield of 9% to quell the inflation of the 1970s when he put the rates at 22% when the price inflation was 13%. The solution of monetary tightening through higher interest rates that Paul Volcker achieved during his tenure starting in 1979 is almost out of the question now. It worked back then on account of the much lower levels of debt in the system.

Today, even the current Fed Funds rate of 5.25% would lead to the bursting of the HB2.0 and take down the banking system along with it. As was explained in Section 4.C, it takes time for the interest rate hikes to work through the system and for the market participants to recognize the reality of excessive valuations. The floodgates of selling eventually opens and cause the bursting of the bubble and a collapse of the value of the MBS holdings.

But if the US Fed is going to provide a backstop to the value of the MBS through its BTFP program, then why can't the interest rates be increased further to dampen the growth in National debt?

As economist Peter Schiff has explained, ZIRP and QE were the monetary equivalent of "Roach Motels." It is indeed easy to enter into these programs but almost impossible to exit. The success of ZIRP & QE have to be gauged not upon bringing stability to the markets after a bubble burst, but only upon central banks successfully exiting these programs of monetary inflation. So the US Fed needs to normalize monetary policy without destabilizing the markets for us to conclude that ZIRP and QE indeed worked as a solution to the GFC 2008. However, as we have explained in this chapter, that's an impossibility as all that ZIRP and QE have done is to replace HB1.0 with a bigger bubble.

This time around, we have an even bigger problem if the US Fed attempts the Volcker solution. Not only will the banking system need a bail-out, the Fed itself would require a bail-out. Fig 4.41 shows the losses incurred by the Federal Reserve for FY 2023, a first since 1916.

The loss of the US Fed is on account of an Asset-Liability mismatch in its balance sheet. It owns long-term securities purchased over the last decade at low interest rates and owes short-term liabilities at current higher interest rates. Any increase in the Fed Funds rate would only widen these losses. So realistically speaking, the US Fed is not going to put itself in a situation where it has to report losses year after year.

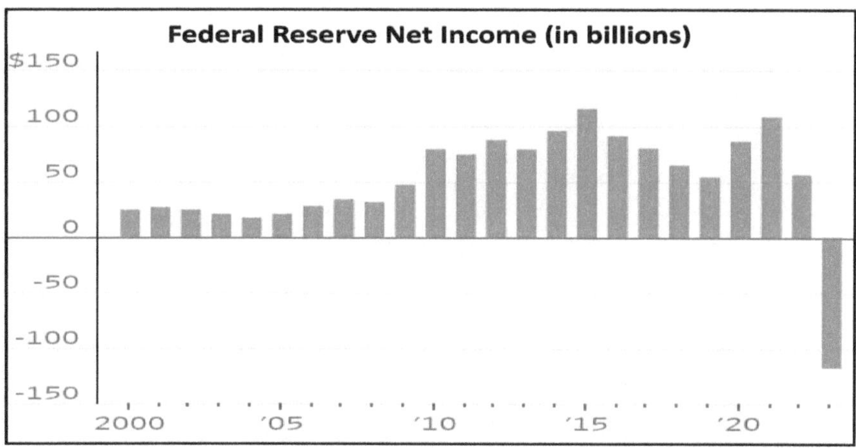

Fig 4.41 – The Federal Reserve had a loss of $114 billion for 2023 tied to expenses related to managing short-term interest rate target.

The "supercore inflation" was 4.8% y-o-y in March and at more than 8% at a 3-month annualized rate. If the primary mandate of the US Fed is price stability, then they ought to double down on the interest rate hikes and the QT program. Yet, it has already acknowledged that the QT might be on its last legs.

Just imagine the losses of the US Fed if the Fed Funds rates are at 10%. After taxes on the interest, that would still be a negative real yield using the US Fed's preferred measure of supercore inflation. Even at the above mentioned 10%, the losses for the US Fed would near a trillion dollars. Can the Fed continue to pretend that these losses do not have any detrimental effect on its monetary policy tools as they are doing today?

In summary, the quantum of debt is way too high for the monetary policy tools to work without completely wrecking the economy. The solution, as will be outlined in the next chapter, has to come from the fiscal front.

Chapter 4 - Suggested Reading

1. *"The Forgotten Depression: 1921: The Crash that Cured Itself"* by James Grant

2. *"Money, Inflation and Business Cycles - The Cantillon Effect and the Economy"* ** by Arkadiusz Sieron

3. *"The Real Crash: America's Coming Bankruptcy"* by Peter Schiff

4. *"The Money Bubble: What to do before it Pops"* by John Rubino and James Turk

5. *"Mr.Market Miscalculates: The Bubble Years and Beyond"* by James Grant

6. *"Inflation and Income Inequality"* ** - Prague Economic Papers by Arkadiusz Sieron

** - For the scholars

CHAPTER 5

The Way Forward

Given the amount of national debt and the current rate of increase (at $3+ trillion/year), there is no conceivable combination of fiscal and monetary policy that can help the US avoid an economic depression when the HB2.0 bursts. There is going to be a tremendous decline in the standards of living of the average citizen during the years and indeed the decade ahead. The only realistic proposition today is to forget the economy and save the dollar. The 1970s was a similar trade-off though the scale of the problem was substantially lower than what the US government faces today.

However, doing the "right things" would bring stability to the US dollar and within a few years the US could return to the path of gaining its economic supremacy. The US is endowed with tremendous natural advantages as well as a highly-skilled / disciplined labor pool that the recovery ought to be faster than what the Weimar Republic post 1923 had.

Few realize that the US has been the largest oil producer in the world since 2018 and has been a net exporter of crude oil since 2020. For the year 2022, the US produced about 17.8mbpd (million barrels per day) out of a total world production of 93.85mbpd. It was also the 4th largest exporter during 2022 and it is this cheap energy that was one of the reasons for the US dominance in agriculture as well as manufacturing during the latter half of the nineteenth century. All those natural advantages continue to this day, though the manufacturing culture has been hollowed out by a combination of loose monetary policy and the burden of government regulations.

So what are these "right things" that would put the US economy and the US dollar on the road to recovery? On the very top would be balanced budgets, normalizing monetary policy, a non-interventionist foreign policy and restoring individual liberty. All four of the mentioned acts are well within the exclusive purview of the US government and not dependent on some external factors. There are no trade-offs within these policies and they are all intellectually / philosophically consistent with one another. For example, a non-interventionist foreign policy would dramatically reduce the "National Defense" expense which would help towards balancing the budgets. Balancing the budgets would help normalize monetary policy etc.

Incidentally, these are not radical thoughts, and in fact, are the very ideals that the US was founded upon. In every sense of the word, it is just a proposition for the US government to return to the founding principles that made it the richest

> *Peace, commerce, and honest friendship with all nations – entangling alliances with none.*
>
> *– **Thomas Jefferson, Washington Doctrine of Unstable Alliances.***

country in the world. Yet, not only is the political consensus of the two parties in favor of the exact opposite, but even the public opinion is nowhere near the above. Public choice, guided by short-term self-interests and ignorance of the economic consequences, ensures that the incentives are structured for the political actors to make the wrong choice.

We are of course at the very early stages of the currency crisis. It's so early that the US government and the Federal Reserve are not even "thinking about thinking" about such outcomes. However, assuming that the government embarks on the correct path as outlined above, and the earlier they start the better, what are the market signposts that the reader should look to determine that the economic recovery is around the corner?

But before that, an introduction to the gold market, central bank gold holdings and how minuscule a role that gold has been reduced to would be useful to understand. This would help the readers appreciate better why forecasts of a 10 or 20 fold increase in the price of gold as shown in the subsequent sections are well within the realms of probabilities. In fact, near certain as I see it.

5.A – Size of the Gold Market

As a prelude to the details of Central Bank holdings of gold and their purchases, some basic numbers are presented below for the readers to understand the scale of the market and that of the various participants.

i. Central Bank gold holdings are reported in tonnes. How much is a ton of gold worth in dollar terms?

- A tonne (or Metric ton) is equal to 1000 kgs or 2204.6 pounds. A short Ton (or Ton) is the normal US standard and that is 2000 pounds.

- Gold prices are reported in US dollars per troy ounce. A troy ounce is 31.1035 grams. The normal US standard of the ounce is 28.3495 grams. In discussions concerning gold prices, an "oz." as it is shown always refers to the troy ounce.

- A tonne of gold therefore has 32,150 troy ounces. At a price of $2000/oz., this is about $64M.

ii. Mining companies usually report their annual production in troy ounces. The large mining companies typically produce in the order of 1 to 2 million ounces/year. A million ounce is about 28.35 tonnes.

iii. The world's annual mine supply has been about 3500 tonnes for the last decade as shown in Fig 5.1. At a price of $2000/oz., the value of gold annually produced by the mines would be about $225 billion.

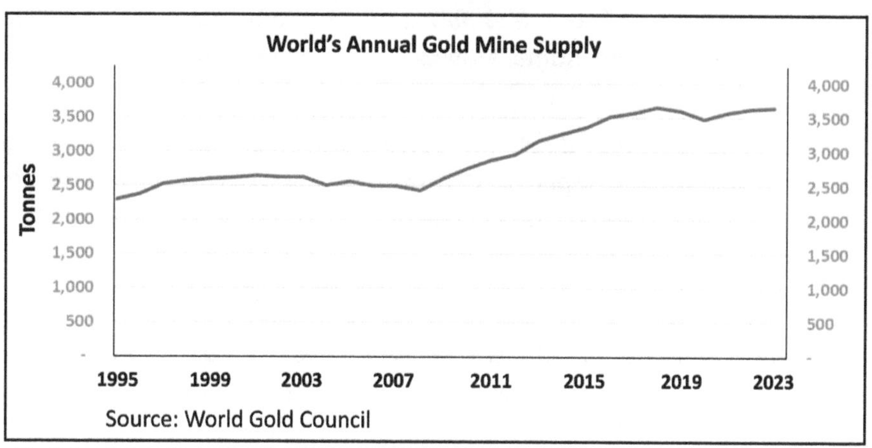

Fig 5.1 – Annual Supply of Gold from Mines.

iv. Saudi Aramco and Apple (the two most profitable companies in the world) combined had $221 billion of net profits for the TTM (Trailing Twelve Months) ending March 2024. So these two companies combined can buy the world's annual mine supply of gold from their operating profits.

- o Saudi Aramco declared dividends of nearly $100 billion in 2023. Only using the dividends of Saudi Aramco, 45% of the annual mine supplies can be purchased.

v. China had a trade surplus of $576 billion in 2022. Under the classical gold standard, more than 250% of the annual mine supplies would have gone to China.

vi. The US had a trade deficit of $945 billion in 2022. The Federal Reserve has about 8133 tonnes of gold in its reserves translating into a value of $522 billion. Under the classical gold standard, Fort Knox would have been emptied of its entire gold holdings with just 7 months of trade deficits.

vii. The world's above ground reserves of gold are estimated at 212,500 tonnes of gold as of Dec 2023 (source: World Gold Council). Using the Warren Buffett style of expression, the entire above ground world's supplies would fit into a cube of sides measuring 22 meters. This is virtually all of the gold that has been mined over thousands of years. At a price of $2000/oz., this would be about $13.6 trillion. Given below are some statistics to indicate how small the gold market is.

- o As of March 2024, the combined market capitalization of just the top 6 companies (Microsoft, Apple, NVIDIA, Saudi Aramco, Amazon and Alphabet/Google) is $13.8 trillion.

- o The national debt of the US Federal government is $34 trillion. The household debt in the US is an additional $18 trillion.

- o The world's bond market is about $133+ trillion of which the US accounts for $51+ trillion. The value of all the listed US companies would be $50+ trillion.

- o The US Government is currently increasing the national debt at an annualized $3 trillion rate. Further, as explained in section 4.B.II, the new issuance of debt securities by the US Federal Government would be nearly $10 trillion for each of the years 2024 and 2025.

viii.   Gold mining is a very fragmented industry. Only about 6 companies globally produce more than a million ounces/year (a million ounce is about 28.35 tonnes). The top 10 gold mining companies produce a combined 360 tonnes annually - or just about 10% of the world's annual production.

- Newmont which is the largest gold mining company in the world has an annual gold production of about 70 tonnes (less than 2% of the world's annual gold production). Their operations are spread across 9 countries and they produce from more than 80 operating mines.

- In comparison, Saudi Aramco, the largest crude oil producer is responsible for nearly 15% of the world's annual production. Most of their output comes from just 5 oil fields in Saudi Arabia.

- The top 10 listed gold mining companies in the world have a combined market capitalization of less than $ 200 billion (as of March 2024). Saudi Aramco can purchase all the top 10 companies with just 2 years of their operating profits.

Gold, which is money and should be one-half of all monetary transactions, is just a minuscule and completely ignored asset in the world's market. *"Irrational Depression"* would be the most appropriate expression for gold despite the current nominal all-time high prices - especially in light of the macroeconomic conditions as explained in Chapter 4. The inverse of the gold trade, by definition, is the US dollar trade and this is in a state of *"Irrational Exuberance."*

5.A.I - Central Banks' Gold Reserves

The Central Banks should have been the largest players in the gold market by far. But as Fig 5.2 indicates, the total gold holdings of the top 10 countries account for just under 25,000 tonnes or less than 1/8th of the estimates of above-ground stock of gold. Even including the top 50 countries, the IMF, and the BIS (Bank of International Settlements - the unofficial Central Bank for all Central Banks), the estimate is less than 36,000 tonnes.

Central Bank Gold Holdings – Top 10 Countries

Country	Gold Holdings by Central Banks (tonnes)
USA	8,133.46
Germany	3,352.65
Italy	2,451.84
France	2,436.97
Russian Fed.	2,332.74
China	2,235.39
Switzerland	1,040.00
Japan	845.97
India	803.58
Netherlands	612.45

China is the world's largest gold producer and also imports significant quantities of gold every year. Also, China's foreign exchange reserves is more than $3 trillion, but the reported gold holdings of 2,235 tonnes is just 4% of the forex reserves. What explains this low allocation to gold?

A few countries including China and Russia do not report their gold purchases to IMF every quarter. Hence the data as reported by the WGC could be an underestimate.

Private estimates of the gold held within China are at about 30,000 to 35,000 tonnes. Most of this gold is held by the state owned banks outside of the People's Bank of China (the Chinese Central Bank).

Source: World Gold Council (WGC)

Fig 5.2 – Top 10 Gold holdings of the Central Banks as of December 2023

i.   The 8,133 tonnes held by the Federal Reserve at a price of $2000/oz is worth just about $500 billion – about 50% of current quarterly addition to the National debt

The Central Banks have been asleep at the wheel during the last 15 years wherein we have had massive monetary inflation. At a time when they should have accumulated gold, they have remained silent spectators in the gold market. However, that trend has changed and in the last couple of years, i.e., 2022 and 2023, the Central Banks have purchased more than 1000 tonnes - still less than 1/3rd of the world's annual mine supplies. This is shown in Fig 5.3

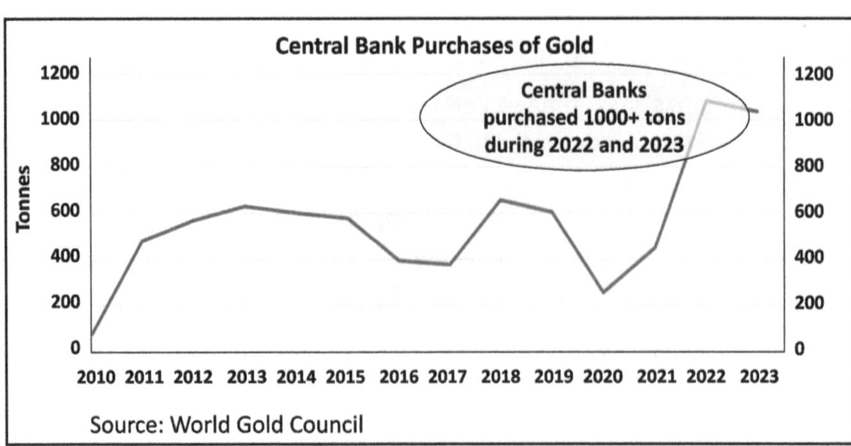

Fig 5.3 – Annual Purchases of Gold by the Central Banks

Many institutions have reported this increase in Central Banks' buying as "colossal." In relative terms compared to the historical purchases, this is indeed a significant change. But the absolute numbers seen in the context of other asset valuations are still very small.

i.   To put these central banks' gold purchases in perspective, the 1000 tonnes purchased during 2022 & 2023 would be about $64 billion. This is only about 11% of the trade surplus of China during 2022. So when the move towards the gold standard starts on a more serious footing, we can expect the central banks to purchase the bulk of the world's annual mine supplies. China can use 40% of its annual trade surplus and buy out the world's annual mining output.

ii. To see it from another perspective, India has annually imported 800 tonnes for the last 10 years. While there was a serious dip during the COVID pandemic of 2020 to 400 tonnes, it has subsequently recovered to the 800+ tonnes annual average. Additionally, India has had an import duty of between 10 to 15% on gold over the years. Consequently, there is not-so-insignificant smuggling of gold on top of the official imports as well.

This significant buying by Indians over the years should be viewed in the context of the per-capita GDP of India which is about $2300/year and India ranks 140th in the world on this front. In comparison, China has a per-capita GDP of $12,500 with both countries having a population size of 1.4 billion. What happens when the Chinese start developing an appetite for gold similar to Indians?

Price has to be the arbitrator amongst the competing entities as supplies are unlikely to increase anytime soon. The point is that gold prices could explode and we would still have significant purchases of gold - both by the central banks and the Chinese consumer even if the Indian consumer gets priced out. That said, there are 1.42 billion Indians and this 800 tonnes of imports is only 0.8 billion grams. **So even with all the fascination for gold in India, on average, Indians are buying less than 1 gram / person / year.**

So a developing country with a per-capita GDP of $2300 is buying almost 25% world's annual mine supply when the average annual purchase in that country is less than 1 gm/person. What will happen to gold prices when a slightly greater allocation to savings in terms of gold happens within India?

& then China? And then the developed markets such as the US where the annual per-capita GDP is $70,000.

Or if Saudi Aramco decides that instead of dividends in national currencies, they will distribute dividends using the BRICS gold-backed currency. An explosion of gold prices is pretty much guaranteed in the years ahead.

5.B - Signposts to a Dollar Collapse / Revival

What is clear from the discussions above is that there will be much greater allocations to gold in the years ahead and this will ensure a substantially higher price of gold. But what are the indicators of the fair value for the price of gold? Are there any historical comparisons that can be done to determine the likely target?

We will use three metrics – Monetary Base to Value of Gold Ratio, Dow-to-Gold Ratio and Goldman Sachs Commodity Index to S&P 500 ratio to determine the course of the bull market ahead. Needless to add, all three of the above indicate substantially higher gold prices.

i. **"Monetary Base M0" to "Value of Gold held by the Federal Reserve" Ratio**

    The above ratio indicates the inverse of the fraction of the money supply (M0) that is covered by the gold reserves at the given market price of gold. For example, a ratio of 5 indicates that only 20% of the money supply in circulation can be redeemed for gold if convertibility were offered to the holders of the currency. So either the gold prices have to go up 5 times or the money supply has to shrink by 80% for convertibility to work at this specified ratio.

    Fig 4.37 indicates the above ratio and it currently stands at about 12. What this means is that at twelve times the current market price of $2000/oz, i.e., $24,000/oz, the Federal Reserve can return to the classical gold standard with 100% backing by gold. There are a few additional factors to be taken into account and these are listed below:

    a. **Future Monetary Inflation:** There will be additional monetary inflation in the years ahead, and unquestionably it is going to be a meaningful increase. This needs to be accounted for in calculating the future price of gold at which this transition can be effected.

b. **Increase/decrease in the stock of gold at the Federal Reserve:** The US has about 8133 tons of gold held at the Federal Reserve, and this has remained constant since 1971.

However, whether all of this gold belongs to the US "Today" has been a topic of much market speculation. GATA (Gold Anti-Trust Action Committee) has produced several papers indicating otherwise. Eric Sprott & team in a paper titled "Do Western Central Banks have any gold left?" have made similar claims. Several analysts including Ted Butler and others have also spoken for decades about the possibility of the US not owning the gold at Fort Knox (assuming it's there in the first place). Given that no verifiable authentic information is there, all these claims are in the realms of speculation.

ii. Dow Index to Gold Ratio

The "Dow Index to Gold" indicates the number of ounces of gold required to buy a unit of the Dow Index at any given point in time. Cyclical lows, which have indicated major historical bottoms for the stock markets have happened in 1933 and 1980 and on both occasions, the price of an ounce of gold has almost been the same as that of the Dow index value.

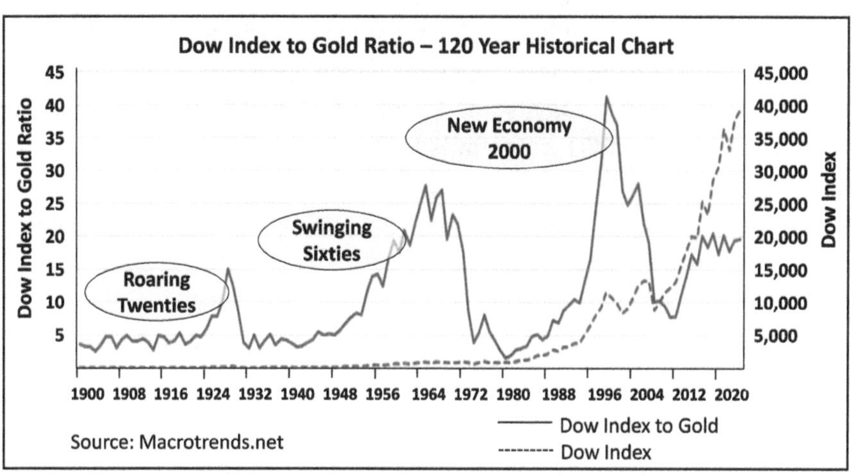

Fig 5.4 – Number of ounces of gold required to buy 1 unit of the Dow at a specified time. Previous cyclical lows have been 1.94 in February 1933 and 1.29 in Jan 1980.

Stock market gains have always been accompanied by a mood of optimism and resurgence in economies. As shown in Fig. 5.4, we witnessed "index gains adjusted for gold prices" move up during the era of the Roaring Twenties, Swinging Sixties, and during the "New Economy 2000." Subsequent to these cyclical peaks, we have witnessed protracted bear markets in stocks where this ratio came down to low single digits. Both during 1933 and 1980, which were the historical bottoms, this ratio was quoting with a "1" handle. The recent bear market cycle of this ratio happened in 2011 when this ratio was below 7. Despite the massive monetary inflation after 2011, due to the phenomenon called Cantillon Effects as explained in Sec 4.D, this ratio currently trades near 20. What this indicates is that either gold prices have to up nearly 20 times or the Dow Index has to decline by about 95%, or some combination of these parameters for the "Dow Index to gold" ratio to go back to the cyclical lows of 1933 and 1980.

iii.   **S&P GSCI to S&P 500 Ratio**

This ratio has been discussed as part of Fig 4.11 and Fig 4.31 and so we will not elaborate on the same here again. This ratio currently trades below "1" and would have to go above "6" to meet the cyclical historical peaks of the GS commodity Index vis-à-vis S&P 500.

In 1971, starting from a higher base as compared to today and under conditions of monetary tightening, gold delivered a near 23X and such a return is not inconceivable in the decade ahead. There are no Reagan's and Volcker's around to end the reign of monetary inflation as well during the years ahead. If anything, Powell has already indicated that the current QT program is likely to be slowed down and interest rate cuts are on the horizon as well. Therefore, a substantive price increase for gold is on the immediate and most certainly the long-term time horizon.

Summary of Gold Projections

A summary of the gold projections using the above three economic indicators is given in Fig 5.5. These are projections for the decade ahead and while the specific numbers could change a lot depending on the policy decisions, the directions and the magnitude of the increase is are what is relevant.

Economic Indicator	Gold Price Projections & Comments
Monetary Base to Value of Gold with the Federal Reserve Ratio	**Gold Price Projection - $24,000/oz** The future monetary inflation is not included in the above price projection.
Dow-to-Gold Ratio	**Gold Price Projection - $30,000 to 40,000/Oz** The Dow to Gold Ratio has ranged between 1 and 1.5 at the bottom of the previous cycles
GSCI to S&P Ratio	**Gold Price Projection - $40,000 to 50,000/Oz** Extrapolating the move that happened during the 1970's. Of course conditions are much worse today.

Source: Author's compilations

Fig 5.5 – A compilation of various economic Indicators and gold price projections for the decade ahead.

All three indicators point towards a substantial increase in the price of gold in the range of 10 to 25X. These numbers are also consistent with what could be inferred from Sec 5.A, which shows how minuscule the "market for money" has become. A move of the magnitude indicated above would make the valuations of gold more aligned with the other assets.

The 1971 to 1980 gold bull market delivered a 23X in terms of gold price increases, while the 2001 to 2011 bull market delivered a 6.5X. In my opinion, the one just ahead is likely to be closer to the 1970s bull market in terms of returns.

At the cost of repetition, it needs to be emphasized that whether the specific numbers indicated are final destinations before a currency turnaround or just intermediate steps towards the eventual destruction of the US dollar would depend on the corrective measures taken by the government. A few of the parameters that we have used in Chapter 4 that could indicate if the US government is proceeding in the right direction would be the following:

i.   A significant reduction in the debt-to-GDP ratio from the current 120+%

ii. Reduction in the unaccounted liabilities of Social Security and Medicare

iii. Reduction / Normalization of the Federal Reserve balance sheet.

This brings us to a pivotal moment in the US dollar's history. All through the decades, other countries have supported the dollar by using it as a reserve currency and thus propping up its value by creating additional demand. The cost to other countries was significant, but bearable. The more important point was that the US Economy was in an overwhelmingly strong position that the other countries had no choice but to listen to the dictates of the US.

That is no longer the case today. Additionally, the price inflation of the decade ahead will make the costs of supporting the US dollar unjustifiably large and other countries will have no option but to cut the umbilical cord they maintain to the US dollar today.

So now for another trillion-dollar question - "Which currency is going to replace the US Dollar?" The answer shouldn't be surprising if the reader has followed the thread of reasoning so far - it is not going to be another fiat currency that is a bit less flawed as compared to the US dollar. It's going to be gold that will replace the impostor that has undeservingly ruled the world's monetary system for the last 50 years.

5.C - The Most Likely Way Forward

The basic issue as we have explained above is that none of the fiat currencies in circulation today are backed by money (gold) and hence have no intrinsic value. They function today because of the legal tender laws as well as the faith of the citizens that these will not be monetarily inflated out of existence.

But as we have explained in Chapter 4, the above faith has no basis or evidence. There is plenty of evidence that the US government and the Federal Reserve have been doing the exact opposite - explosion in money supply, federal deficits and the national debt - since the US went off the gold standard in 1971.

So any solution that is proposed has to address the above flaws. For these very reasons, some of the solutions that have been discussed in public forums will fail and these will be explained in brief below:

i. **Central Bank Digital Currencies (CBDCs):** These have the same flaws as the currently existing national currencies i.e. no desirability other than its function as a currency. Additionally, quite unlike bitcoin which at least cannot be easily created, CBDCs can be created easily and hence have the same risk of "monetary inflation."

    However, a very important reason why CBDCs would be a preferred instrument for the central banks is that they can exercise complete control over the citizens with these digital currency instruments.

    > *Those who would give up essential liberty to purchase a little temporary safety deserve neither liberty nor safety.*
    >
    > *— **Benjamin Franklin**

    We have observed that under conditions of economic crises, a transition of power happens towards totalitarian regimes. The rise of the Nazi party in Germany could be attributed to the hyperinflation in the Weimar Republic. It would be very easy for the governments to lay the blame for hyperinflation on the greedy capitalists / currency speculators and offer CBDCs as a solution as a means of tracking their activities. This of course would be another Faustian bargain for the hapless citizens!!!

ii. **IMF Special Drawing Rights (SDRs):** This is supposed to be an international currency whose value is derived from a basket of national currencies. But once again, these national currencies have no intrinsic worth and so SDRs have the very same disadvantages that national currencies have.

There could be other similar alternatives, but any proposed currency that is NOT anchored to gold will have very low acceptability outside of the geographical boundaries where it is proposed. Within a country or an economic union such as the EU, citizens may not have much of a choice but to use these currencies because of the legal tender laws. It is to be remembered that the earlier international selling proposition of the dollar was that **"The US dollar is as good as gold."**

While I have said the above two alternatives will not work, I am also reasonably certain that these would be tried. The intellectual justification will come from a misdiagnosis of the fundamental problem of monetary inflation. In the light of the understanding of the concepts as explained in Chapters 3 and 4, if one reads through the reports on the GFC 2008 written well after the events - by both governments as well as private agencies - it will be clear that the Federal Reserve is the equivalent of "Caesar's Wife" (from the phrase "Caesar's wife must be above suspicion"). The role of the Federal Reserve has never been under the scanner when a post-mortem analysis of the bubbles is done.

Every conceivable secondary factor listed and not listed in Fig 4.14 was discussed at length and how these contributed to the HB 1.0; yet, the singularly necessary condition of monetary inflation deliberately created by the US Federal Reserve would either be completely ignored or just mentioned in passing. I expect similar reports after the bursting of the HB2.0 as well. After the crisis, we should not be surprised to see reports suggesting that if central banks can exercise greater control over the market speculators, these issues can be monitored and controlled.

5.C.I - The Reserve Currency Status Under Threat

During World War II and 1971, the US was the dominant economic force in the world with no close competitor. These were the only points in time when the status of the US dollar as the reserve currency could have been questioned in the past. That unquestioned economic dominance is no longer the case today and so when a choice of the alternative to the dollar is discussed, the default answer is not TINA (There Is No Alternative) as was the case earlier.

Economy Rankings	1971 GDP (USD in billions)	2023 GDP (USD in billions)
First	US - 1,164	US - 27,357
Second	USSR - 445	China - 17,886
Third	Germany - 250	Germany - 4,456
Fourth	Japan - 245	Japan - 4,237
Fifth	France - 165	India - 3,389
$\sum$ (2nd to 5th) GDP	1,105	29,968
US Vs. $\sum$ (2nd to 5th)	105 %	91 %
US Vs. 2nd Largest	261 %	151 %

Source: countryeconomy.com

Fig 5.6 – The relative decline of the US Vs. other economies between 1971 and 2023

There has been a significant deterioration in the relative economic strength of the US between 1971 and 2023 as indicated in Fig 5.6. To summarize the differences in one word, it would be "China."

1. In 1971, the US GDP was larger than the next four largest economies combined. That is no longer the case today.

2. Even more importantly, the relative strength of the US vis-à-vis the second largest economy has declined substantially. It was more than 2.5 times the size of the second largest economy i.e., the USSR. Today, it's only 50% larger than the second largest economy China.

3. The USSR was a declining power during the 1970s and the situation is the exact opposite today. Most projections indicate that China's GDP will overtake that of the US by the mid-2030s. I estimate that it will happen before the end of the current decade primarily on account of the US dollar losing substantial value against the Chinese RMB.

For the US citizens, the above raises a serious concern and points to the growing influence of China and the declining relative influence of the US.

But the above Fig 5.6 hides the extent of decline in the US economy over the decades. The "Trade Balance" reflects the changes more accurately and shows how China has become the dominant economic force in the world today.

What is the Trade Balance and why is it relevant?

Trade Balance refers to the balance of exports of goods and services minus the import of goods and services. A trade deficit implies greater imports as compared to exports and is indicative of a weakening economy. As can be seen from Fig 5.7, the US has been running trade deficits to the tune of $500 billion for almost the last 20 years. During the days of the gold standard and even under the Bretton Woods agreement, the above would have caused an outflow of gold from the US and this would have significantly weakened the US Economy. Because the imports would have to be paid with gold rather than the US Dollar, the deficits could not have continued for an indefinite period as has been the case with the current monetary system.

On a gold standard, the deterioration of the fundamentals of the US economy would have been obvious decades ago and the problem of the lack of US competitiveness would have been halted in its infancy.

Year	China (USD in billions)	United States (USD in billions)
1960	(0.07)	(2.76)
1970	0.03	3.95
1980	(1.15)	(13.06)
1990	9.76	(77.85)
2000	28.79	(381.07)
2005	124.63	(739.90)
2010	222.40	(532.31)
2015	358.84	(526.20)
2020	355.15	(627.50)
2022	576.65	(945.30)

Source: macrotrends.net

Fig 5.7 – Trade balance of China and US from 1960

2022 US Trade in Goods

(1.18) trillion. Imports – 3.27 & Exports – 2.09 trillion

2022 US Trade in Services

- 0.23 trillion. Imports – 0.696 & Exports – 0.92 trillion

Not only has the US deteriorated in competitiveness, but even the bulk of the meager exports of the US to China today are basic commodities. China exports "value-added" manufactured products including nuclear reactors, boilers, electronics, and other consumer durables to the US. The primary US exports to China are the agricultural commodities of soybeans and corn.

2022 China and US Bilateral trade – Who exports What?		
2022 Exports	**China Exports to US (USD in billions)**	**US Exports to China (USD in billions)**
First	Electrical & Electronics - 142.56	Soybeans and Corn - 23.14
Second	Machinery & Nuclear Reactors - 109.64	Electronic Intg Circuits - 9.42
Third	Toys, games and sports requisites - 36.96	Crude Oil - 6.76
Fourth	Furniture, lightings, Prefab Units - 34.54	Blood, Vaccines - 5.93
Fifth	Plastics - 27.27	Civilian aircraft and parts - 5.52
% of Raw materials / Commodities exported by the US in the top 5 Exports to China		**58.9 %**

Source: tradingeconomics.com, USAfacts.org

Fig 5.8 – The quality of exports of China and US. China exports finished manufactured products while nearly 60% (in the top 5) of the US exports are basic commodities.

After studying Fig 5.7 and Fig 5.8, it would be natural for readers to conclude that the USA of 2024 resembles the USSR of 1971, as portrayed in Fig 5.6. The primary exports of the former Soviet Union were grain and crude oil, while they imported manufactured goods with the dollars earned through their "commodity" exports. Similarly, the US today exports soybeans/corn and crude oil, with imports paid for using dollars created out of thin air.

It's not just the deteriorating trade competitiveness with China. In the list of the top 5 exports (to all countries) of the US by value for 2023 are crude oil ($117 b), civilian aircraft parts ($113 b), gasoline and other fuels ($113 b),

LNG and other petroleum gases ($68 b), and passenger vehicles ($63 b). About 2/3rd of all US exports as basic commodities.

But how did the US reach this state of manufacturing morass? Almost mirroring the history of money, the story of US manufacturing is largely forgotten. The US was a manufacturing powerhouse, and its rise as a superpower was almost solely due to the manufacturing base and the riches it created for both investors and society alike.

Even today, despite the emphasis on the US being a services economy, two-thirds of US exports are goods. Without a revival in manufacturing, it's almost inconceivable for the US to return to its former economic glory.

The Rise of the US and its Manufacturing Base (Post-Civil War to 1950)

The US had developed and adopted technology extensively during the first few decades of the nineteenth century. The Civil War of 1861 to 1865 could be described as the first major battle that utilized technology extensively - telegraph, railroads, ironclad warships, and mass-produced weapons. The trend of developing and adopting technology only intensified subsequently. Post the Civil War, many new industries such as petroleum refining, steel mills, and electrical power emerged. Railroads were also expanded, connecting most parts of the country into one national economy. The transcontinental railroads that connected the east and west coasts were developed, and five such transcontinental systems were in place by 1900. This opened the way for the settlement of the West and created new economic opportunities as well.

Manufacturing thus was the reason for the transformation of the US from an agrarian society into a wealthy country. It also created an industrious and prosperous middle class. Till that period, agriculture was the predominant occupation, and the "middle class" was almost an unknown entity - there were wealthy landowners and lowly peasants.

An American born during the middle of the nineteenth century, around 1850, would have experienced a major transformation in living standards during his lifetime. Transportation, food, quality of housing, and electricity all changed dramatically over the subsequent few decades.

The change in transportation/connectivity was particularly impressive. Horses had been domesticated around 4000 BC and had been the primary mode of transport at least from around 1500 BC. So for almost 3300 years leading up to the year 1850, horses had been the primary mode of transportation. From horse-drawn carriages to steam engines to electric locomotives to gasoline-powered automobiles and finally the airplane - all within a human lifespan was an unparalleled change.

This manufacturing boom incentivized two types of migrations - from rural townships within the US and immigration from other countries. Between 1880 and 1890, an estimated 40% of the townships lost population due to migration to the cities. About 12 million migrants moved to the US from Europe and China in the decades leading up to 1900, seeing the US as the land of economic opportunity and individual liberty.

This manufacturing-led prosperity gained momentum during the early part of the twentieth century as well. In what is referred to as "Fordism," the unmistakable trend was towards large-scale manufacturing with higher productivity-linked wages, shorter working hours, and higher product quality at lower prices. The assembly line, one of the landmark innovations of Ford, ensured that car prices fell from $825 in 1908 to $260 by 1925.

Ford had also almost doubled wages to $5/day (using gold prices as a proxy, this is the equivalent of $500/day in terms of today's dollars), and their Model T was now within the purchasing grasp of his assembly line workers. Despite multiple attempts, trade unions

> *We believe in making 25,000 men prosperous & contented rather than follow the plan of making a few slave drivers in our establishment multi-millionaires.*
>
> *– Henry Ford*

could never successfully organize against corporations due to continuously improving wages and working environments. It was not until the Great Depression that unions were able to make decisive inroads into the labor force.

It was this manufacturing boom that resulted in the US Dollar becoming the world's reserve currency. Products made in the US were widely recognized for their superior quality and low prices. Countries started using the dollar as the reserve currency as they could buy products produced by the US using the same.

The Switch in Reserve Currency

The US overtook the UK as the largest economy during the 1880s by flooding the world with its manufactured exports. This was in addition to the large agricultural output of the US due to the vast land holdings. China had a large economy during 1900 primarily due to its agricultural output, and the decline of the relative share of China's GDP would coincide with the emergence of manufacturing around the world.

The Reserve Currency Switch – US Dollar and Great British Pound				
Year	US GDP Share (in %)	UK GDP Share (in %)	Other Countries GDP Share (in %)	Share of Global Stock Markets (in %)
1900	18.0	9.2	China – 11.4 Germany – 7.6	US – 14.4, UK – 24.2 China – 0.4, Germany – 12.6
1910	23.3	9.0	China – 10 Germany – 8.8	US – 23.1, UK – 16.8 China – 0.9, Germany – 11.9
1920	24.2	7.1	China – 10.4 Germany – 6.6	US – 31.5, UK – 21.5 China – 1.9, Germany – 2.0
1930	23.3	7.0	China – 8.7 Germany – 7.3 Japan – 3.8	US – 56.6, UK – 12.7 China – 1.0, Germany – 2.7 Japan – 12.7
1940	25.1	8.0	China – 7.0 Germany – 8.9 Japan – 5.2	US – 44.7, UK – 13.2 China –0.2, Germany – 7.6 Japan – 9.3
1950	27.7	6.6	China – 5.3 Germany – 5.1 Japan – 3.1	US – 63.9, UK – 9.5 China –0.0, Germany – 0.7 Japan – 0.2

Source: Visual Capitalist

Fig 5.9 – GDP / Stock Markets Patterns that resulted in the USD becoming the Reserve Currency. Although the official change happened during 1944 at Bretton Woods, the US Dollar was more used as a Reserve Currency than the GBP from the 1920's. What happened at Bretton Woods was just a formal recognition of the *de facto* standard.

Though the US GDP was almost twice the size of the UK GDP by 1900, the British Pound continued to be the reserve currency for historical reasons. Besides, London continued to be the financial capital of the world, and the UK's share of the global stock market capitalization was almost 50% higher than that of the US.

However, the US economy was ascending while the UK was descending on a relative basis, as shown in Fig 5.9. It was a natural corollary that the stock markets would follow the pattern of the global GDP share. At the end of WWI, it was clear that the US was the dominant force in both aspects - GDP size and share of global stock market capitalization. Military domination added to the economic dimension to make it an unrivaled force by 1920.

So, the transfer of power from the UK to the US would start in a not-so-subtle fashion after World War I. Starting in 1920, the US dollar was used almost as much as the reserve currency by most countries around the world, although the British pound was still the official reserve currency. This would continue despite the Great Depression, and by the time of WWII, the US had unquestionably overtaken the UK as the financial and military power center. The US economy as well as the stock market capitalization by 1940 was three times that of the UK. So, the replacement of the GBP by the USD as the world's reserve currency was only a matter of time.

The dramatic weakening of the UK's economy during WWII ensured this near-seamless switch. The US did not enter World War II until 1942 (the Pearl Harbor incident happened in December 1941), and before that, the UK had to bear the brunt of German blitzkrieg and Luftwaffe air-raids. By the time WWII ended, most economies, including that of the UK, had been decimated. As Fig 5.9 shows, by the year 1950, the GDP of the US was greater than the next 4 countries combined by a wide margin, and its stock market represented almost 2/3rds of the world's total stock market capitalization.

By 1950, as an outcome of WWII, the combined market capitalization of China, Germany, and Japan was less than 1% of the total share, while that of the UK would fall below 10% for the first time. The UK would gradually continue to weaken through the next few decades, and by 2020, the UK's share of the world GDP was just 3%, and its share of the stock markets would be 4.2%.

The dominance of the US would continue for the next decade, and by 1960, the US share of the global stock market capitalization would be more than 2/3rds. The GDP share would slightly decline to 24.3% from 27.7% during 1950. Incidentally, the top 5 companies by revenue in the world during 1960 were General Motors, Exxon Mobil, Ford Motor, General Electric, and US Steel. Manufacturing completely dominated the landscape of the US economy and created a thriving middle class that was the envy of the world.

From a situation of complete dominance by 1960, how did the US lose so much of its competitiveness over the next few decades to a near-bankrupt stage today?

It is indeed a very deep question, and we will attempt to answer the same more comprehensively in Section 5.D. However, we will start with the history of the decline in US manufacturing from 1960.

The Decline of US Manufacturing (1960 - ?)

The contributions of manufacturing to US dominance are largely a forgotten story, and the emergence of the large middle class could be attributed to the high-paying manufacturing jobs in the US during the early to mid-part of the twentieth century. Process innovations like Ford's assembly line helped to improve productivity and the pay of workers while reducing the price of end products simultaneously. Manufacturing contributed more than 25% to the GDP during the 1950s through the late 1960s, as shown in Fig 5.10.

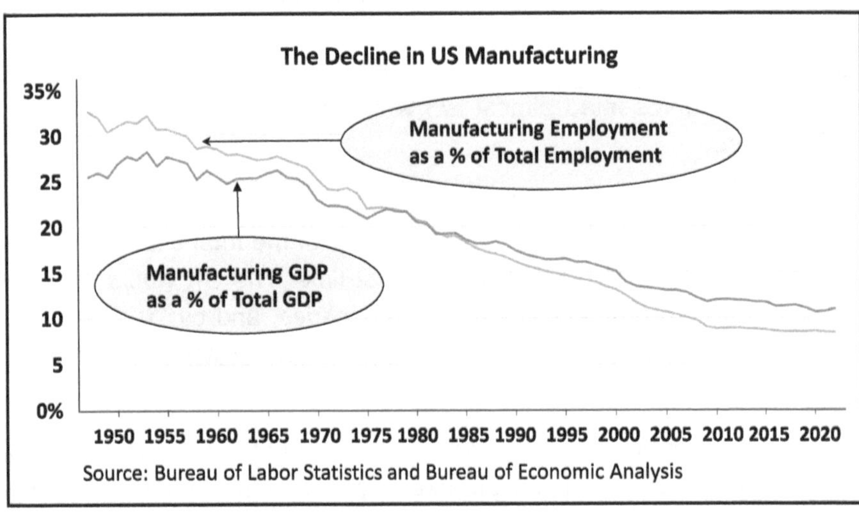

Fig 5.10 – From more than 30% of the total employment during the 1950s, today the share has declined to less than 10%.

Manufacturing has experienced a steady decline subsequently, and today it contributes just 11% of the GDP. The surge in Chinese manufacturing did not start until the 1990s, and it acquired a reasonable scale only post-2000, as can be inferred from Fig 5.7. The problems are far more structural than the emergence of China as a competing manufacturing powerhouse. China simply occupied the space vacated by US manufacturing.

The decline of the share of US GDP

The loss of manufacturing capacity within the US has also resulted in a steady decline of the US GDP as a percentage of the World GDP. The period of the 1950s and 1960s was the peak of the US Economy in terms of the share of the world GDP. The post-World War II induced manufacturing boom of consumer durables coupled with limited government ensured the above, and the US GDP share stayed at more than 25% through the 1950s.

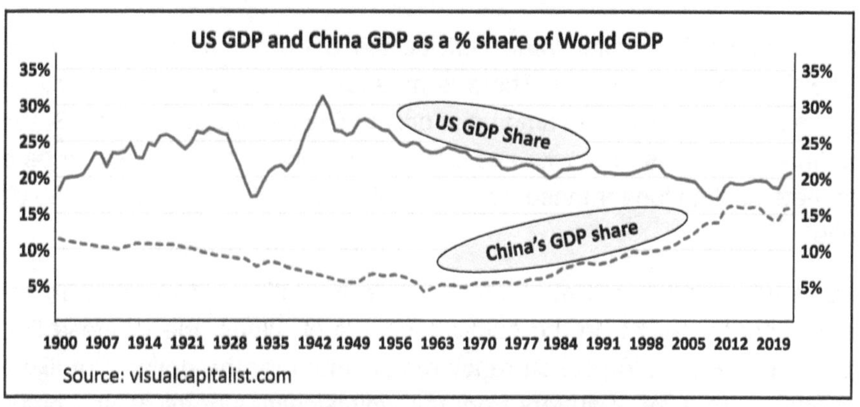

Fig 5.11 – Excluding the WW-II period, the 1950's and early 1960's is the peak of the US share of the World GDP at above 25%. By 2010, this had declined to 17%. The subsequent strengthening of the DXY has caused the share to climb up to 20% by 2022.

Post the 1960s, the US GDP share declined to about 20% by the late 1970s, and it remained at that level until about 2000 as shown in Fig 5.11. This further declined to about 17% by 2010 and has subsequently increased to about 20% by 2022. In comparison, China's share of GDP has grown from less than 5% in 1960 to more than 16% by 2022.

The US Dollar Reserve Currency Status – Way Past Expiry Date

As can be concluded from the previous section, the dollar became the reserve currency for the world for two reasons.

1. The US was the dominant economy for a prolonged period starting during the 1880s and had a relative peak during the early 1960s. Even today, it is the largest economy in the world, though it owes that position primarily to the reserve currency status of the dollar. The consequence has now become the cause.

2. When the US dollar was crowned the reserve currency after the Bretton Woods agreement, the promise was that it was convertible at a fixed rate of $35/oz. There was a risk-free interest from the treasuries and so it was even better than gold as far as the foreign central banks were concerned.

With annual trillion-dollar trade deficits, the US dollar no longer deserves to be the reserve currency. There is no supply of goods from the US that can be purchased with the amount of dollars floating outside of the US. With the financial assets of stocks and bonds in a bubble, there needs to be an alternate destination for these dollars circulating outside the US, and there is none.

The world governments at this stage have no option but to return to gold as the reserve asset. In the current scheme of things, the Chinese RMB would be the most logical currency replacement for the dollar. But like all national currencies, it suffers from the whimsicalities of its central banks. It is just too early, and the world is not going to jump from placing its trust in the Federal Reserve to the People's Bank of China. Especially when it realizes how the privilege has been misused by the US at the cost of the rest of the world.

So the US dollar is not going to be replaced by the Euro, the RMB or any combination of regional currencies. It is gold that will replace the dollar. The only question is the timelines and the structure of the gold standard. & of course the price.

The Emerging BRICS Gold Standard

The obvious solution that has been discussed for a few years now is the BRICS gold-backed currency. It is much closer to implementation than what is generally perceived in the US.

While I have no inside information on the structure of the BRICS currency, it is possible to make some postulates on the possible implementation roadmap.

1. The BRICS currency would be defined in much the same way as the dollar was done before 1971 i.e., at a fixed exchange rate with gold. The specific convertibility rate for the BRICS currency to gold is not so relevant for our purpose other than to state that the convertibility of BRICS currency to gold will be offered to all the central banks.

2. The individual national currencies will be on a free-floating standard with the BRICS gold currency. The option for countries to move towards a fixed exchange rate with the BRICS currency will be "on the table," and this would incentivize the participating countries to move towards a gold standard for their national currencies as well. I believe the Chinese RMB and the Russian Rouble would be amongst the first set of currencies to move towards this fixed exchange rate, at which point they would have to offer convertibility to their citizens as well for their national currencies.

3. The inclusion of Saudi Arabia, UAE, and Iran as part of the BRICS group is an important indicator that "Petro BRICS" could well be on the cards. But quite unlike the "Petro Dollar" that created an artificial demand for the paper US Dollars, the "Petro BRICS" would enlarge the legitimate use of gold for international transactions.

Not being tied to one country, no single country will have the power to unilaterally suspend convertibility as Nixon did during 1971. That I think is the single most important advantage that BRICS would have over any one country offering a gold convertible currency.

The more other countries (BRICS or otherwise) move towards a gold standard themselves, greater would be the integration of the world economy. To that extent, BRICS will incentivize their members to move towards a fixed exchange rate with the BRICS currency and make convertibility of national currencies for the citizens a prerequisite for the same.

Of course, I am contemplating the future roadmap for the next few decades and it appears as if the world would go back to the classical gold standard in much the same stages / path it moved away from it i.e., in stages with each subsequent step having a closer bond to gold.

5.D - A Hard Look at Reviving the US Dollar

The path to reviving the US Dollar is not easy, and the solutions are not just economic changes to the currency and regulatory system. The US of today is a far cry from the nation that made it to be a superpower and the envy of every other nation on the planet.

It was a country built with sheer industry offering equality of opportunities. "Give me liberty or give me death" is one of the phrases that is so uniquely American and it encapsulated the attitude of the citizens to the concept of liberty and self-reliance. Today, it's just another country on the face of the planet spoilt by government bureaucracy and the social fabric corrupted by giveaways.

When did the decline of the US start?

It's a difficult question as the answer would vary depending on how we define "decline." While it is quite natural to use GDP as indicated in Fig 5.11 as an indicator for measuring the above, it is a basic lesson of history that the decline in the moral fabric of the society and the civil liberties of citizens starts several decades or even centuries before these start showing up in the measurable numbers.

This basic philosophical fact cannot be overemphasized - The invisible decay of a society from within far precedes the externally visible decline.

There are many parallels between the historical decline of the Roman Civilization and the US today. While many consider the invasion of the barbarians as having caused the downfall of the Roman Empire, that specific event was nothing more than the final nail in the coffin. Max Weber outlined the above in his chronicle on the decline of the Roman Civilization in his essay "The Social Causes of the Decay of Ancient Civilization."

> *The Roman Empire was not destroyed from without; its destruction was not caused by the numerical superiority of its opponents nor by the inadequacy of its political leaders. In the last century of its existence Rome had her iron chancellors: heroic figures, like Stilicho, men who combined Teutonic boldness with the art of cunning diplomacy, were at the head of the state.*
>
> *...(but) the Empire had, long before, undergone a change in its very essence; when it disintegrated, it did not suddenly collapse under one powerful blow. The Teutonic invaders brought to its logical climax a development that had been long in the making.*
>
> *But most important: the decay of ancient civilization was not caused by the destruction of the Roman Empire. The Empire as a political structure survived by centuries the acme of Roman culture. This culture had vanished much earlier.... (finally, with) the extinction of the office of the emperor in the West, the books are closed, it becomes obvious that barbarism, long ago, has conquered the Empire from within.*

Quite similar to the decline of the Roman Civilization, the decline of the US started much earlier than the visible decline in the GDP share. The two events that signaled the definitive beginning of the decline of the US happened during the final months of 1913:

i. The introduction of the income tax as part of the Revenue Act in October 1913.

ii. The formation of the US Fed with the Federal Reserve Act in December 1913.

It would take nearly 50 years for the impact of the above two Acts to start showing in the US competitiveness and dominance in the global GDP. While the formation of the Federal Reserve and how it enabled deficit spending and the build-up of the national debt has been explained

> *Income taxes are responsible for the transformation of the Federal government from one of limited powers into a vast leviathan whose tentacles reach into almost every aspect of American life.*
>
> *– Ron Paul*

extensively in Chapter 4, the effect of the income tax has not been dealt with earlier. Primarily because the impact is more from a philosophical perspective. However, in some sense, this is more fundamental as Max Weber explains in his essay cited above.

It was the income tax that enabled the growth of the "Cradle-to-Grave Nanny state" where citizens came to be dependent on the government. This was not the intention of the founding fathers, and the US was founded on the principles of rugged individualism and a very limited Federal government. The onus was on the individual to take care of his family, health, education, and other necessities of life. The rights granted to citizens under the *"Declaration of Independence"* were limited to *"life, liberty, and the pursuit of happiness"* and not "social security, medicare, and education."

Most individuals in the US today believe that payment of the income tax contributes to the overall welfare of the society while the actual impact is the exact opposite. Citizens would have been far better off retaining their earnings and planning their retirements, health/medical budgetary allocations, and other such requirements. Citizens are going to realize in a short few years that all the payments they have made to the US Federal government aren't going to really return much or perhaps even nothing at all. On the contrary, the misadventures of the military-industrial complex and the Federal bureaucracy are a direct outcome of the income tax.

5.D.I - The Income Tax in the US - A Brief History

The income tax incidentally was positioned as a way to reduce the tariffs that impacted every citizen. The average tariff was about 40%, and this was reduced to 25% as a trade-off for the income tax. The lowest income tax slab was set at $20,000 in 1913 (adjusting for inflation, that would be the equivalent of $440,000 by 2010 dollars), and the income tax rate was only 2% for these individuals. The highest slab was 7%, and the income tax was positioned as a mechanism in which the "rich" would pay for the reduction in tariffs that would benefit everybody.

Revenue Act of 1913		
Income 1913 Dollars	Total Tax Rate	Income Adjusted for 2010 Dollars
< 20,000	1%	
> 20,000	2%	$ 440,400
> 50,000	3%	$ 1,101,000
> 75,000	4%	$ 1,651,600
> 100,000	5%	$ 2,202,100
> 250,000	6%	$ 5,505,300
> 500,000	7%	$ 11,010,700
Source: Wikipedia		

Fig 5.12 - Income Tax was introduced in lieu of a reduction in Tariffs

"Soak-the-Rich" schemes usually sail through in democracies as citizens don't realize the Faustian bargain involved. Deficit financing is one such bargain as has been explained earlier. In all these cases, the starting point appears innocuous, indeed helpful to the average citizen. For example, under the Act of 1913, very few citizens would pay the income tax, and even then the average payment was just a little more than 1%. What could be harmful about such a system when the trade-off was a steep reduction in tariffs? The Revenue Act of 1913 was indeed another instance of the "camel's nose under the tent" and the real effects of permitting the income tax would show up a few decades later.

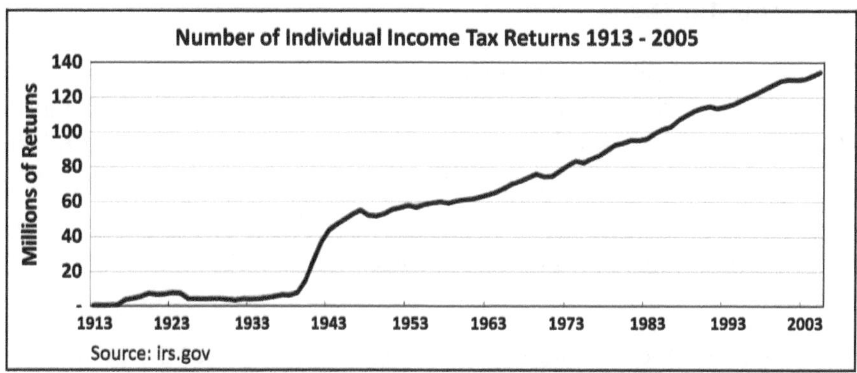

Fig 5.13 – Introduction of the Income Tax in the year 1913. For the first 3 decades, the number of income tax filers was limited i.e. much less than 5% of the total population. Today it is almost 50% of the total population that files tax returns.

The population in the US was nearly 100 million during the year 1913 and the number of people filing tax returns was much less than 0.5% that year. The number of individual income tax returns filed till 1916 stayed well under 0.5 million as shown in Fig 5.13. Due to a series of tax law changes on the rates and other conditions, the number of returns filed rose almost 10-fold to 3.5 million by 1917. The number of returns filed would continue with a marginal increasing trend till 1940.

The introduction of the lower income filing requirements during 1940 would cause another near 10-fold increase and the number would touch 50 million by 1946. Since that time, the growth in the number of individual filers mirrored the population growth crossing 100 million by 1985. This number would continue to gradually grow over the years and would touch 135 million by 2005.

There were two periods of a near 10X increase in the number of individuals filing their Income tax returns. Both these 10X increases happened during the World War years. Coincidence?

Governments can get away with very detrimental regulations under the banner of "Patriotism."

For 2022, the number of individual return filings was about 160 million. Out of a total population of about 330 million, this means almost 48.5% of the population are filing their returns.

The Income Tax Rates

The 1940s would witness two steep changes in the income tax front. One is the number of individuals filing their income tax as can be observed in Fig 5.13. The other significant change was in the income tax rate paid. While the highest rate would touch 77% by 1918 (from 7% in 1913) and would be above 80%+ between 1940 and 1964, these were not indicative of the average tax rates due to the tax brackets for which these were set and exemptions provided.

The Federal income tax rate would average around 4% for the period 1913 to 1941 as shown in Fig 5.14. Throughout the 1940's, several tax laws were passed to increase individual income tax rates and these resulted in a more than tripling of the rates to 12%. These rates have stayed between 12 and 16% from the 1970s till date with a marginally upward trending bias.

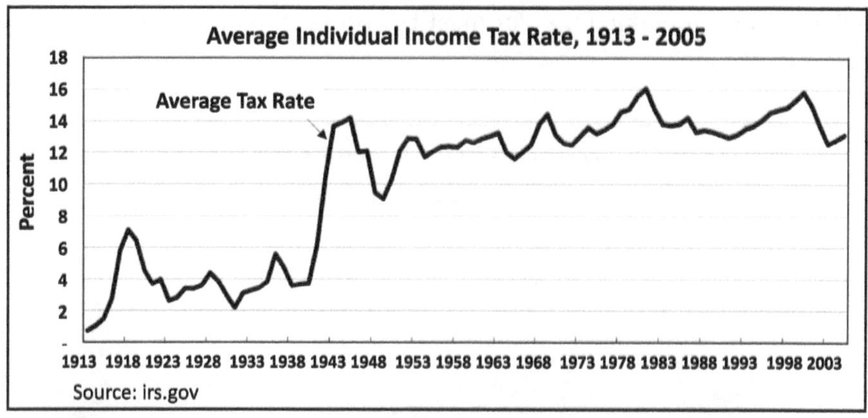

Fig 5.14 - Income Tax Rate changes since 1913. The average rate would stay at around 4% for the first 3 decades. By the mid 1940's, this would increase to 12%. Between 1970 and now, the rates have ranged between 12 and 16%.

Starting with the condition wherein less than 0.5% of the population paid less than 2% of their incomes as taxes in 1913, we are in a situation today wherein nearly 48.5% of the population pays around 14% as Federal income tax. There really can't be a better example of the idiom "camel's nose under the tent."

The Consequences of the Income Tax and the Inflation Tax

The above-discussed Income Tax started imposing a serious burden on the population starting in the 1940s. Another form of taxation - the monetary inflation tax - started during the 1960s and accelerated during the 1970s. How did Americans cope with these two additional forms of taxation? Both these represented a significant drain on the net purchasing power, and the average US family should have witnessed a declining standard of living as a consequence. How did the US continue to enjoy higher living standards over the subsequent decades?

A two-part explanation - the first is to dispel a conventional myth about productivity gains linked to improvements in real wages, and two - the real reason.

It is usually assumed that productivity gains have resulted in real wage gains for US workers. While we can see sharp wage gains for those near the top and in specific sectors like finance, technology, and pharmaceutical research, it is entirely unacknowledged that for most US workers, real wages have barely moved in decades.

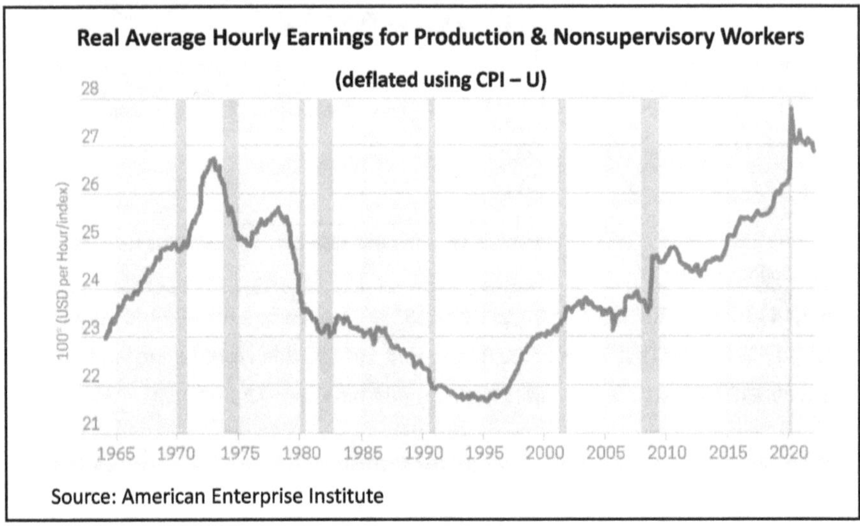

Fig 5.15 – Average Real Wages starting 1971 has increased only marginally after 50 years.

Fig. 5.15 shows the real wages for US production workers, which have been non-existent at best since 1971. Of course, if we change the base years to a more favorable situation (like 1990), some improvements are visible, but then there is a big question mark over the deflator used and whether these numbers are even close to accurate. As part of Fig. 3.17, it has been explained how the inflation numbers have been understated in a significant way starting in the mid-1990s. So even these gains could well be an illusion of monetary inflation.

So if it's not the productivity gains and the associated real wage increases, what has caused the improvement in living standards?

It is the women entering the labor force in a big way starting from the 1920s. The labor force participation rate among women would continuously increase from 1920 until the year 2000. Fig. 5.16 shows the labor force participation rate for women from 1948 to date. The period that witnessed the steepest increase would be the 1940s and 1960-80, coinciding with the steep increase in income tax rates during the 1940s and the inflation tax during the 1960s and 1970s.

Fig 5.16 – Increasing trend of labor force participation amongst women.

During the 1920s, the labor force participation rate among women was quite low at 22.7%, as can be observed from Fig. 5.17. The peak of women's labor force participation was in the age group of 20-24, which could be just before the period they were married and started raising a family. For the age group 25 to 64, men's labor force participation was almost five times that of women.

Labor Force Participation Rates by Age and Gender

Age Group	1920		2015	
	Men	Women	Men	Women
Total, > 14 years	84.6	22.7	69.1	56.7
14 – 19 years	51.5	28.4	34.2	34.4
20 – 24 years	89.9	37.5	73.0	68.3
25 – 44 years	95.6	21.7	89.5	73.8
45 – 64 years	90.7	16.5	78.1	66.1
> 65 years	55.6	7.3	23.4	15.3

The labor force participation rate amongst men was 3.7 times of women during 1920. In the peak working age group of 25 to 64, the ratio was even higher at 5.1 times.

By 2015, the gender difference had substantially narrowed down to just 22% in the workforce. In the peak working age group, this drops below 20%.

Source: Bureau of Labor Statistics

Fig 5.17 – Increase in the labor force participation by Women.

So it was women entering the labor force in a large way that helped American families combat the twin attacks of the income tax and the inflation tax.

The labor force participation of women peaked at around 60% during 2000 and has stayed between 55% and 60% since then.

Leisure and raising kids (instead of the daycare option) are legitimate end goals for all of us. It was the dwindling purchasing power of the US dollar that made women take up the median job. While some jobs are intellectually challenging / inherently motivating and is a legitimate goal for some individuals, for the vast majority, it is the lack of earning power that made the life partner become a wage earner as well.

Post-2000, families have also increased their debt (from less than $5 trillion in 2000 to nearly $18 trillion in Q1 2024) in much the same way as the US government. The US consumers also appear creditworthy and have increased their living standards by using additional debt. The reasons should be very easy to guess for the reader, i.e., falling interest rates and ZIRP from 2008 onwards have allowed for the buildup of an enormous amount of consumer debt. It is only with the recent increase in the Fed funds rate that the interest obligations would begin to reflect on the financial health of the US consumer in the years ahead.

This, of course, is the end of the road for the US consumer. All of the silver arrows have been utilized, and the quiver is empty. The extended rope that the reserve currency status of the US dollar has given has been abused beyond limits by the US government and citizens alike. The payback time is around the corner, and it isn't a pretty picture if you can peep ahead!

How to Revive the US Dollar after the Collapse?

I think it's a fair assumption to make that the required radical changes will not be attempted until the crisis in the US dollar is well underway. I also have no doubts that similar to Romans pointing fingers at the barbarians, some external sources to blame would be found.

Readers should know by now that these are self-inflicted wounds dating perhaps at least to 1971 if not 60 years before that. Any revival in the US has to recognize that it has veered away from the path that made it an economic powerhouse and a return to the basics of limited government and sound money is essential.

Rome never regained the glory once the decline started, and it was a slow and gradual decline spanning centuries. The decline of the UK would be a more recent example of an empire losing its pre-eminent status and never gaining it back. From the largest economy during the 1880s and the world's reserve currency about 80 years ago, today the UK is just about 3% of the world economy. The decline of the UK's GDP as a share of the world has been a gradual and continuous event as shown below. The dethroning of the status of the British Pound as the world's reserve currency with Bretton Woods during 1944 has only hastened this decline.

UK's share of Global GDP						
1900	1920	1940	1960	1980	2000	2020
9.2%	7.2%	7.5%	5.4%	3.6%	3.1%	2.9%

Can the UK reverse this 120-year-old trend of declining economic prominence? There is no chance for a revival under the current socialistic system of governance that has a broad consensus between the two main political parties. This trend toward even greater socialism is also a growing one given the compulsions of democratic politics and this guarantees a stagnation / decline in the global GDP share during the decades ahead. Again, it is the bipartisan consensus amongst the political parties that is driving the UK towards bankruptcy, albeit at a much slower rate as compared to what the US is currently on.

For the US, the decline started at least during the 1960s if not earlier. A definitive signal for the end of the dominance of the US dollar could be the dethroning of the reserve currency status. But I guess that it may not even be an explicit change like what happened at Bretton Woods, and it could well be a decision by OPEC to trade oil for gold using the BRICS currency. The very launch of the BRICS currency could be a 1920s-type event wherein the market started using the US dollar as the reserve currency rather than the then "official reserve currency," which was the British pound. Similar to that, countries might start using the BRICS currency as their main reserve asset quite independent of the official reserve currency. We are not far off from the day in which the US pays for its imports using another currency.

It is only at that point that the inevitability of radical change "might" dawn upon the policymakers. While this is certainly not the forum to sketch out the details, a few lines indicating the possible directions might help:

1. A policy of balancing the budget within a couple of years with limits on additions to the national debt on an annualized basis explicitly specified.

2. A staged five-year policy towards the abolition of income tax while freeing the current generation of workers from the mandatory Social Security and Medicare obligations.

3. A plan to offer a gold-backed currency with convertibility to citizens. The BRICS gold currency would have been launched by then, but it would be very difficult for the BRICS countries to offer convertibility to citizens at least to start with. The US can up the ante on the convertibility front by offering the same to their citizens for the US dollar.

4. Abolishing the Federal Reserve and permitting private banks to issue their dollar currencies with convertibility to gold at fixed rates. Competition is always good for all products/services, and it is no different for the currency market.

Radical as the above suggestions might seem, these are indeed the very principles that the US was founded upon. Both the Income tax and the Federal Reserve were non-existent till 1913 and by then, the US was already the dominant economic power in the world. It was the introduction of these practices that started the degradation of the US economy.

It is also not the case that the founding fathers of the US were not aware of the concept of a "Central Bank" or the "National Debt" that it perpetrates. They were well aware of the dangers of allowing the Federal government to borrow, of central banks monetizing Government debt and the dangers posed by the paper money system as can be inferred from their observations.

I wish it were possible to obtain a single amendment to our Constitution. I would be willing to depend on that alone for the reduction of the administration of our Government to the genuine principles of its constitution; I mean an additional article, taking from the Federal Government the power of borrowing.

– Thomas Jefferson, 1798

The Bank of the United States is one of the most deadly hostilities existing, against the principles and form of our Constitution.

– Thomas Jefferson, 1803 *(comments on the First Central Bank of the US that existed between 1791- 1811)*

Paper money has had the effect in your state that it will ever have, to ruin commerce, oppress the honest, and open the door to every species of fraud and injustice.

– George Washington, 1787

Paper money is unjust. It is unconstitutional for it affects the rights of property as much as taking away equal value in land.

– James Madison

All the perplexities, confusion and distress in America arise, not from defects in their Constitution or Confederation, not from want of honor or virtue, so much as from the downright ignorance of the nature of coin, credit and circulation.

– John Adams

What are the chances for the above plans to be implemented? Sadly, not too high. In fact, very close to "zero" would be my estimate.

What is certain is that China will overtake the US as the largest economy very soon. But the social ideas / freedom that China represents (in economic terms of having a limited government, China is more capitalistic than the US today) would be far from being praiseworthy or worth emulating. Having said that, if one were to choose between emigrating the US or to China today, the latter would have to be considered an informed choice. This is true for both individuals and businesses. The land of opportunity for the next century is going to be China notwithstanding its near-term economic troubles. Remember that the US transition into a superpower included a civil war, two economic depressions and a number of recessions.

The one wrong conclusion that self-seeking governments the world over would make is this - having a single-party system as China has today is necessary to achieve the economic ends of prosperity. The fact that the US achieved an even greater economic dominance while having a "free society" would be completely forgotten or would be rationalized away as impractical under the current circumstances.

The US was indeed a very unique experiment in world history with the idea of individual liberty and limited government taking center stage. The US of today is a far cry from those ideals and a return to those principles will not be easy. Can the US citizens endure the interim temporary hardship and force the government to take the "road already traveled" 250 years ago?

John Adams had observed "Liberty, once lost, is lost forever." I do fondly hope John Adams is proven wrong in the not-too-distant future. He would do too.

A Glossary of Terms

1. **CRB Index:** Commodity Research Bureau Index also known as the Thomson Reuters Core Commodity Index is a mathematical average of 19 commodity prices. Agricultural commodities (corn, cotton, coffee, sugar etc.) have the highest weightage with 41% followed by Energy (crude oil, natural gas etc.) at 39%. Precious metals (gold and silver) accounts for 7% and base metals (aluminum, copper etc.) for the remaining 13%.

2. **DXY Index:** Pronounced as "Dixie," the DXY is the US Dollar Index and tracks the strength of the dollar against a basket of 6 major currencies. The Euro has the highest weightage with 57.6% followed by the Japanese yen at 13.6%. The other currencies are the Pound sterling, Canadian dollar, Swedish krona and the Swiss franc.

3. **Expansion of the Federal Reserve Balance Sheet:** Refer "Quantitative Easing."

4. **Federal Finances**

    a. **Federal Revenues:** This is the amount received by the US federal government from taxes and other sources during a Fiscal Year which runs from October to September. For example, the FY2023 revenues refers to the amount collected during the period Oct 01, 2022, to Sep 30, 2023.

    The primary sources of revenue are the individual income taxes, Social Security and Medicare taxes, and the corporate income tax. The federal revenue for FY2023 was $4.44 trillion and individual Income tax contributed 49%, Social Security and Medicare taxes contributed 36% and corporate Income tax contributed about 9%.

    b. **Federal Expenses:** The federal government spends money on a variety of goods, services and programs for the support and welfare of the American public. In addition, they also have to pay interest on the debt.

The federal expenses for FY2023 was 6.13 trillion and the major expenditure categories for the US government are Social Security, Health, National defense, Net Interest and Medicare.

c. **Federal Deficit / Surplus:** This refers to the excess of Federal Expenses over Federal Revenues. When the expenses are greater, then this referred to as Fiscal Deficit. When revenues is greater than expenses, this is referred to as a fiscal surplus. In FY2023, the US had a federal deficit of nearly $1.70 trillion ($6.13 - $4.44 trillion).

d. **Federal Debt or National Debt:** The federal or national debt is the total amount of outstanding borrowings by the US federal government accumulated over the nation's history.

Technically, the national debt should be the summation of all the federal deficits / surpluses. But there are a few expenditure line items that are not explicitly accounted for in the US budgetary expenses. So the growth in national debt over the fiscal year is a better indicator of the true fiscal deficit. For example, the growth in national debt over the time period FY2023 was $2.24 trillion through the fiscal deficit over this period was $1.7 trillion.

5. **Federal Reserve Funds Rate (Fed funds rate):** The term refers to the target interest rate (or a range) set by the Federal Reserve at which commercial banks borrow / lend their reserves to each other overnight.

The Fed funds rate can be considered to be the base rate over which other types of short-term loans (credit-cards, auto loans etc.) are charged a premium. Long-term rates (e.g., 30-year mortgage) are also affected by the movement in the Fed funds rate although the impact is not so well correlated as compared to the rates on the short-term loans.

a. **Federal Discount rate:** The discount rate is the interest rate set by the Federal Reserve on loans extended by the central banks to commercial banks or other eligible participants. The discount rate is usually marginally higher than the Fed funds rate, and is intended to be used as a last resort for banks who are not able to borrow in the interbank market at the Fed funds rate.

6. **GFC 2008:** Global Financial Crisis of 2008 refers to the period of extreme stress in the global banking and financial system. This was started by a burst of the housing bubble in the US that triggered a wave

of bank closures. This was the biggest economic crisis that the world faced since the onset of the Great Depression in 1929.

7. **Malinvestments:** This is a terminology that is specific to Austrian Economics. It refers to the wrong allocation of capital, usually as an entire sector, such as the housing market or the technology industry. According to the Austrian Business Cycle Theory this is caused by the additional flow of credit that is not backed by real savings and is caused by central banks artificially reducing interest rates within the system.

8. **Money Supply:** The money supply is the sum total of all the currency and liquid assets with an economy on a given date. There are different components of the Money Supply as defined as M0, M1, M2 and M3. These definitions are nested i.e., M3 includes M2, M2 includes M1 and M1 includes M0. The main distinguishing feature is the liquidity of these components or how easily these can be converted into cash.

    a. **M0:** Also referred to as the "monetary base." This is the currency in circulation + reserves of the commercial banks at the Federal Reserve banks.

    b. **M1:** Also referred to as "narrow money." Includes M0 + demand deposits at commercial banks and other liquid deposits.

    c. **M2:** M1 + savings accounts + time deposits under $100,000 and retail money market funds.

    d. **M3:** Also referred to as "broad money." Includes M2 + large time deposits and institutional money market funds. The Federal Reserve discontinued reporting the M3 numbers in 2006.

9. **NASDAQ 2000 / dot com bubble:** This was a stock market bubble that occurred during the late 1990's and peaked by March 2000. Between 1995 and 2000, the NASDAQ index would give a 400% return only to fall by 2/3rd from the peak over the subsequent 30 months.

10. **National Debt:** Also known as Federal Debt. Refer to 4.d for the explanation.

11. **Quantitative Easing:** This is the practice of Central Banks purchasing government bonds and financial instruments, such as Mortgage-backed securities (MBS) to prop up the asset prices. In the normal course, there is market place for the purchase and sale of the above securities. But when the supply of these are much greater than the demand from

investors (at the current market price), then the Central Bank step in to purchase these securities with the objective of propping up asset prices.

For example, in the absence of Federal Reserve buying would have led to an increase in the interest rate on the government bonds and a fall in the prices of MBS.

Quantitative Easing is of course monetary inflation disguised under technical terminology. This leads to an expansion in the balance sheet of the Federal Reserve and makes the Federal Reserve vulnerable as the liabilities are increased while assets of questionable value (given the lack of market demand) are added as a matching transaction.

12. **Trade Surplus / Deficit:** This is the balance of trade i.e., exports - imports of goods and services. An excess of exports over imports results in a trade surplus while the converse results in a trade deficit.

13. **ZIRP:** Refers to "Zero Interest Rate Policy" administered by the US Federal Reserve on the Fed funds rate after the GFC 2008.

Annexure I – Gold and Economic Freedom

Alan Greenspan, 1967

An almost hysterical antagonism toward the gold standard is one issue which unites statists of all persuasions. They seem to sense - perhaps more clearly and subtly than many consistent defenders of laissez-faire - that gold and economic freedom are inseparable; that the gold standard is an instrument of laissez-faire, and that each implies and requires the other.

In order to understand the source of their antagonism, it is necessary first to understand the specific role of gold in a free society.

Money is the common denominator of all economic transactions. It is that commodity which serves as a medium of exchange, is universally acceptable to all participants in an exchange economy as payment for their goods or services, and can, therefore, be used as a standard of market value and as a store of value, i.e., as a means of saving.

The existence of such a commodity is a precondition of a division of labor economy. If men did not have some commodity of objective value which was generally acceptable as money, they would have to resort to primitive barter or be forced to live on self-sufficient farms and forgo the inestimable advantages of specialization. If men had no means to store value, i.e., to save, neither long-range planning nor exchange would be possible.

What medium of exchange will be acceptable to all participants in an economy is not determined arbitrarily. First, the medium of exchange should be durable. In a primitive society of meager wealth, wheat might be sufficiently durable to serve as a medium, since all exchanges would occur only during and immediately after the harvest, leaving no value-surplus to store. But where store-of-value considerations are important, as they are in richer, more civilized societies, the medium of exchange must be a durable commodity, usually a metal. A metal is generally chosen because it is homogeneous and divisible: every unit is the same as every other and it can be blended or formed in any quantity. Precious jewels, for example, are neither homogeneous nor divisible. More importantly, the commodity chosen as a medium must be a luxury. Human desires for luxuries are unlimited and, therefore, luxury goods are always in demand and will always be acceptable. Wheat is a luxury in underfed civilizations, but not in a prosperous society. Cigarettes ordinarily would not serve as money, but they did in post-World War II Europe where they were considered a luxury. The term "luxury good" implies scarcity and high unit value. Having a high unit value, such a good is easily portable; for instance, an ounce of gold is worth a half-ton of pig iron.

In the early stages of a developing money economy, several media of exchange might be used, since a wide variety of commodities would fulfill the foregoing conditions. However, one of the commodities will gradually displace all others, by being more widely acceptable. Preferences on what to hold as a store of value will shift to the most widely acceptable commodity, which, in turn, will make it still more acceptable. The shift is progressive until that commodity becomes the sole medium of exchange. The use of a single medium is highly advantageous for the same reasons that a money economy is superior to a barter economy: it makes exchanges possible on an incalculably wider scale.

Whether the single medium is gold, silver, seashells, cattle, or tobacco is optional, depending on the context and development of a given economy. In fact, all have been employed, at various times, as media of exchange. Even in the present century, two major commodities, gold and silver, have been used as international media of exchange, with gold becoming the predominant one. Gold, having both artistic and functional uses and being relatively scarce, has significant advantages over all other media of exchange. Since the beginning of World War I, it has been virtually the sole international standard of exchange. If all goods and services were to be paid for in gold, large payments would be difficult to execute, and this would tend to limit the extent of a society's divisions of labor and specialization. Thus, a logical extension of the creation of a medium of exchange is the development of a banking system and credit instruments (banknotes and deposits) which act as a substitute for, but are convertible into, gold.

A free banking system based on gold is able to extend credit and thus to create banknotes (currency) and deposits, according to the production requirements of the economy. Individual owners of gold are induced, by payments of interest, to deposit their gold in a bank (against which they can draw checks). But since it is rarely the case that all depositors want to withdraw all their gold at the same time, the banker need only keep a fraction of his total deposits in gold as reserves. This enables the banker to loan out more than the amount of his gold deposits (which means that he holds claims to gold rather than gold as security of his deposits). But the amount of loans which he can afford to make is not arbitrary: he has to gauge it in relation to his reserves and to the status of his investments.

When banks loan money to finance productive and profitable endeavors, the loans are paid off rapidly, and bank credit continues to be generally available. But when the business ventures financed by bank credit are less profitable and slow to pay off, bankers soon find that their loans outstanding are excessive relative to their gold reserves, and they begin to curtail new lending, usually by charging higher interest rates. This tends to restrict the financing of new ventures and requires the existing borrowers to improve their profitability before they can obtain credit for further expansion. Thus, under the gold standard, a free banking system stands as the protector of an economy's stability and balanced growth.

When gold is accepted as the medium of exchange by most or all nations, an unhampered free international gold standard serves to foster a worldwide division of labor and the broadest international trade. Even though the units of exchange (the dollar, the pound, the franc, etc.) differ from country to country, when all are defined in terms of gold, the economies of the different countries act as one -- so long as there are no restraints on trade or on the movement of capital. Credit, interest rates, and prices tend to follow similar patterns in all countries. For example, if banks in one country extend credit too liberally, interest rates in that country will tend to fall, inducing depositors to shift their gold to higher-interest-paying banks in other countries. This will immediately cause a shortage of bank reserves in the "easy money" country, inducing tighter credit standards and a return to competitively higher interest rates again.

A fully free banking system and fully consistent gold standard have not as yet been achieved. But prior to World War I, the banking system in the United States (and in most of the world) was based on gold and even though governments intervened occasionally, banking was more free than controlled. Periodically, as a result of overly rapid credit expansion, banks became loaned up to the limit of their gold reserves, interest rates rose sharply, new credit was cut off, and the economy went into a sharp, but short-lived recession. (Compared with the depressions of 1920 and 1932, the pre-World War I business declines were mild indeed.) It was limited gold reserves that stopped the unbalanced expansions of business activity, before they could develop into the post WW-I type of disaster. The readjustment periods were short and the economies quickly reestablished a sound basis to resume expansion.

But the process of cure was misdiagnosed as the disease: if shortage of bank reserves was causing a business decline-argued economic interventionists -- why not find a way of supplying increased reserves to the banks so they never need be short! If banks can continue to loan money indefinitely -- it was claimed -- there need never be any slumps in business. And so the Federal Reserve System was organized in 1913. It consisted of twelve regional Federal Reserve banks nominally owned by private bankers, but in fact government sponsored, controlled, and supported. Credit extended by these banks is in practice (though not legally) backed by the taxing power of the federal government. Technically, we remained on the gold standard; individuals were still free to own gold, and gold continued to be used as bank reserves. But now, in addition to gold, credit extended by the Federal Reserve banks ("paper reserves") could serve as legal tender to pay depositors.

When business in the United States underwent a mild contraction in 1927, the Federal Reserve created more paper reserves in the hope of forestalling any possible bank reserve shortage. More disastrous, however, was the Federal Reserve's attempt to assist Great Britain who had been losing gold to us because the Bank of England refused to allow interest rates to rise when market forces dictated (it was politically unpalatable). The reasoning of the authorities involved was as follows: if the Federal Reserve pumped excessive paper reserves into American banks, interest rates in the United States would fall to a level comparable with those in Great Britain; this would act to stop Britain's gold loss and avoid the political embarrassment of having to raise interest rates.

The "Fed" succeeded; it stopped the gold loss, but it nearly destroyed the economies of the world in the process. The excess credit which the Fed pumped into the economy spilled over into the stock market -- triggering a fantastic speculative boom. Belatedly, Federal Reserve officials attempted to sop up the excess reserves and finally succeeded in braking the boom. But it was too late: by 1929 the speculative imbalances had become so overwhelming that the attempt precipitated a sharp retrenching and a consequent demoralizing of business confidence. As a result, the American economy collapsed. Great Britain fared even worse, and rather than absorb the full consequences of her previous folly, she abandoned the gold standard completely in 1931, tearing asunder what remained of the fabric of confidence and inducing a world-wide series of bank failures. The world economies plunged into the Great Depression of the 1930's.

With a logic reminiscent of a generation earlier, statists argued that the gold standard was largely to blame for the credit debacle which led to the Great Depression. If the gold standard had not existed, they argued, Britain's abandonment of gold payments in 1931 would not have caused the failure of banks all over the world. (The irony was that since 1913, we had been, not on a gold standard, but on what may be termed "a mixed gold standard;" yet it is gold that took the blame.) But the opposition to the gold standard in any form -- from a growing number of welfare-state advocates -- was prompted by a much subtler insight: the realization that the gold standard is incompatible with chronic deficit spending (the hallmark of the welfare state). Stripped of its academic jargon, the welfare state is nothing more than a mechanism by which governments confiscate the wealth of the productive members of a society to support a wide variety of welfare schemes. A substantial part of the confiscation is effected by taxation. But the welfare statists were quick to recognize that if they wished to retain political power, the amount of taxation had to be limited and they had to resort to programs of massive deficit spending, i.e., they had to borrow money, by issuing government bonds, to finance welfare expenditures on a large scale.

Under a gold standard, the amount of credit that an economy can support is determined by the economy's tangible assets, since every credit instrument is ultimately a claim on some tangible asset. But government bonds are not backed by tangible wealth, only by the government's promise to pay out of future tax revenues, and cannot easily be absorbed by the financial markets. A large volume of new government bonds can be sold to the public only at progressively higher interest rates. Thus, government deficit spending under a gold standard is severely limited. The abandonment of the gold standard made it possible for the welfare statists to use the banking system as a means to an unlimited expansion of credit. They have created paper reserves in the form of government bonds which -- through a complex series of steps -- the banks accept in place of tangible assets and treat as if they were an actual deposit, i.e., as the equivalent of what was formerly a deposit of gold. The holder of a government bond or of a bank deposit created by paper reserves believes that he has a valid claim on a real asset. But the fact is that there are now more claims outstanding than real assets. The law of supply and demand is not to be conned. As the supply of money (of claims) increases relative to the supply of tangible assets in the economy, prices must eventually rise. Thus, the earnings saved by the productive members of the society lose value in terms of goods. When the economy's books are finally balanced, one finds that this loss in value represents the goods purchased by the government for welfare or other purposes with the money proceeds of the government bonds financed by bank credit expansion.

In the absence of the gold standard, there is no way to protect savings from confiscation through inflation. There is no safe store of value. If there were, the government would have to make its holding illegal, as was done in the case of gold. If everyone decided, for example, to convert all his bank deposits to silver or copper or any other good, and thereafter declined to accept checks as payment for goods, bank deposits would lose their purchasing power, and government-created bank credit would be worthless as a claim on goods. The financial policy of the welfare state requires that there be no way for the owners of wealth to protect themselves.

This is the shabby secret of the welfare statists' tirades against gold. Deficit spending is simply a scheme for the confiscation of wealth. Gold stands in the way of this insidious process. It stands as a protector of property rights. If one grasps this, one has no difficulty in understanding the statists' antagonism toward the gold standard.

www.ingramcontent.com/pod-product-compliance
Lightning Source LLC
Chambersburg PA
CBHW020841150726
48196CB00002B/170